The First
Legal Answer Book
for Fund-Raisers

WILEY NONPROFIT LAW, FINANCE, AND MANAGEMENT SERIES

The Art of Planned Giving: Understanding Donors and the Culture of Giving by Douglas E. White

Beyond Fund Raising: New Strategies for Nonprofit Investment and Innovation by Kay Sprinkel Grace

Budgeting for Not-for-Profit Organizations by David Maddox

Charity, Advocacy, and the Law by Bruce R. Hopkins

The Complete Guide to Fund Raising Management by Stanley Weinstein

The Complete Guide to Nonprofit Management by Smith, Bucklin & Associates

Critical Issues in Fund Raising edited by Dwight Burlingame

Developing Affordable Housing: A Practical Guide for Nonprofit Organizations, Second Edition by Bennett L. Hecht

Faith-Based Management: Leading Organizations That Are Based on More Than Just Mission by Peter C. Brinckerhoff

Financial and Accounting Guide for Not-for-Profit Organizations, Fifth Edition by Malvern J. Gross, Jr., Richard F. Larkin, Roger S. Bruttomesso, John J. McNally, PricewaterhouseCoopers LLP

Financial Empowerment: More Money for More Mission by Peter C. Brinckerhoff

Financial Management for Nonprofit Organizations by Jo Ann Hankin, Alan Seidner, and John Zietlow

Financial Planning for Nonprofit Organizations by Jody Blazek

The First Legal Answer Book for Fund-Raisers by Bruce R. Hopkins

The Fund Raiser's Guide to the Internet by Michael Johnston

Fund-Raising Cost-Effectiveness: A Self-Assessment Workbook, by James M. Greenfield

Fund-Raising: Evaluating and Managing the Fund Development Process, Second Edition by James M. Greenfield

Fund-Raising Fundamentals: A Guide to Annual Giving for Professionals and Volunteers by James M. Greenfield

Fund-Raising Regulation: A State-by-State Handbook of Registration Forms, Requirements, and Procedures by Seth Perlman and Betsy Hills Bush

Grantseeker's Toolkit: A Comprehensive Guide to Finding Funding by Cheryl S. New and James Quick

Grant Winners Toolkit: Project Management and Evaluation by James Quick and Cheryl S. New

High Performance Nonprofit Organizations: Managing Upstream for Greater Impact by Christine Letts, William Ryan, and Allen Grossman

Intermediate Sanctions: Curbing Nonprofit Abuse by Bruce R. Hopkins and D. Benson Tesdahl

International Fund Raising for Nonprofits by Thomas Harris

International Guide to Nonprofit Law by Lester A. Salamon and Stefan Toeplar & Associates

Joint Ventures Involving Tax-Exempt Organizations, Second Edition by Michael I. Sanders

The Law of Fund-Raising, Second Edition by Bruce R. Hopkins

The Law of Tax-Exempt Healthcare Organizations by Thomas K. Hyatt and Bruce R. Hopkins

The Law of Tax-Exempt Organizations, Seventh Edition by Bruce R. Hopkins

The Legal Answer Book for Nonprofit Organizations by Bruce R. Hopkins

A Legal Guide to Starting and Managing a Nonprofit Organization, Second Edition by Bruce R. Hopkins

Managing Affordable Housing: A Practical Guide to Creating Stable Communities by Bennett L. Hecht, Local Initiatives Support Corporation, and James Stockard

Managing Upstream: Creating High-Performance Nonprofit Organizations by
Christine W. Letts, William P. Ryan, and Allan Grossman

Mission-Based Management: Leading Your Not-for-Profit Into the 21st Century by
Peter C. Brinckerhoff

*Mission-Based Marketing: How Your Not-for-Profit Can Succeed in a More Competitive
World* by Peter C. Brinckerhoff

Nonprofit Boards: Roles, Responsibilities, and Performance by Diane J. Duca

Nonprofit Compensation and Benefits Practices by Applied Research and
Development Institute International, Inc.

Nonprofit Compensation, Benefits, and Employment Law by David G. Samuels and
Howard Pianko

The Nonprofit Counsel by Bruce R. Hopkins

The Nonprofit Guide to the Internet, Second Edition by Michael Johnston

The Nonprofit Handbook, Second Edition: Volume I—Management by Tracy
Daniel Connors

The Nonprofit Handbook, Second Edition: Volume II—Fund Raising by James M.
Greenfield

Nonprofit Investment Policies: A Practical Guide to Creation and Implementation by
Robert Fry, Jr.

The Nonprofit Law Dictionary by Bruce R. Hopkins

Nonprofit Litigation: A Practical Guide with Forms and Checklists by Steve Bachmann

The Nonprofit Manager's Resource Dictionary by Ronald A. Landskroner

Nonprofit Mergers and Alliances: A Strategic Planning Guide, by Thomas A.
McLaughlin

Nonprofit Organizations' Business Forms: Disk Edition by John Wiley & Sons, Inc.

The NSFRE Fund Raising Dictionary by The National Society of Fund Raising
Executives

Planned Giving: Management, Marketing, and Law by Ronald R. Jordan and
Katelyn L. Quynn

Planned Giving Simplified: The Gift, The Giver, and the Gift Planner by
Robert F. Sharpe, Sr.

Private Foundations: Tax Law and Compliance by Bruce R. Hopkins and Jody Blazek

Program Related Investments: A Technical Manual for Foundations by Christie I. Baxter

Reengineering Your Nonprofit Organization: A Guide to Strategic Transformation by
Alceste T. Pappas

Reinventing the University: Managing and Financing Institutions of Higher Education
by Sandra L. Johnson and Sean C. Rush, PricewaterhouseCoopers LLP

The Second Legal Answer Book for Nonprofit Organizations by Bruce R. Hopkins

Special Events: Proven Strategies for Nonprofit Fund Raising by Alan Wendroff

*Strategic Communications for Nonprofit Organizations: Seven Steps to Creating a
Successful Plan* by Janel Radtke

Strategic Planning for Nonprofit Organizations: A Practical Guide and Workbook by
Michael Allison and Jude Kaye, Support Center for Nonprofit Management

Streetsmart Financial Basics for Nonprofit Managers by Thomas A. McLaughlin

A Streetsmart Guide to Nonprofit Mergers and Networks by Thomas A. McLaughlin

Successful Marketing Strategies for Nonprofit Organizations by Barry J. McLeish

The Tax Law of Charitable Giving, Second Edition by Bruce R. Hopkins

The Tax Law of Colleges and Universities by Bertrand M. Harding

*Tax Planning and Compliance for Tax-Exempt Organizations: Forms, Checklists,
Procedures, Third Edition* by Jody Blazek

*The Universal Benefits of Volunteering: A Practical Workbook for Nonprofit
Organizations, Volunteers and Corporations* by Walter P. Pidgeon, Jr.

*Values-Based Estate Planning: A Step-by-Step Approach to Wealth Transfers for
Financial Planners* by Scott C. Fithian

The Volunteer Management Handbook by Tracy Daniel Connors

The First
Legal Answer Book
for Fund-Raisers

Bruce R. Hopkins

JOHN WILEY & SONS, INC.
New York • Chichester • Weinheim • Brisbane • Singapore • Toronto

This publication is designed to provide accurate and authoritative information in regard to the subject matter covered. It is sold with the understanding that the publisher is not engaged in rendering legal, accounting, or other professional services. If legal advice or other expert assistance is required, the services of a competent professional person should be sought.

Designations used by companies to distinguish their products are often claimed as trademarks. In all instances where John Wiley & Sons, Inc., is aware of a claim, the product names appear in initial capital or all capital letters. Readers, however, should contact the appropriate companies for more complete information regarding trademarks and registration.

Library of Congress Cataloging-in-Publication Data:
Hopkins, Bruce R.
    The first legal answer book for fund-raisers / Bruce R. Hopkins.
        p.   cm.—(Wiley nonprofit law, finance, and management series)
    Includes bibliographical references and index.
    ISBN 0-471-35619-0 (pbk. : alk. paper)
        1. Fund raising—Law and legislation—United States—Miscellanea.
    2. Charitable uses, trusts, and foundations—United States—Miscellanea.
    I. Title.   II. Series.
    KF1389.5.Z9 H66   2000
    344.73   —dc21
                                                                99-052785

"There is a distinction—when it comes to tax planning—between tax evasion (i.e., choosing an impermissible path) and tax avoidance (i.e., choosing the least costly permissible path. But, simply because the [donors] have the right to choose the least costly path (from a tax perspective) upon which to walk, they do not have the right to be free from taxation if they decide to walk the line between what is and what is not permissible, and happen to stray across it, as they have here."
—Ferguson v. Commissioner, 99-1 U.S.T.C. ¶ 50,412 (9th Cir. 1999)

"The federal government discovered one taxpayer who was able to correctly prepare his tax return, causing the House and Senate Joint Tax Mutation Committee to swing into action and make a number of significant changes to the Tax Code, although no one seems to know what those changes are."
—Dave Barry, syndicated column, March 1998

Subscriber Update Service

BECOME A SUBSCRIBER!

Did you purchase this product from a bookstore?

If you did, it's important for you to become a subscriber. John Wiley & Sons, Inc., may publish, on a periodic basis, supplements and new editions to reflect the latest changes in the subject matter that you *need to know* in order to stay competitive in this ever-changing industry. By contacting the Wiley office nearest you, you'll receive any current update at no additional charge. In addition, you'll receive future updates and revised or related volumes on a 30-day examination review.

If you purchased this product directly from John Wiley & Sons, Inc., we have already recorded your subscription for this update service.

To become a subscriber, please call **1-800-225-5945** or send your name, company name (if applicable), address, and the title of the product to:

mailing address: **Supplement Department**
John Wiley & Sons, Inc.
One Wiley Drive
Somerset, NJ 08875

e-mail: **subscriber@wiley.com**
fax: **1-732-302-2300**
online: **www.wiley.com**

For customers outside the United States, please contact the Wiley office nearest you:

Professional & Reference Division
John Wiley & Sons Canada, Ltd.
22 Worcester Road
Rexdale, Ontario M9W 1L1
CANADA
(416) 675-3580
Phone: 1-800-567-4797
Fax: 1-800-565-6802
canada@jwiley.com

Jacaranda Wiley Ltd.
PRT Division
P.O. Box 174
North Ryde, NSW 2113
AUSTRALIA
Phone: (02) 805-1100
Fax: (02) 805-1597
headoffice@jwiley.com.au

John Wiley & Sons, Ltd.
Baffins Lane
Chichester
West Sussex, PO19 1UD
ENGLAND
Phone: (44) 1243 779777
Fax: (44) 1243 770638
cs-books@wiley.co.uk

John Wiley & Sons (SEA) Pte. Ltd.
2 Clementi Loop #02-01
SINGAPORE 129809
Phone: (65) 463-2400
Fax: (65) 463-4604; (65) 463-4605
wiley@singnet.com.sg

About the Author

Bruce R. Hopkins is a lawyer in Kansas City, Missouri, having practiced law in Washington, D.C., for 26 years. He specializes in the representation of charitable and other nonprofit organizations. His practice ranges over the entirety of legal matters involving nonprofit organizations, with emphasis on fund-raising law issues, charitable giving (including planned giving), the formation of nonprofit organizations, acquisition of recognition of tax-exempt and public charity status, unrelated business planning, application of intermediate sanctions, use of nonprofit and for-profit subsidiaries, and review of annual information returns.

Mr. Hopkins served as chair of the Committee on Exempt Organizations, Tax Section, American Bar Association; chair, Section of Taxation, National Association of College and University Attorneys; and president, Planned Giving Study Group of Greater Washington, D.C. He was accorded the Assistant Commissioner's (IRS) Award in 1984. He also teaches a course on nonprofit organizations at the University of Missouri–Kansas City School of Law.

Mr. Hopkins is the series editor of Wiley's Nonprofit Law, Finance, and Management Series. In addition to *The First Legal Answer Book for Fund-Raisers*, he is the author of *The Law of Fund-Raising, Second Edition*; *The Tax Law of Charitable Giving, Second Edition*; *The Legal Answer Book for Nonprofit Organizations*; *The Second Legal Answer Book for Nonprofit Organizations*; *The Law of Tax-Exempt Organizations, Seventh Edition*; *Charity, Advocacy, and the Law*; *The Nonprofit Law Dictionary*; *A Legal Guide to Starting and Managing a Nonprofit Organization, Second Edition*; and is co-author, with Jody Blazek, of *Private Foundations: Tax*

Law and Compliance, with D. Benson Tesdahl, of *Intermediate Sanctions: Curbing Nonprofit Abuse*; and with Thomas K. Hyatt, of *The Law of Tax-Exempt Healthcare Organizations*. He also writes *The Nonprofit Counsel*, a monthly newsletter, published by John Wiley & Sons. He is hard at work on *The Second Legal Answer Book for Fund-Raisers*.

Mr. Hopkins earned his J.D. and LL.M. degrees at the George Washington University and his B.A. at the University of Michigan. He is a member of the bar of the District of Columbia and the state of Missouri.

How to Use This Book

The First Legal Answer Book for Fund-Raisers is designed for fund-raising professionals, nonprofit executives, board members, lawyers, accountants, and others who need quick and authoritative answers concerning the law governing fund-raising for charitable purposes. It is designed to help the reader not only better understand this law, but, more important, to show how to work with it and within its boundaries while maintaining and enhancing fund-raising programs. This book uses simple, straightforward language and avoids technical jargon when possible. This question-and-answer format offers a clear and useful guide to understanding the complex, but extremely important, area of the statutes, regulations, and other law governing the raising of funds. Citations are providing as research aids for those who need to pursue particular items in greater detail.

Numbering System: The question numbering system has been designed for ease of use. The questions are numbered consecutively within each chapter (e.g., 5:1, 5:2, 5:3).

Listing of Questions: The detailed List of Questions that follows the Table of Contents in the front of this book helps the reader locate areas of immediate interest. This listing serves as a detailed table of contents that provides both the question number and the page on which it appears.

Index: The index at the back of this book provides a further aid to locating specific information. All references in the index are to question numbers rather than page numbers.

Preface

The First Legal Answer Book for Fund-Raisers is the third in Wiley's Legal Answer Book Series. (Yes, more are coming, including *The Second Legal Answer Book for Fund-Raisers*.) The first two of these books—*The Legal Answer Book for Nonprofit Organizations* and *The Second Legal Answer Book for Nonprofit Organizations*—reflect my attempt to summarize, using the question-and-answer format, the broad sweep of the law of tax-exempt organizations and charitable giving.

With this book, I focus on these areas of the law from the unique standpoint of those who are charged with the difficult task of raising money for charitable ends. That task is arduous, indeed, due in no small part to the law that the federal and state governments keep heaping on the fund-raising process. Much of this law directly affects and shapes—often burdens—the administrative aspects of fund-raising.

I am a lawyer, not a fund-raiser—and I like things that way. I would much rather advise as to the law than have to raise charitable dollars in an environment dictating compliance with all of these requirements. In other words, my sympathies are extended to you charitable fund-raisers. Having said that, I feel compelled to raise a rather sensitive point. Some of you are easing the compliance burden by the tried and true technique of . . . noncompliance. Most of this, I hasten to add (and believe), is inadvertent.

My take on this situation, however, is that it is getting harder to sustain this approach to fund-raising law compliance. The issues are mounting, regulators are growing more knowledgeable, donors are more sophisticated, and then there is this matter of modern technology.

It's a different fund-raising world where a prospective donor can call up your organization's most recent Form 990 by computer and ask penetrating questions while you are straining to secure a gift. Thus, in short, there is a lot of law out there for you, the fund-raiser, and you and/or your organization is expected to adhere to it. My goal with this Legal Answer Book is to help you understand the law and appropriately comply with it—and to make this process as palatable as possible for you. (I have done many seminars for associations of fund-raisers over the years on the subject of the law applicable to fund-raising professionals, and I know that the vast majority of you would much rather be elsewhere—and you often are.)

The book opens with a look at the basics: what the fund-raiser should know about the federal and state law applicable to charitable fund-raising. Chapter 1 ranges over some basic definitions pertaining to the fund-raiser and the organization(s) he or she serves, and some basic law concepts applicable to most charitable entities. This is not law school for fund-raisers; it is an attempt to create a framework as to the minimum amount of law the fund-raiser should master fairly early in the career.

Next is explored the matter of public charity status. Charitable organizations that engage in fund-raising are not likely, of course, to be private foundations. Yet, my experience with fund-raisers has led me to conclude that most of you do not know the public charity status of the charity you are raising money for—or, if you do, you do not fully understand the advantages and disadvantages of that status or if that status should be changed (or perhaps worse, has been lost). If you are in this position, Chapter 2 is for you.

Some fund-raisers work with newly formed entities. This means that the organization may be seeking its recognition of tax-exempt (and public charity) status during the time the fund-raiser is in the picture. Chapter 3 identifies the portions of the application to be filed with the IRS that are of principal concern to fund-raisers.

Chapters 4 and 5 are the ones the typical fund-raiser is likely to first turn to and dwell on (partly, perhaps, as a reason for delay of review of other portions of the book). Chapter 4 is a summary of the federal law charitable contribution tax deductibility rules. Chapter 5 is a summary of the tax law concerning the planned giving techniques. This information is, it goes without saying, essential for the fund-raiser.

Believe it or not, the unrelated business rules can apply in many ways in the fund-raising setting. Chapter 6 leads the fund-raiser through the basic rules and then concentrates on those that are unique to charitable fund-raising.

In Chapter 7, I wander about in an area that many fund-raisers don't like to consider: the law aspects of their compensation. Here, I explore some current developments as to the basic requirement of the standard of reasonableness. Also examined is this pesky matter of percentage-based compensation. For those of you who are not employees, I offer some thoughts on the elements of the fund-raiser's contract.

Another aspect of all this that has troubled me over the years is the process of preparation of charitable organizations' annual information returns (usually, Form 990). I am continually dismayed at the lack of involvement in this process by the fund-raiser. Thus, Chapter 8 looks at the annual information return from the fund-raiser's perspective—and contains a plea for including the fund-raiser in the preparation of the return. (If you can't be part of the process, please at least read these returns.)

The book ends with the state law rules. In this context, we have a big chunk of the law that causes fund-raisers (and charities) compliance headaches and that is the basis for considerable noncompliance. Chapter 9 surveys the contents of these laws and offers some advice about complying with them.

I feel compelled now to bring up an aspect of this book that is illustrative of the state of the law pertaining to fund-raising: not all of the applicable law is in here. In fact, as the reference to the *First Legal Answer Book* in this area reflects, there was only room to include a discussion of about one-half of it. To remedy this deficiency, as noted, *The Second Legal Answer Book for Fund-Raisers* will be forthcoming. Subjects to be treated include the intermediate sanctions rules, estate planning, property valuation, gift substantiation, the quid pro quo contribution rules, special events, postal law, securities law, antitrust law, the IRS's audit perspective, and various disclosure requirements. (If you have questions relating to any of these areas, send them to me at bhopkins@pwvs.com.) The way the law in this field is evolving, there may be some material in there that can't be conceived of at this writing.

Your author is finishing up his 30th year of law practice. A goodly amount of what is in this book is reflective of answers to questions that arise year in and year out, from clients and seminar attendees. Also, I often draw on responses to questions that should be asked . . . and are not. Some perspectives and commentary have been included.

The end product has real value only if those who need it can use it to promptly resolve a problem or answer a question before them. To facilitate its usefulness, all of the questions answered in the book are listed at the beginning. There is also an index. Endnotes have been kept to the minimum. (For more, see "How to Use This Book" on page xi.) Those who need additional information on a matter can turn to one or more of the books in Wiley's Nonprofit Law, Finance, and Management

Series. One of my favorites for you is *The Law of Fund-Raising*, in its second edition and annually supplemented.

I want to thank my editor at Wiley, Martha Cooley, who has been so supportive of this and other Answer Books. Her tolerance of the inability of those who write tax regulations and rulings, and court opinions, on subjects pertaining to charitable fund-raising to match the timing of issuance of their documents with Wiley's publishing schedule is greatly appreciated. I also want to thank Robin Goldstein, an associate managing editor at Wiley, for her fine work on this book.

Kansas City, Missouri   Bruce R. Hopkins
December, 1999

Contents

List of Questions

CHAPTER 2 Public Charity Status

CHAPTER 3   Tax Exemption Application

CHAPTER 5   Planned Giving

CHAPTER 7   Fund-Raisers' Compensation

The First
Legal Answer Book
for Fund-Raisers

CHAPTER 1

The Basics: What Every Fund-Raiser Should Know About the Law

Professional fund-raisers and the law all too frequently intertwine. Yet, an individual may *think* he or she is not (or is) a *professional fund-raiser* or that he or she is (or is not) serving a *charitable* cause, but the law—federal and/or state—may see it differently.

Many professional fund-raisers do not understand some of the basic legal concepts pertinent to their field. For example, some do not understand or appreciate the distinctions between *nonprofit* organizations, *charitable* organizations, and *public* charitable organizations. Some fund-raisers cannot explain the public charity status of their charitable organization(s) to prospective donors. Many fund-raisers do not comprehend the *private inurement doctrine*, or concern themselves with what they perceive as irrelevant facts, such as a charity's involvement in lobbying, politics, partnerships, joint ventures, and subsidiaries. A "charitable" gift to an organization may not be deductible if the "charitable" organization has had its tax-exempt status revoked.

Here are the questions most frequently asked by professional fund-raisers (or that should be asked by them) about the basic principles of law applicable to their field—and the answers to them.

Q 1:1   What is a *professional fund-raiser*?

This is certainly a pertinent question to start things off. The professional fund-raiser is the individual to whom these answers are primarily directed. Nonetheless, the law has a more elegant definition of the term *professional fund-raiser*. This topic, by the way, is almost uniquely a matter of state law.

The most popular definition used by state law views the professional fund-raiser as a consultant to one or more charitable organizations, rather than as an employee of one of them. This definition is as follows: "any person who for a flat fixed fee under a written agreement plans, conducts, manages, carries on, advises or acts as a consultant, whether directly or indirectly, in connection with soliciting contributions for, or on behalf of, any charitable . . . organization, but who actually solicits no contributions as a part of such services." This definition, or a similar version of it, is utilized in 29 states.[1]

In many instances, the law is clear that this term does not embrace employees and salaried officers of charitable organizations. Frequently, these laws also exclude from the ambit of professional fund-raiser those who advise individuals to contribute to a charitable organization, such as lawyers, investment counselors, and bankers.

Thus, this definition, in addition to contemplating a consultancy, focuses on the manner of compensation, the fact of a written contract, and the absence of actual solicitation of gifts. It is predicated on the premise that the professional fund-raiser works with the charity in planning the solicitation effort (such as an annual fund drive or a capital campaign) and that the actual asking for gifts is left to others, such as volunteers, paid staff, or professional solicitors. Nonetheless, some professional fund-raisers do solicit contributions and professional fundraisers (at least in a generic sense) can be employees of charitable organizations.

OBSERVATION: The principal professional association of fund-raisers has settled on the term *fund-raising executive*. The membership of the National Society of Fund Raising Executives (NSFRE) is comprised of both those who are employees and those who are consultants, albeit with a much larger concentration of the former. (An association of consultants is the American Association of Fund Raising Counsel.) Full membership in NSFRE is available to those (1) with at least one year of experience as fund-raising professionals for one or more organizations, as members of counseling firms which are engaged in fundraising management, or as self-employed professionals; (2) who "hold some degree of accountability for income-generation within the philanthropic process"; (3) who estimate that at least 25 percent of their time is spent on fund-raising–related responsibilities; and (4) who are compensated for their services.[2]

Probably the most comprehensive definition of the term (which appears to encompass both employees and consultants) is this state's rule: A professional fund-raiser is "any person who for financial compensation or profit performs for a charitable organization any service in connection with which contributions are, or will be, solicited in this state by the compensated person or by any compensated person the person employs, procures, or engages to solicit; or any person who for compensation or profit plans, manages, advises, consults, or prepares material for, or with respect to, the solicitation in this state of contributions for a charitable organization."[3]

In truth, the law on this point is a mess. Despite the frequency of use of the term *professional fund-raiser*, it is utilized in only nine states. Other comparable terms are *professional fund-raising counsel* or *professional fund-raiser consultant*. Some states don't use the word *professional* and others omit the hyphen.

One of the principal difficulties in this regard is the blurring of the distinction between a professional fund-raiser and a *professional solicitor* (Q 1:2). The essential difference between the two is that the fund-raiser does not solicit contributions. In real life, however, that distinction does not always hold up.

As the comprehensive definition of the term *professional fund-raiser* reflects, it sometimes embraces the function of soliciting gifts. The confusion is enhanced in those states that use the term *professional fund-raiser* to mean precisely what the term *professional solicitor* means in other states. Other terms meaning *professional solicitor* include *professional commercial fund-raiser, independent paid fund-raiser,* and *professional fund-raising firm.*

Thus, today, the phrase *professional fund-raiser* can—as a matter of law—mean just about what anyone wants it to mean. An individual's (or company's) status in this regard can change, depending on the state or states in which the fund-raising is taking place. Basically, then, a fund-raiser is a person who assists, to varying extents, one or more charitable organizations in soliciting and receiving contributions (including grants).

Professional fund-raisers are subject to state law regulation (Q 9:4).

Q 1:2   What is a *professional solicitor?*

The term *professional solicitor* is defined under state law in one of two ways.[4]

The most common of these definitions (employed in 34 states) essentially provides that a professional solicitor is any person involved in the solicitation process other than the consultant generically referred to as a *professional fund-raiser* (Q 1:1). Thus, one state's law defines a solicitor as a "person who, for a financial or other consideration, solicits contributions for, or on behalf of, a charitable . . . organization, whether such solicitation is performed personally or through his agents, servants, or employees or through agents, servants, or employees specially employed by or for a charitable . . . organization, who are engaged in the solicitation of contributions under the direction of such person, or any person who, for a financial or other consideration, plans, conducts, manages, carries on, advises, or acts as a consultant to a charitable . . . organization in connection with the solicitation of contributions but does not qualify as a professional fund-raising counsel."[5]

This type of definition is usually accompanied by the same exclusions that are available with respect to the definition of professional fund-raisers: those for officers, employees, lawyers, and the like (Q 1:1).

The other definition (used in eight states) casts the professional solicitor as a person who is employed or otherwise retained for compensation by a professional fund-raiser, rather than directly by a charitable organization, to solicit charitable contributions.

Q 1:3   What is the significance of these distinctions?

There can be great consequences associated with these distinctions. However, as noted (Q 1:1), in real life, the distinctions are often blurred. That is, many consultants are also involved in gift solicitation and many who solicit gifts are also involved in the solicitation planning process.

The evaporation of the once relatively easy-to-define dichotomy between professional fund-raisers and professional solicitors started with direct mail fund-raising. In that setting, those who consult about the design of the solicitation literature also often physically introduce it into the postal system, thereby becoming part of the gift solicitation process.

Many in the fund-raising field find the term *solicitor* to be pejorative. Yet even this is changing. Soliciting by telephone has come out of the boiler room and become respectable. Telemarketing as a means of fund-raising is common. Gift solicitation over the Internet is growing.

Still, in many quarters today, being cast as a solicitor means image problems. Solicitors are seen as those who pursue gifts by going door to door, harassing passers-by on street corners, or making telephone calls interrupting dinners. They are also portrayed as those who consume a large portion of the contributions intended for charitable ends.

— 4 —

A self-respecting fund-raising consultant is likely to be offended if labeled a *solicitor*—"professional" or otherwise.

OBSERVATION: Several years ago, a task force was drafting a prototype charitable solicitation act. The group was comprised of government regulators, lawyers, accountants, executives of charitable organizations, and fund-raising consultants. Someone suggested adding a paid solicitor to the group, to gain his or her perspective, but none of the task force members seemed to know one.

From a law viewpoint, professional solicitors are generally treated more harshly under the state charitable solicitation acts than professional fund-raisers. Solicitors usually have more extensive registration and reporting requirements, greater disclosure responsibilities, and may have to be bonded even though fund-raisers may not (Q 9:5).

In general, then, the professional fund-raiser—employee or consultant—should strive to avoid categorization as a professional solicitor. Of course, the law of each state in which a solicitation takes place will govern the fund-raiser's status in that jurisdiction.

Q 1:4   What is a *commercial co-venture*?

Commercial co-venturing occurs when a for-profit commercial business enterprise is conducting a promotion, announced to the general public, by which a portion (sometimes stated as a specific amount or a specific percentage) of the purchase price of a product or service will, during or at the close of a fixed period of time, be paid to a charitable organization.[6] This arrangement usually results in a charitable contribution (although often deducted as a business expense) by the business enterprise, the amount of which is dependent on the extent of consumer response to the promotion. This "venture" produces gift revenue to the beneficiary charity (but no charitable deduction for the purchasers) and positive publicity for the business sponsor. The foregoing definition of a commercial co-venture is in the law of six states.

It has become more common, however, to define a commercial co-venture as a *charitable sales promotion*. One state defines a charitable sales promotion as "an advertising or sales campaign, conducted by a commercial co-venturer, which represents that the purchase or use of goods or services offered by the commercial co-venturer shall benefit, in whole or in part, a charitable trust or purpose."[7] In this setting, the term *commercial co-venturer* is defined as a "person who for profit is regularly and primarily engaged in trade or commerce other than in connection with soliciting for charitable trusts or purposes and who conducts a charitable sales promotion."

NOTE: Read literally, a definition like this excuses a professional fund-raising firm from the scope of these laws, although it would be rare indeed for a business of this nature to conduct a charitable sales promotion.

These definitions, or versions closely akin to them, are used in 11 states.

By the way, the term *commercial co-venture* is an unfortunate one. First, it suggests that the charitable organization involved is engaging in a joint venture with a for-profit entity. This is not entirely the case, inasmuch as the charity usually has a relatively passive role in the activity. Worse, the term connotes participation by the charitable organization in a *commercial* enterprise, which it is not. Thus, the term can easily lead the public or the IRS to thinking that the charity is conducting an unrelated business (Chapter 6), rather than being involved in a fund-raising effort. This is why the phrase *charitable sales promotion*, while less than artful, is preferable.

These promotions may be subject to state law regulation (Q 9:7).

Q 1:5   What is considered *fund-raising*?

Whether an activity is considered fund-raising will depend on the views of the individuals involved and the legal setting. The concept of fund-raising may be defined in terms of an activity or it can play off the word *fund* (which suggests revenue).

As to activities, fund-raising clearly embraces annual fund campaigns, capital campaigns, planned giving programs, direct mail revenue-raising, telemarketing, door-to-door canvasses, street-corner solicitations, and the seeking of grants. But, does fund-raising include efforts such as dues solicitations and the generation of exempt function revenue (the latter being revenue derived from the sale of goods or services as a related business)? For that matter, does fund-raising include the process of deriving unrelated business income (Chapter 6)?

The fund-raising purist is likely to contend that *fund-raising* is one or more activities restricted to the solicitation of gifts and grants. The law, however, often transcends the bounds of purity in this context.

Federal law rarely defines the term *fund-raising*. In one of these infrequent instances, for example, the term is used in connection with the *expenditure test*, which is an elective standard most public charities can follow to determine the range of permissible legislative activities (Q

1:16). Under this test, allowable lobbying is measured by applying certain percentages to increments of an organization's expenditures, other than fund-raising expenditures.[8] For this purpose, the term *fund-raising* includes not only the solicitation of contributions and grants (including grants from governmental units), but also the solicitation of dues (including the solicitation of those whose dues are in arrears).[9]

These distinctions are manifested in another legal context: that involving the service provider type of publicly supported charity (Q 2:6). This type of charitable organization can receive *public support* in one of two basic ways. One is contributions, grants, and membership fees.[10] These forms of revenue are generally the product of fund-raising by anyone's definition (although, as noted, some may balk at the thought that dues solicitation is fund-raising). The other type of public support is gross receipts (within certain limits) from exempt function activities, specifically, money from admissions, sales of merchandise, performance of services, or furnishing of facilities.[11] There can be disagreement as to whether this type of revenue is that generated as the result of fund-raising.

NOTE: The very concept of *public support* would seem to connote the financial consequences of fund-raising. Indeed, that is the case with respect to the donative type of publicly supported charity, where only gifts and grants amount to public support (Q 2:5). But, in the setting of the service provider organization, the overlay of the concepts of *fund-raising* and *public support* is debatable.

Thus, in its broadest sense, *fund-raising* means the generation of revenue (including property) for charitable purposes. Whether the phrase is to be more narrowly defined than that is, as noted, dependent on the views of those involved and the character of the applicable law.

Q 1:6   What is a *nonprofit* organization?

The term *nonprofit* organization is a misleading one; regrettably, the English language lacks a preferable (clearer) word. This term does *not* mean that the organization cannot earn a profit (an excess of revenue over expenses). Many nonprofit organizations, in fact, enjoy substantial profits. An entity, whether nonprofit or for-profit, cannot long exist without revenues that at least equal expenses.

The easiest way to define a nonprofit organization is to first define its antithesis: the *for-profit* organization. A for-profit organization exists to operate a business and to generate profits from that business for the benefit of those who own the enterprise. As an example, the owners of a for-profit corporation are stockholders, who take their profits in the form of dividends. Thus, when the term *for-profit* is used, it refers to profits acquired by the owners of the business, not by the business itself. The law, therefore, differentiates between profits at the *entity level* and profits at the *ownership level*.

Both for-profit and nonprofit organizations are allowed by the law to earn profits at the entity level. But, only for-profit organizations are permitted profits at the ownership level. Nonprofit organizations rarely have owners; in any event, these organizations are not permitted to pass along profits (net earnings) to those who control them.

Profits permitted to for-profit entities but not nonprofit entities are forms of *private inurement* (Q 1:10). The term private inurement refers to ways of transferring an organization's net earnings to persons in their private capacity. The very purpose of a for-profit organization is to engage in private inurement. By contrast, nonprofit organizations may *not* engage in acts of private inurement. (Economists are fond of calling this fundamental standard the *nondistribution constraint.*) Nonprofit organizations are required to use their profits for their program activities. In the case of tax-exempt nonprofit organizations, these activities are termed their *exempt functions*.

NOTE: The prohibition on private inurement does not mean that a nonprofit cannot pay compensation to its employees and other service providers. This law requires, however, that these payments be reasonable.

Consequently, the doctrine of private inurement is the essential dividing line, as a matter of law, between nonprofit and for-profit organizations.[12]

Q 1:7   What is a *tax-exempt* organization?

The term *tax-exempt* organization usually is used to mean an organization that is exempt, in whole or in part, from the federal income tax.[13] To be tax-exempt, it is not sufficient that an organization merely be structured as a nonprofit organization (Q 1:6). Rather, the organization must meet specific statutory and other regulatory criteria to qualify for tax-exempt status.

Indeed, some nonprofit organizations cannot qualify as certain types of tax-exempt organizations under the federal tax law. For example, a nonprofit organization that engages in a substantial amount of lobbying cannot be a tax-exempt charitable organization (Q 1:16). Likewise, an organization that provides a substantial amount of commercial-type insurance cannot be an exempt charitable organization.[14] Some nonprofit organizations are ineligible for any category of tax exemption.

There are other federal taxes for which there may be an exemption, such as certain excise and Social Security taxes. Yet, despite the term, a tax-exempt organization is not completely free from the prospect of taxation. Nearly all exempt organizations are subject to tax on their unrelated business income (Chapter 6). Public charities can be taxable if they undertake a substantial amount of lobbying activities (Q 1:16) or if they participate or intervene in a political campaign (Q 1:17). A charitable organization can be taxable if it engages in certain types of political activities, other than campaigns (*id.*). Private foundations must pay an excise tax on their net investment income and are susceptible to a host of other excise taxes.[15]

State laws have several bases enabling an organization to qualify for a tax exemption. Taxes may be levied, at the state level, on income, franchise, sales, use, tangible property, intangible property, and real property. The law varies dramatically from state to state as to the categories of exemptions that are available.

Q 1:8   What is a *charitable* organization?

For these purposes, a *charitable* organization is one that qualifies as a charitable entity under the federal tax law. There are two definitions in this regard: a broad, overarching definition and a narrower, more technical definition. Both of these definitions rest on the provision in the Internal Revenue Code that is the basis for this category of tax exemption: the well-known Section 501(c)(3).

Code section 501(c)(3) encompasses eight categories of exempt organizations: entities that are religious, charitable, scientific, public safety testing, literary, educational, amateur sports competition fostering, and cruelty prevention (for children or animals) in nature. All of these organizations are known as *charitable* organizations. There are three reasons for this.

One reason is that most of these concepts for exemption emanate from the nation's history; they are part of the English common law precepts of charity as it evolved over the centuries in the law of charitable trusts and property. Second, most of these entities are subject to the *public policy doctrine* applicable to charities, which means that an organization cannot qualify as a charitable one if it engages in an activity that is contrary to federal public policy.[16] The third of these reasons is that, with one minor exception, these entities are eligible to receive deductible charitable contributions (Chapter 4).

NOTE: The exception is that organizations that test for public safety are exempt as charitable organizations but may not be the recipient of deductible charitable gifts.

The narrower definition of the term *charitable* focuses on that word as it relates to only one of the eight categories of entities referred to in Section 501(c)(3). There are, today, 15 discrete ways for an organization to be charitable. These rationales for charitability originated with English and American common (court-made) law; most of them are now recognized in tax regulations and/or IRS rulings. By the way, the tax regulations state that the term *charitable* is defined using its "generally accepted legal sense,"[17] which means that it is a constantly evolving concept, accommodating new understandings of what is meant by the word *charitable* as the needs of society grow and change.[18]

The 15 definitions of the term *charitable* are relief of the poor, promotion of health, lessening the burdens of government, advancement of religion, advancement of education, advancement of science, promotion of social welfare, promotion of the arts, protection of the environment, promotion of patriotism, promotion of amateur sports, local economic development, public interest law, care of orphans, and maintenance of public confidence in the legal system.

Relief of the poor, including the distressed and underprivileged,[19] is the most basic and historically founded type of charitable activity. Assistance in this regard can be in the form of money or services. For example, low-income housing programs can qualify as charitable ones pursuant to this rationale.[20] Another traditional definition of the term *charitable* is lessening of the burdens of government,[21] which includes the provision of services that a governmental unit would otherwise have to perform.

NOTE: In a unique application of the rule that lessening the burdens of government is charitable, the IRS ruled that it was a charitable undertaking for charitable organizations in Kansas City, Missouri, to purchase and hold ownership in the Kansas City Royals (a for-profit professional baseball club). This was done to prevent the team from moving from Kansas City; the charities owned the club until it was sold to a group pledged to keep the team in that town. The state of Missouri and Kansas City had worked strenuously to retain the Royals and was failing in that task. By investing in the Royals for this purpose, the charities were ruled to have lessened (indeed, eliminated) what previously was a burden assumed by the two governments.[22]

Other forms of charitable activity are far more modern, such as environmental protection.[23] Some of the contemporary applications of the concept of *charity* are found as elements of the principle that promotion of social welfare can be charitable.[24] Under this rationale, charitable undertakings include the elimination of discrimination, defense of human and civil rights, lessening of neighborhood tensions, and combating community deterioration.

Some activities recognized as charitable under a particular rationale were previously regarded as charitable under another rationale. The most prominent example of this is health care activities. The charitability of these functions once rested on the precept that the poor were being relieved (such as by free health care in nonprofit hospitals) or that education was being advanced (teaching hospitals). With the advent of Medicare, Medicaid, and private medical insurance, however, most patients had the ability to pay, directly or indirectly, for health care services, and the rationale that the "poor" were being served became untenable. Thus, promotion of health was recognized by the IRS as a charitable undertaking in and of itself (giving rise to a wide range of issues as the era of managed care settled in soon thereafter).[25]

NOTE 1: This act of the IRS, which occurred in 1969, came on the eve of the advent of the era of managed care. Thirty years ago, the principal health care provider was the freestanding hospital. Today, many exempt hospitals are parts of an array of entities that directly and indirectly promote health (networks), and the health care delivery system involves organizations that were not thought about when the IRS made its move, such as varying types of clinics, health maintenance organizations, preferred provider organizations, integrated delivery systems, and assisted-living facilities. Enormous controversies still rage over the eligibility of these entities for tax exemption (federal and state). Even charitable hospitals, surrounded by so many for-profit ones, are struggling to convince skeptical lawmakers, regulators, and members of the public that they are, indeed, still worthy of classification as *charitable* organizations.

NOTE 2: Despite the distinctions between these two definitions, the use of the term *charitable* throughout includes educational, scientific, religious, and like activities and purposes, unless the context indicates otherwise.

For charitable giving purposes—as opposed to tax-exempt organizations law purposes—charitable organizations include qualified veterans' and fraternal groups, cemetery companies, and governmental entities.[26]

Q 1:9   What is the *primary purpose rule*?

To be tax-exempt, an organization must have purposes and engage in activities that qualify it for that category of exemption. These activities need not, however, be the entity's exclusive undertakings; there can be some—often termed *incidental*—nonexempt functions. Thus, for example, an otherwise tax-exempt organization can engage in a limited amount of unrelated business activities (Chapter 6).

Read literally, the federal tax statutory law requires that a charitable organization be organized and operated *exclusively* for charitable purposes.[27] That is not the actual law, however; the Supreme Court has made it clear that the word *exclusively* in fact means *substantially* or *primarily*.[28] This, then, is also the law as respects other tax-exempt organizations where the federal statutory law provides that they be organized and operated exclusively for exempt functions. This rule of law is generally referred to as the *primary purpose* rule.[29]

Measuring what is *primary* is not easy to do; there is no mechanical formula. The measurement is done on the basis of what the law likes to term the *facts and circumstances*. The IRS—uniformly supported by the courts—heartily rejects the thought of using any particular percentage in ascertaining primary activities, and applies this principle of law on a case-by-case basis.[30]

TIP: Percentages are used in this and comparable contexts all the time, if only as a guide. The term *primary* has been assigned specific percentages in other federal income tax law settings; for example, for unrelated business income purposes, it can mean at least 65 percent. By comparison, the term *substantial* is sometimes defined as at least 85 percent; *substantially all* is sometimes set at 90 percent. *Incidental* is sometimes defined as up to 15 percent.

Not only are percentages informally used at best, it is often not a formal rule as to the base to which any percentage is to be applied. Usually, the matter is a function of money; sometimes it is a matter of time. In the lobbying setting, for example, where a variant of the primary purpose rule is applied in the case of charitable organizations, the term *primary* can mean as low as 80 percent (that is, non-exempt function activity (lobbying) can be as much as 20 percent) (Q 1:16). By contrast, in the unrelated business context (Chapter 6), the IRS may emphasize the percentage of time expended by an organization for related activities, rather than the percentage of its unrelated business income—particularly where the unrelated income is passive in nature.

NOTE: In one instance, a charitable organization was permitted by the IRS to retain tax exemption, even though the percentage of its unrelated income for the years audited was 98 percent. The unrelated income was passive and the time expended by the organization for charitable undertakings exceeded 40 percent.[31]

The statement that there is no mechanical formula for measuring what is *primary* is not precisely accurate. In the case of tax-exempt title-holding companies, the maximum amount of unrelated business income that they can earn in a year without endangering their tax exemption is 10 percent.[32] This rule does not apply, however, with respect to any other type of tax-exempt organization. For most exempt organizations, including charitable ones, 10 percent is too narrow a limitation on permissible non-exempt activities.

OBSERVATION: Fund-raising (Q 1:5) is not usually a charitable activity. The solicitation of gifts and grants is not inherently an exempt function. Yet the generation of exempt function revenue can be an exempt activity (patient care revenue for a hospital, tuition for a school, or admission fees of a theater). Some charities find it difficult to regard fund-raising as a non-exempt function. Likewise, there can be controversy over whether a particular undertaking is a program or fund-raising; a single activity can partake of both. This distinction can be quite meaningful when a charity's fund-raising expenses are being evaluated.

Q 1:10   What is *private inurement*?

As noted (Q 1:6), in its most sweeping form, the doctrine of private inurement embodies the fundamental distinction between nonprofit organizations and for-profit organizations. *Private inurement* means the transfer of an entity's profits (net earnings) from the organization to persons in their private capacity (often the owners of the organization). Private inurement is supposed to occur with for-profit organizations; nonprofit organizations are not to engage in forms of private inurement—that is the essence of the term *nonprofit*.

The doctrine exists to preclude application of a nonprofit organization's income or assets to private ends. The specific phraseology refers to inurement (transfer) of *net earnings*.[33] On its face, this language suggests that private inurement transactions are akin to the payment by a corporation of dividends. That is not the case, however; the law has evolved to the point where many types of transactions are considered forms of private inurement even though there is no transmission of net earnings in a formal accounting sense.

Thus, private inurement is a term used to describe a variety of ways of transferring some or all of an organization's resources (income and/or assets) to individuals or other persons in their private capacity. A private inurement transaction must involve a person who is an *insider* with respect to the organization. This relationship arises when the person (he, she, or it) has a special relationship with the organization; a person who is in a position to exercise a significant amount of control over the affairs of the organization is an insider. Usually, the special relationship arises out of a governance arrangement; that is, an organization's insiders include its trustees, directors, and officers. Key employees can be embraced by the term if their duties and responsibilities are akin to those of an officer.

A person can be an insider because of some other relationship with the organization. A founder of the entity, a substantial contributor to it, or a vendor of goods or services to it may be an insider, particularly where he, she, or it has a significant voice in the policy making or like operations of the organization.

NOTE: In a very significant and certainly pertinent development, a federal court concluded that a fund-raising company was an insider with respect to a charitable organization, because of elements of control. The court also found private inurement, in the form of excessive compensation and manipulation of the resources of the charity (chiefly its donor list) for the company's private ends.[34] Although this decision was reversed,[35] the case is currently being evaluated in light of the private benefit doctrine (Q 1:11) and illustrates how a fund-raiser may be considered an insider with respect to a charitable organization.

There are attribution rules in this area. Controlled businesses and family members may also be treated as insiders.

TIP: Although they are not formally controlling outside their specific contexts, the rules concerning *disqualified persons* in the law of excess benefit transactions[36] and private foundations[37] can provide useful analogies in determining who are insiders, in that they define *substantial contributors, members of the family,* and other affiliated persons, such as corporations, trusts, and estates.

The IRS not too long ago provided its view of the contemporary meaning of the term *private inurement:* it "is likely to arise where the beneficial benefit represents a transfer of the organization's financial resources to an individual solely by virtue of the individual's relationship with the organization, and without regard to accomplishing exempt purposes."[38] On another occasion, the IRS was not quite so dainty: the prohibition on inurement means that an individual "cannot pocket the organization's funds."[39]

As the first of these quotes indicates, one of the ways the law ascertains the presence of private inurement is to look to the ultimate purpose of the organization. If the organization is benefiting individuals in their private capacity and not doing so in the performance of exempt functions, private inurement is likely to be present. If so, the organization may not qualify as a charitable organization or, for that matter, a nonprofit organization.

The law as to private inurement does not prohibit transactions with insiders. (These transactions, however, may well be accorded greater scrutiny by the IRS or a court.) Thus, a charitable organization can pay an insider a salary or a fee, rent, interest on loans, and the like. At the same time, the amount paid must be reasonable—that is, it must be comparable to similar payments made in similar circumstances, including those in the commercial setting.

NOTE: This aspect of private inurement is the same as the excess benefit rules, yet differs from the self-dealing rules applicable to private foundations. As to the latter, in general, there is no arm's-length standard. Even transactions with insiders that are beneficial to a private foundation are largely prohibited under the self-dealing rules.

Although it is the view of the IRS that the private inurement doctrine is absolute (that is, there is no lenience for minor indiscretions),[40] some courts have suggested that there is some form of de minimis floor underlying it.[41] Nonetheless, any such de minimis threshold—if there is one—may not be as generous as the insubstantiality test that is part of the private benefit doctrine (Q 1:11).

The sanction for violation of the private inurement doctrine is revocation or denial of the charitable organization's tax exemption. This is seen as a draconian punishment and the IRS rarely invokes the doctrine in that way. When, however, the facts are egregious, the IRS will not hesitate to revoke the exemption, sometimes retroactively.[42] With the advent of the intermediate sanctions rules, it may be expected that the IRS will withdraw fewer tax exemptions and instead impose the tax penalties for excess benefits received by disqualified persons (insiders).

TIP: Charitable organizations are not the only types of tax-exempt organizations that are subject to the private inurement doctrine. Others
include social welfare organizations (Q 1:18) and membership associations (Q 1:19); altogether, there are nine categories of tax-exempt organizations that have the private inurement doctrine engrafted onto
their exemption rules. Therefore, a development in the law where a
transaction involving one of these other types of organizations is or is
not found to be private inurement is precedent for application of the inurement rules in the charitable entity context.

Q 1:11   What is *private benefit*?

The term *private benefit*, unlike *private inurement*, is not part of the definition of a nonprofit organization (Q 1:10). Rather, private benefit is derived from the operational test, which looks to determine whether a
charitable organization is being operated primarily for exempt purposes.[43] The essence of the private benefit requirement is that the entity is not supposed to be operated for private ends, other than
insubstantially.

The law as to what constitutes private benefit is unusually vague.
There is little law on the point. There is one principal court opinion in
this area—and it was wrongly decided. The case involved the tax status
of a nonprofit school, the purpose of which was to train individuals to
be political campaign managers and consultants. The court was dismayed by the fact that all of the graduates of the school ended up working for candidates of the same political party. Although the school's
programs did not constitute political campaign activities (Q 1:16), nor
violate any other then-existing rule barring tax exemption, the court
nonetheless endeavored to deny tax-exempt status to the school. It con-
jured up two levels of private benefit. One is *primary private benefit*: the
benefits accorded the students of the school, which could not be the
basis for denial of exemption because they are also educational functions. The other is *secondary private benefit*, which is private benefit
that flows to one or more persons as the consequence of the provision
of private benefit to the primary beneficiaries. In the case, the private
benefit that was found to preclude tax exemption for the school was the
benefit to the candidates for political office who received the services
of the school's graduates.[44]

COMMENT: The concept of secondary private benefit is troublesome
because of its reach. Every nonprofit school has secondary beneficiaries: those who employ its graduates and thus acquire the benefits of
the knowledge and skills taught by the school. For example, the part-

---

ners of a law firm who bill for the services of newly graduated associates are secondary private beneficiaries of exempt law schools to a far greater economic and other extent than political candidates who hire trained campaign managers and consultants.

Generally, then, the private benefit doctrine is a fall-back, catch-all concept that is used to prevent the resources of a charitable organization from being misapplied—that is, applied for noncharitable ends. The sanction for violation of the private benefit doctrine is revocation or denial of tax-exempt status.

Q 1:12 What is the difference between *private inurement* and *private benefit*?

There are three principal differences between *private inurement* and *private benefit*:

1. The private inurement doctrine is applicable to charitable and eight other categories of tax-exempt organizations (Q 1:10). To date, the private benefit doctrine has been applied only when evaluating the tax-exempt status of public charities.

2. A private inurement transaction must involve an *insider* (Q 1:10). A private benefit transaction can be with any person. Thus, the private benefit doctrine has a much broader sweep than does the private inurement doctrine. Indeed, any transaction or arrangement that may constitute private inurement is also a form of private benefit.

3. In the view of the IRS, the private inurement doctrine is absolute, although some courts have suggested that the law may be otherwise (Q 1:10). By contrast, insubstantial private benefit does not cause any violation of the private benefit limitation.

Q 1:13 What is a *gift*?

From the standpoint of a professional fund-raiser, this obviously is a fundamental aspect of the law. This should be a simple concept—but it isn't.

Basically, however, a *gift* is a transfer of money or property that is voluntary and is motivated by something other than consideration. The law today places more emphasis on the second element than on the first one. Thus, the income tax regulations state that a transfer is not a contribution when it is made "with a reasonable expectation of financial return commensurate with the amount of the donation."[45]

COMMENT: In the context of charitable fund-raising, the words *gift*, *contribution*, and *donation* basically have the same meaning.

Instead, this type of payment is a purchase of a product or service. In another context, the IRS stated that a contribution is a "voluntary transfer of money or property that is made with no expectation of procuring financial benefit commensurate with the amount of the transfer."[46]

Q 1:14 What is a *charitable gift*?

A *charitable gift* is a *gift* (Q 1:13) made to a charitable organization (Q 1:8). As discussed, for charitable giving purposes, the concept of the charitable organization goes beyond that of entities traditionally regarded as charitable, educational, religious, and the like.

Q 1:15 Is it possible for a donor, when making a gift to a charitable organization, to cause private inurement or realize a private benefit from the gift?

Generally, neither private inurement (Q 1:10) nor private benefit (Q 1:11) arises out of a charitable gift transaction. Certainly, unwarranted private gains are not inherent in this type of transaction, even where the donor is an insider with respect to the charity. The benefits that flow from forms of conventional donor recognition, for example, are not private inurement or benefit that would adversely affect the charity's tax-exempt status. Thus, a gift transaction where a building or scholarship fund is named after a contributor does not involve an extent of private inurement or benefit that would threaten the donee's tax exemption. It either is not considered this type of private inurement or benefit at all or is regarded as so incidental as to be ignored for these purposes. The same may be said for the receipt of income interests in instances of planned gifts (Chapter 5).

Nonetheless, it is quite possible for a donor to receive a private benefit in exchange for a contribution. Although the charity's tax exemption may not be implicated, the extent of the charitable contribution deduction may be affected. This type of benefit would be a good or service and thus would probably have to be accommodated as part of the substantiation of the gift.[47] The deduction may have to be reduced by the value of the goods or services provided.[48]

OBSERVATION: Determining whether there is a private benefit in a contribution context and placing a value on it can be difficult. An illustration of

---

this is one of the hot fund-raising endeavors of the day: the charitable split-dollar insurance plan. Pursuant to this plan, a donor contributes money to a charitable organization, taking a full charitable deduction for the transfer; the donee invests the money in a life insurance policy which, upon the donor's death, provides benefits to the charity and the donor's heirs. The charity pays some or all of the policy premiums to keep the insurance in force. Questions of the day include these: Are these plans giving rise to private benefit, that is more than insubstantial, and are the non-charitable benefits provided by the insurance a "service" that must be valued in determining (and reducing) the charitable deduction? Or, is the gift an unrestricted one, with the charity free to spend the gift proceeds as it wishes? Are these split-dollar insurance plans tax shelters that may trigger imposition of the tax shelter penalties? (Q 5:35)

Q 1:16   Can a charitable organization engage in lobbying?

Yes, although there are limitations on the extent of allowable lobbying.[49] A public charity may engage in lobbying activities but only to the extent they are not substantial.[50] Private foundations are essentially constrained from any lobbying at all.[51]

A public charity that engages in substantial attempts to influence legislation is considered an *action organization*[52] and can have its tax exemption denied or revoked for that reason. In general, there is no precise formula for measuring whether lobbying activities are substantial. It is common practice, however, to evaluate the extent of lobbying in terms of a percentage of total funds expended over a period of time or of total time expended over a particular period. Nonetheless, the IRS will not commit to the use of any specific percentages in this area.

Generally, the law regards lobbying as being *direct lobbying* or *grass roots lobbying*. Direct lobbying occurs when the lobbying organization communicates, for purposes of influencing legislation, with a member of a legislative body, an individual who is on the staff of such a member, or an individual who is on the staff of a committee of a legislative body.[53] This communication can be in many forms, including personal contact, correspondence, telegram, facsimile, electronic mail, video, telephone, position paper, other publication, or formal testimony. Grass roots lobbying takes place when the lobbying organization communicates, for purposes of influencing legislation, with the general public, or a segment of it, in an effort to induce the persons contacted to communicate with a legislative body.[54]

The general prohibition on substantial lobbying by public charities is known as the *substantial part test*.[55] This test is applicable on a year-to-year basis. Expenditures of both money and time can be taken into account in determining whether there is substantial lobbying. This test does not differentiate between direct lobbying and grass roots lobbying.

The *expenditure test* is an electable alternative to the substantial part test. This scheme allows public charities to ascertain how much lobbying is allowable by use of precise percentages of total expenditures of money.[56] The test permits a public charity to expend, for lobbying, 20 percent of its first $500,000 of total expenditures, 15 percent of the next $500,000, 10 percent of the next $500,000, and 5 percent of the remaining expenditures. There is an annual ceiling of $1 million for lobbying outlays. Grass roots lobbying may not exceed 25 percent of total allowable lobbying. These limitations are known as the *direct lobbying allowable amount* and the *grass roots lobbying allowable amount*. The percentages are applicable to an organization's expenditures of funds over its most recent four years.

Activities that are *educational* in nature[57] usually are not considered lobbying, nor is the mere monitoring and reporting on the status of legislation. Also, a public charity is not considered to be engaged in impermissible lobbying when it presents testimony as the result of an invitation from a legislative body or a committee of that body.[58]

The following categories of activities are excepted from the scope of lobbying for purposes of the expenditure test:

1. Making available the results of nonpartisan analysis, study, or research.
2. Providing technical advice or assistance to a governmental body or legislative committee in response to a written request by the body or committee.
3. Appearing before, or communicating with, any legislative body with respect to a possible decision by that body that might affect the existence of the organization, its powers and duties, its tax-exempt status, or the deduction for contributions to it. This is known as the *self-defense exception*.
4. Effecting communications between the organization and its members with respect to legislation that is of direct mutual interest.
5. Communicating in a routine manner with government officials or employees.[59]

If a public charity subject to the substantial part test engages in a substantial amount of legislative activities in a year, it can have its tax exemption revoked. The organization can also be liable for a 5 percent excise tax on the lobbying expenditures.[60] A tax in this amount may also be imposed on the managers of the organization, who are held responsible for knowing that the expenditures would likely result in loss of the organization's tax-exempt status.

If a charitable organization under the expenditure test exceeds the direct lobbying allowable amount or the grass roots lobbying allowable amount, it is subject to a 25 percent excise tax on the excessive portion of the outlay.[61] If an organization exceeds either lobbying expenditure limitation by 150 percent or more, it can have its tax exemption revoked.[62]

Some charitable organizations that undertake a considerable amount of lobbying do so by means of related social welfare organizations, rather than engage in the legislative activities directly (Q 1:18).

Q 1:17   Can a charitable organization engage in political campaign activities?

No. One of the fundamental requirements for tax exemption as a public charity is that the entity is not allowed to participate in or intervene in any political campaign on behalf of or in opposition to any candidate for a public office.[63] A charitable organization that engages in political campaign activities is considered an *action organization*.[64] Unlike the constraint on legislative activities, which tolerates insubstantial lobbying (Q 1:16), the prohibition on electioneering is absolute. There is another absolute limitation in this regard applicable to private foundations.[65]

The key words in this context are *participation* and *intervention*. These words mean essentially the same thing: an involvement in some way in a political campaign for public office. These types of activities include the solicitation or making of political campaign contributions, the use of resources of an organization to benefit or thwart the candidacy of an individual in a political campaign, the volunteering of services for or against a candidate for a public office, and the publication or distribution of literature in support of or in opposition to a candidate for public office. The IRS and the courts traditionally broadly define these terms.

NOTE: In one instance, these rules were applied in the setting of direct mail fund-raising. An organization sent solicitation letters to its supporters, suggesting that some of the resulting contributions would be used to support the campaigns of candidates for Congress whose views on issues were those of the organization. During the resulting examination, the IRS was told by the organization that this was merely "puffery"—that the organization did not actually intend to make political contributions with the money but was merely trying to "energize" its donor base. The IRS was not persuaded of that view, however, and held that the mere mention of campaign contributions in the fund-raising letters was participation or intervention in the political campaigns.[66]

A *candidate for public office* is "an individual who offers himself, or is proposed by others, as a contestant for an elective public office, whether such office be national, state, or local."[67] Certainly an individual becomes a candidate for a public office as of the date he or she announces his or her candidacy for that office. The IRS refuses to commit itself to any specific rule in this regard, leaving the matter to a facts-and-circumstances test; it has been known to assert the candidacy of an individual well before any official announcement. Mere speculation in the media that an individual may campaign for an office can be the basis of an IRS insistence that the individual has become a candidate.

The tax law is silent as to when there is commencement of a political *campaign*.[68] Again, it is the practice of the IRS to utilize a facts-and-circumstances test. The IRS has been known to assert the launching of a campaign for public office far in advance of a formal announcement of candidacy. A *public office* basically is a policy-making position in the executive, legislative, or judicial branch of a government; it means more than simply public employment.[69]

OBSERVATION: This aspect of the tax law currently is embroiled in controversy, largely because of the involvement of churches in political campaigns, including the presidential campaigns in 1992 and 1996. The IRS is believed to be studying in excess of 50 cases of churches in politics, such as candidates speaking during church services and endorsements from pulpits. This matter is exacerbated by the view of some that the IRS is biased in this regard, acting against only religious organizations on the political right and ignoring politicking by religious entities on the left; the staff of the Joint Committee on Taxation is investigating these charges. A church recently had its tax exemption revoked for engaging in political campaign activity; it failed to convince the court that there was IRS bias in this context.[70]

A public charity's participation in a political campaign is a ground for denial or revocation of tax-exempt status. Also, it is the basis for assessment of an initial 10 percent excise tax on the organization and a $2^1/_2$ percent tax on each of the organization's managers, and additional taxes of 100 percent on the organization and 50 percent on its managers.[71]

CAUTION: Grass roots lobbying can also amount to political campaign activity; these activities are said to have a *dual character*. This duality can arise where the timing of the lobbying is such that it is coincident with an imminent election and the positions taken in the lobbying effort further the candidacy of one or more candidates for public office.[72]

Q 1:18   What is a *social welfare* organization?

Federal tax law is skimpy when it comes to defining the term *social welfare organization*. The Internal Revenue Code, in providing for tax exemption for these entities, blandly references them as "[c]ivic leagues or organizations not organized for profit but operated exclusively for the promotion of social welfare."[73] These basic criteria are embellished somewhat by the tax regulations, which state that the promotion of social welfare does not include activities that primarily constitute "carrying on a business with the general public in a manner similar to organizations which are operated for profit."[74] These regulations also contain a prohibition on political campaign activity[75] and state that an organization is not operated primarily for the promotion of social welfare "if its primary activity is operating a social club for the benefit, pleasure, or recreation of its members."[76]

In this context, *social welfare* is commensurate with the "common good and general welfare" and "civic betterments and social improvements."[77] For an entity to qualify as an exempt social welfare organization, its activities must be those that will benefit a community as a whole, rather than benefit merely the organization's membership or another select group of individuals or organizations.

There are many types of social welfare organizations, including certain kinds of health care and advocacy entities.[78] From a fund-raising standpoint, an important aspect of this subject is that social welfare organizations may engage in attempts to influence legislation without adversely affecting their tax-exempt status. That is, other than the general requirement that the lobbying be in furtherance of the organization's exempt purposes, there is no limitation on the amount of lobbying that the organization may do. The fund-raiser, therefore, may be involved in one or more situations where there is a public charity with an affiliated social welfare organization as a lobbying arm of the charity. Or, the arrangement may be reversed: the "parent" entity is a social welfare organization and there is a related charitable or educational foundation (Q 1:19).

Q 1:19   What is a *business league*?

The federal tax law uses the term *business league* to describe what is known today as a trade, business, or professional association. The purpose of these entities is to improve business conditions for their members, although many associations also have programs that benefit the public. Some professional associations are termed *societies* (Q 1:1).

A business league, assuming it meets all of the tax law requirements, is a tax-exempt organization.[79] These organizations usually have a membership; they are what the tax regulations term an *association of persons*. Also, the persons who are associated must have some *common business interest.*[80]

The fund-raiser may be involved with one or more of these types of associations. Generally, contributions to these entities are not tax deductible, so a fund-raising program directly for them is not practical. Nonetheless, may associations operate related charitable organizations, usually termed *foundations*. These organizations are often used for fund-raising purposes.

COMMENT: Some foundations have fund-raising as their only function; the funds are granted to the association for use in charitable, educational, and like programs. Other foundations operate programs of this nature directly. Other foundations function as a blend of these two approaches.

NOTE: Despite use of the term *foundation*, these organizations are not private foundations (or at least they should not be). They are either publicly supported charities (Q 2:7, Q 2:8) or supporting organizations (Q 2:15, Q 2:22).

Q 1:20   What is a *C corporation*?

The term *C corporation,* sometimes referred to as a *regular corporation*, is wholly a tax law concept (that is, it is not a type of corporation in a non-tax law setting). It is a corporation that is recognized as a separate taxable[81] entity for federal tax purposes. These corporations are so named because they are subject to the body of law found in Subtitle A (relating to income taxes), Chapter 1, Subchapter C, of the Internal Revenue Code.[82]

Fundamentally, a C corporation is, with respect to a tax year, a corporation that is not an S corporation (Q 1:21) for that year.[83]

Q 1:21   What is an *S corporation*?

The term *S corporation* is also wholly a tax law concept. It means a corporation (sometimes termed *small business corporation*) that is subject to the body of law found in Subtitle A (relating to income taxes), Chapter 1, Subchapter S, of the Internal Revenue Code.[84] It is this reference in this subchapter that has given rise to this term. A corporation, to be an S corporation, must elect that status;[85] this election is a fundamental requirement for qualification as an S corporation.[86]

An S corporation may not have more than 75 shareholders, may not have a nonresident alien as a shareholder, and may not have more than one class of stock.[87] Traditionally, the shareholders of an S corporation were confined to individuals (as well as estates and certain trusts). Since 1998, however, a tax-exempt charitable organization (and a qualified pension, profit-sharing, or like plan) may be a shareholder in an S corporation.[88]

This type of corporation is a *pass-through entity*, which means that it is not taxable on its net income. Instead, items of income, deductions, and credits are attributed to the shareholders for tax purposes.[89]

Q 1:22   Can a charitable organization have a tax-exempt subsidiary?

Absolutely; this practice is common. There are several instances of this.

One of the prevalent examples of the use by a charitable organization of a tax-exempt subsidiary arises in the fund-raising context: the *supporting organization*. This is a form of public charity that derives that classification from the relationship—usually a governance interlock—it has with one or more other types of public charities (Q 2:12–2:14). The fundamental function of a supporting organization is to support or benefit one or more supported organizations (Q 2:15). There are many ways to provide the requisite support; a contemporary way is by the conduct of programs, where these operations inherently benefit the supported organization(s). More traditionally, supporting organizations are fund-raising vehicles for public charities, often colleges, universities, and hospitals; they are sometime referred to as *foundations*. In these instances, the fund-raising and development functions are those of the foundation. Also, the foundation may be used, as its sole function or one of several, to house the endowment fund that is held for the benefit of the supported organization.

Another type of tax-exempt subsidiary is the *social welfare organization* (Q 1:18). While generally a social welfare organization operates to promote the social welfare of a community, a social welfare organization also includes advocacy entities. Thus, there are no tax law restrictions on the ability of social welfare organizations to engage in lobbying. Consequently, a public charity that wishes to engage in more lobbying than the tax laws allow (Q 1:16) may find that its only alternative is to utilize a social welfare organization subsidiary for the conduct of the legislative activities.[90]

A third type of tax-exempt subsidiary is the *political organization*.[91] Generally, a public charity cannot have a related political organization, such as a political action committee (PAC), because the functions of a PAC are attributed to the affiliated public charity, probably causing the charity to pay the excise tax on political expenditures and/or forfeit its tax exemption (1:17). This use of a PAC is permissible, however, where the political activities engaged in by the committee are other than political campaign activities. These activities must be exempt functions of political organizations but not the type of political campaign activities that public charities are forbidden to engage in, such as efforts to defeat the nomination by a president of an individual to become a member of the Supreme Court.[92] This use of a PAC would also preclude the charity from having to pay the political organization tax on expenditures associated with that political activity.[93]

Another type of tax-exempt subsidiary is the *title-holding company*.[94] Just about any type of tax-exempt organization is permitted to utilize an affiliated title-holding entity. The function of a title-holding company is a passive one: hold title to property, collect any rent or other income, and periodically remit any net amount to the parent. Management considerations may dictate the titling of property in a separate entity; sometimes the title-holding entity is used in an effort to limit the liability of the parent organization.

> **TIP:** When the parent entity is a public charity and a title-holding company is being considered, thought should also be given to using a supporting organization instead. Supporting organizations offer more flexibility in terms of the scope of their activities than title-holding companies and can often do precisely what the title-holding entity would do. Also, supporting organizations can receive deductible gifts and grants.

Still another tax-exempt subsidiary is the employee benefit fund.[95] The funds underlying forms of pension, retirement, and other types of employee benefit funds are tax-exempt organizations. They are not often regarded as subsidiaries but in fact that is what they are: separate yet controlled exempt entities.

Q 1:23   Can a charitable organization have a for-profit subsidiary?

Yes. For the most part, a charitable organization establishes a for-profit subsidiary because of the existence, or planned existence, of an unrelated business, or set of unrelated businesses, that is too extensive to be conducted in the parent entity without jeopardizing the parent's tax-exempt status.[96] Some charitable organizations incubate unrelated businesses within themselves and then transfer them (*spin them off*) to a for-profit subsidiary. Others create a subsidiary at the outset.

There is no limit in the law as to the type of business activity that can be conducted in a for-profit subsidiary; the charitable organization can devise any type of business activity it wants as a means to generate revenue (which, as discussed below, is likely to be taxed). Also, there is no limit in the law as to the size of subsidiaries, either absolutely or in relation to the parent, or the number of for-profit subsidiaries a charitable organization may have.

NOTE: To be tax-exempt, the charitable parent entity must function primarily in furtherance of charitable ends (Q 1:9). The structure and operation of one or more for-profit subsidiaries must be such that it does not cause the charitable organization to deviate from that end. This means that the subsidiary must be a legitimate business entity (not a sham) and that the exempt parent not be involved in the day-to-day management of the subsidiary. If these legal formalities are not attended to, the IRS may collapse the entities for tax purposes, which could adversely impact the charity's tax-exempt status.

In its broadest sense, the term *fund-raising* includes the generation of monies by means of an unrelated business in a for-profit subsidiary (Q 1:5). In this connection, some tax-exempt organizations place an unrelated business in a for-profit subsidiary even where the tax laws do not require it (that is, where the business is relatively small). This is done for reasons of *politics* and *perception*, particularly where the business is competitive with commercial businesses in the community. As an illustration, a college began using its printing facilities, devoted primarily to its educational activities, for occasional jobs for outside purchasers of the service. This unrelated business grew; as it did, some of the commercial printers in the community complained about the competition. To appease these critics, the college transferred its commercial printing operation to a wholly owned for-profit subsidiary. The competition continued, of course, but the commercial printers were mollified once it came from a for-profit entity.

CAUTION: *Competition* can be synonymous with controversy and sensitivity, particularly among small businesses. When a charitable organization is in competition with a commercial business, the business often views the competition as being *unfair*, in that the charitable organization may not be paying tax on the business's net income; with taxes not a cost of doing business, the charitable entity is (at

---

least in theory) able to underprice the commercial business. Despite plaintiffs' attempts, the courts have held that for-profit businesses do not have standing to challenge the tax-exempt status of their non-profit competitors.[97] Nonetheless, small businesses are making some headway in this regard in Congress, which is pressuring the Treasury Department and the IRS to toughen their regulatory policies concerning competitive, commercial practices by charitable and other exempt organizations. The hot issues of the day are travel tours[98] and fitness centers.[99]

Another use of a for-profit subsidiary by a charitable organization is as a partner in a partnership, in lieu of the charity's direct participation (Q 1:24). The charitable parent may fear the potential of liability or that participation in the partnership (usually as a general partner) might adversely affect the parent's tax-exempt status.

TIP: This is another aspect of the fact that it is crucial that the bona fides of the subsidiary be adhered to (see above). Use of a subsidiary in a partnership works only when the legal form of the subsidiary is respected. In one instance, the IRS (without explanation) ignored a tax-exempt organization's use of a for-profit subsidiary as the general partner in a partnership and applied the law as though the exempt organization was directly involved in the partnership.[100]

One of the controversial aspects of the use of a taxable subsidiary by an exempt organization is the matter of the taxation of the revenue flowing out of the subsidiary to the parent. Generally, income such as dividends, interest, rent, annuities, and royalties is not taxable when received by a tax-exempt organization.[101] Were it not for a special rule, an exempt organization could place unrelated business activities in a subsidiary and cause the resulting net income to flow to it in one or more of the tax-sheltered forms. To avoid this gambit, however, the law causes all revenue from a controlled subsidiary (other than dividends) to be taxed as unrelated business income.[102]

NOTE: These rules were significantly revised in 1997 and generally apply to payments received in tax years beginning after August 5 of that year. The law revisions include alteration of the control test and addition of constructive ownership rules.[103]

For this purpose, a for-profit subsidiary is considered *controlled* by a tax-exempt organization if the parent owns more than 50 percent of the interests (such as stock in the case of a corporation) in the subsidiary.[104] Preexisting constructive ownership rules[105] also apply.[106] The revenue from the controlled subsidiary must be treated as unrelated business income to the extent the payment reduces the net unrelated income of the controlled entity or increases any net unrelated loss of the controlled entity.[107] The controlling organization may deduct expenses that are directly connected with amounts that are treated as unrelated business income under this rule.[108]

Another matter of some controversy concerns termination of a for-profit subsidiary and liquidation of its assets into the tax-exempt parent. This can happen if the exempt organization becomes much larger in scope than was the case when the subsidiary was established, so that the activities of the subsidiary can be absorbed into the exempt parent without endangering the parent's tax exemption; those activities become unrelated business within the tax-exempt parent organization. Liquidation can also seem prudent if the business in the subsidiary does not materialize and management decides to abandon the project. The tax issue in this regard concerns any appreciation in value in capital assets in the subsidiary; the event of the liquidation is treated as if the assets were sold by the subsidiary to the parent, potentially triggering capital gains taxes.

The tax consequences of this type of liquidation produce results that may seem counterintuitive. If the assets coming out of the subsidiary continue to be used by the parent in an unrelated business, there is no capital gain taxation. If the assets are used by the parent in a related business, the capital gains tax must be paid. The capital gains tax must also be paid if the assets are initially used in an unrelated business but subsequently converted to related use; the tax is due for the year of the conversion.[109]

NOTE: If there is a liquidation of a for-profit entity into a tax-exempt organization, and the relationship is *not* that of parent and subsidiary, the tax results are the same. Worse, if a for-profit entity is simply *converted* into a nonprofit entity that qualifies for tax exemption, the conversion is treated as a liquidation (asset sale), with the potentiality for tax.[110]

Q 1:24   Can a charitable organization be a partner in a partnership?

Yes. As a general rule, a charitable organization can be either a general partner or a limited partner in a partnership. Usually, liability for the consequences of a partnership's operations rests with the general partner or general partners. Moreover, a general partner is liable for satisfaction of the ongoing obligations of the partnership and can be called upon to make additional contributions of capital to it. A limited partner is a person whose exposure to liability for the functions of the partnership is confined to the amount of that person's contribution to (investment in) the partnership.[111]

Every partnership must have at least one general partner. A partnership with only general partners is a *general partnership*. A partnership with both general and limited partners is a *limited partnership*. Both types of partnerships are usually manifested by a partnership agreement.

As a general proposition, the partnership is used as a business enterprise because the parties bring unique resources to the relationship, and they want to blend those resources for the purpose of beginning and conducting a business. Another reason for the partnership form—particularly the limited partnership—is to attract financing (usually from the limited partners) for one or more projects. In some instances, the partnership vehicle is favored because it is not taxed—they are *pass-through entities*. This means that the partnership's income, deductions, and credits are passed along to the partners.[112]

The principal tax law issues are, however, whether involvement in the partnership jeopardizes the charitable organization's tax-exempt status and/or causes it to receive unrelated business income. The most critical aspect of this subject is the impact of involvement in a limited partnership by a charitable organization as a general partner on the charity's exempt status. For years, the IRS has had great concerns on this point. Indeed, it was not until 1998 that the IRS formally stated that a charitable organization may form and participate in a partnership and be or remain tax-exempt.[113]

NOTE: Nonetheless, the IRS has issued dozens of private letter rulings, technical advice memoranda, and general counsel memoranda stating that a public charity's involvement in a limited partnership as a or the general partner will not endanger its exempt status.[114] Indeed, on one occasion, the IRS ruled that the exempt status of a charitable organization should not be revoked because of its participation as a general partner in seven limited partnerships.[115] Moreover, except in the early years when it was attempting to maintain a hard-line stance, the IRS has *never* issued a published private determination that involvement in a limited partnership would cause loss or denial of a charity's exempt status.

CAUTION: As to this last observation, there have been ruling requests in which the facts were altered to gain the IRS's approval in this regard. There also have been ruling requests involving charities in limited partnerships that have been withdrawn in the face of an adverse ruling.

The concern of the IRS and some courts is that substantial economic benefits are being provided to the for-profit participants in a limited partnership (usually the limited partners as investors) involving a charitable organization as the or a general partner. Following considerable litigation in this area,[116] the IRS's position has evolved into a three-part test.

Under this test, the IRS first looks to determine whether the charitable organization/general partner is advancing a charitable purpose by means of participation in the partnership. If involvement in the partnership is serving a charitable purpose, the IRS applies the balance of the test. Should the partnership fail to adhere to that charitability standard, however, the charitable organization/general partner will be deprived of or be denied tax-exempt status.

TIP: The fund-raising professional or anyone else involving a charitable organization in a partnership as general partner should remember a first principle: to be exempt, the charity must adhere to the *operational test*, which is an evaluation of the operations of the organization.[117] In general, for tax purposes, the activities of a partnership are considered to be the activities of the partners.[118] This *aggregate approach* is applied for purposes of the operational test.[119]

The rest of this test is designed to ascertain whether the charity's role as general partner inhibits the advancement of its charitable purposes. The IRS looks to means by which the organization may, under the particular facts and circumstances, be insulated from the day-to-day responsibilities as general partner and whether the limited partners are receiving an undue economic benefit from the partnership. It is the view of the IRS and some courts that there is an inherent tension between the ability of a charitable organization to function primarily in furtherance of its exempt functions (Q 1:9) and the obligation of a general partner to operate the partnership for the benefit of the limited partners.

NOTE: The original position of the IRS was that participation as a general partner in a limited partnership by a public charity would cost the charity its tax exemption.[120] It is not clear as to why the IRS formulated

---

that stance in the first instance, inasmuch as it has long been understood that public charities can be general partners in partnerships—this fact is stated in the Internal Revenue Code in two places. One provision speaks of "a partnership of which an [exempt] organization is a member."[121] Another section references "a partnership which has both a tax-exempt entity and a person who is not a tax-exempt entity as partners."[122] These pronouncements from Congress would be wholly superfluous in the case of public charities if their mere participation as a general partner in a limited partnership would deprive them of their exempt status.

Sometimes a charitable organization attempts to sidestep these concerns by creating a for-profit subsidiary, which then becomes a or the general partner in a limited partnership as a surrogate for the charity (Q 1:23).

The other principal tax law aspect of this matter is the potential for activation of the unrelated business income rules (Chapter 6) when an unrelated business is conducted in a partnership of which a charitable organization is a member. The rule applied in this context is a *look-through rule*: if a business regularly carried on by a partnership, of which a tax-exempt organization is a member, is an unrelated business with respect to the exempt organization, in computing its unrelated business taxable income the exempt organization must include its share (whether or not actually distributed) of the gross income of the partnership from the unrelated business.[123] This rule applies irrespective of whether the tax-exempt organization is participating as a general or limited partner.[124]

From the fund-raising standpoint, the rules as to involvement of a charity in a partnership can arise in one of two fundamental ways. One, as noted, is that the charitable organization creates or otherwise becomes involved in the partnership as a means to generate revenue. The other way is for the charity to receive an interest in a partnership as a gift, either from a partner or the partnership itself (Q 4:13).

In an instance of a contribution of a partnership interest, the fund-raiser or other representative of the putative donee charity should be cautious. The charity should understand exactly what involvement in the partnership entails by reviewing the partnership agreement, any other agreement between the partners, and the partnership's financial statements and annual information returns. The five fundamental questions to ask are:

1. Will participation as a partner in the partnership endanger the charity's tax-exempt status?

2. Will participation in the partnership result in unrelated business income?

> **TIP:** Remember, the charitable organization in a partnership conducting an unrelated business can have unrelated business income in a year even though there is no cash distribution from the partnership. This means, of course, that the unrelated business income tax must be paid out of other resources of the charity.

3. Is the charitable organization liable for any calls for additional capital?
4. What are the restrictions on transferability of the partnership interest and what is the market (if any) for selling that interest?
5. What is the motive of the donor in making this gift? (Is the donor trying to unload an unwarranted liability? Remember the gifts of burned-out tax shelters in the 1980s.)

> **TIP 1:** This is a good time to inject a basic point that is sometimes forgotten: A charitable organization need not accept a gift of property just because it is offered.

> **TIP 2:** These concerns can be worse when the entity involved is a charitable remainder trust, rather than a charitable organization. When a charitable remainder trust receives unrelated business taxable income, directly or by means of a partnership, it automatically forfeits its tax-exempt status for the year involved (Q 5:9, Q 5:10).

Q 1:25   Can a charitable organizations be a member of a joint venture?

Yes. However, the principal tax law issues are—just as in the case of involvement in partnerships (Q 1:24)—whether being in the joint venture jeopardizes the charity's tax-exempt status and/or causes it to receive unrelated business income.[125]

The basic reason a charitable organization wants to participate in a joint venture is to carry out a single project or program, using the efforts, money, and/or expertise of one or more other parties. It is a resource-gathering, resource-sharing operation. Often, the other party or parties are for-profit organizations.

The basic rule is that a charitable organization may enter into a joint venture with a for-profit entity (or other person), without adversely affecting the charity's tax-exempt status, as long as doing so furthers exempt purposes and there are no requirements in the joint venture agreement that prevent it from acting primarily to advance those purposes (Q 1:9). A joint venture usually does not present the private inurement or private benefit problems that are associated with participation by charitable organizations in partnerships, because there are no limited partners receiving economic benefits (Q 1:24). (A joint venture is essentially akin to a general partnership (*id.*).) By contrast, an involvement in a joint venture by a charitable organization can lead to loss or denial of tax exemption if the primary purpose of the organization is participation in the venture and if the function of the venture is unrelated to the charitable purposes of the organization.

A charitable organization may enter into a joint venture with another charitable organization in furtherance of the exempt purposes of both of them.

A charitable organization in a joint venture potentially has the same exposure to unrelated business income taxation as a result that is the case if it was a member of a formal partnership (Q 1:24). That is, the look-through rule applies.

A partnership is a form of joint venture. A venture arrangement has been defined as an association of two or more persons with intent to carry out a single business venture for joint profit, for which purpose they combine their efforts, property, money, skill, and knowledge, but they do so without creating a formal entity, namely, a partnership, trust, or corporation.[126] The law can regard a relationship between two or more persons as a joint venture for tax purposes, even though the parties insist that the arrangement is something else (such as parties to a lease or management agreement). This can have significant consequences in the fund-raising context.

The federal tax law is inconsistent in stating the criteria for ascertaining whether a joint venture exists as a matter of law. According to the Supreme Court, "[w]hen the existence of an alleged partnership arrangement is challenged by outsiders, the question arises whether the partners really and truly intended to join together for the purpose of carrying on business and sharing in the profits or losses or both."[127] The Court added that the parties' "intention is a question of fact, to be determined from testimony disclosed by their agreement considered as a whole, and by their conduct in execution of its provisions."[128] In one instance, a court examined state law and concluded that the most important element in determining whether a landlord-tenant relationship or joint venture agreement exists is the intention of the parties. This court also held that the burden of proving the existence of a joint venture is on the party who claims that that type of relationship exists (such as the IRS).[129]

Yet, another court declared that "it is well settled that neither local law nor the expressed intent of the parties is conclusive as to the existence or nonexistence of a partnership or joint venture for federal tax purposes."[130] This court wrote that this is the test to follow: "whether, considering all the facts—the agreement, the conduct of the parties in execution of its provisions, their statements, the testimony of disinterested persons, the relationship of the parties, their respective abilities and capital contributions, the actual control of income and the purposes for which it is used, and any other facts throwing light on their true intent—the parties in good faith and acting with a business purpose intended to join together in the present conduct of the enterprise."[131]

This latter court added that the "realities of the taxpayer's economic interest rather than the niceties of the conveyancer's art should determine the power to tax."[132] The court continued: "Among the critical elements involved in this determination are the existence of controls over the venture and a risk of loss in the taxpayer."[133] Finally, the court said that it is not bound by the "nomenclature used by the parties," so that a document titled, for example, a lease, may in law be a partnership agreement.[134]

The professional fund-raiser should be cautious on this point in two contexts. One involves the unrelated business income tax (Chapter 6), particularly where the charitable organization is asserting that certain income is not taxable because of a statutory exception, such as the one for royalty income.[135] The IRS's general view in this regard is that, to not be taxable, the income must be passive in nature or otherwise akin to investment income.[136] This means that if the charitable organization has some involvement, other than incidentally, in the activity, such as the rendering of services, the IRS will take the position that the organization is *actively* (rather than passively) involved in the income-producing aspects of the activity and hold that the exception for the income is not available.[137] In some of these instances, the IRS will assert that the charity is actively participating in a joint venture. Two examples of this in the fund-raising setting are mailing list rental arrangements[138] and affinity card programs.[139]

The other area of concern pertains to the tax exemption of the charitable organization. For example, a charity may have a contract with an outside fund-raising firm. If the firm's fees are dependent on or otherwise correlated with the flow and amount of contributions, or similar feature in the relationship, the IRS may contend that the fund-raising firm has an undue amount of control over the charity and that the parties are in fact operating a fund-raising joint venture. In one instance, the IRS argued in court—ultimately unsuccessfully—that a fund-raising company was a disqualified person with respect to a charity, because of a significant extent of control over its affairs, and that the amount of fees paid by the charity to the company and the company's manipulation of the charity's assets (chiefly its donor list) amounted to private inurement (Q 1:10).[140]

CAUTION: This type of fund-raising joint venture—intended or imposed—can also have unfortunate consequences in connection with the intermediate sanctions rules.

As will be discussed (Q 1:26), a joint venture may be structured by use of a limited liability company.

Q 1:26   When can a charitable organization utilize a limited liability company?

Basically, there are two instances in which a charitable organization can utilize a limited liability company.

A *limited liability company* is a legal entity, recently recognized under state law. While not a corporation, the limited liability company has the corporate attribute of limitation against personal liability. These companies are not taxable, being treated as partnerships for tax purposes (Q 1:24).

One of the instances where a charitable organization can use a limited liability company (LLC) is as a joint venture vehicle. As discussed, traditionally, a charitable organization becomes involved in a joint venture when it wants to advance a particular program or project (Q 1:25). Yet, in the health care field (and perhaps in other fields to come), there are instances where the institution, such as a hospital, places itself, in its entirety, into a joint venture; this is known as the *whole-hospital joint venture*. In a typical arrangement of this nature, a hospital and a for-profit corporation form an LLC, with the hospital contributing all of its assets to the venture. Depending on various elements of the venture, including the composition of the board of directors of the LLC and the features of an agreement between the LLC and a management company, the hospital may jeopardize its tax-exempt status.[141] Essentially, the matter comes down to whether, as a consequence of participation in the joint venture, the institution has lost control, and the for-profit party has gained control, over the charitable assets.

Another instance in which a charitable organization can utilize an LLC is to house a separate function. Although most LLCs are employed to conduct for-profit enterprises, they can be used to operate charitable and other tax-exempt functions. In this way, the LLC is used instead of a tax-exempt organization. (As noted, LLCs are not taxed.) In one instance, an exempt health care provider partnered with two public hospitals in a foreign country to establish and operate a hospital in that country; the hospital was structured as an LLC.[142] In these cases, any net income generated by the operations of the LLC is not taxable to the exempt organization venturer(s) because it is related business income which retains that character by virtue of the look-through rule (Q 1:24).

NOTE: One of the issues before the IRS these days is whether an LLC can qualify as a tax-exempt organization, charitable or otherwise. While the IRS has not ruled on the point, it came close to doing so in the above instance, essentially finding that LLC to be an exempt health care provider.

Q 1:27   What is the *step transaction* doctrine and how does it apply in the context of charitable giving?

The *step transaction* doctrine has been developed by the courts to prevent form from prevailing over substance in tax matters. The purpose of the doctrine, then, is to bar taxpayers from escaping tax liability by disguising the true nature of transactions with mere formalisms.

Under this doctrine, interrelated yet formally distinct steps in an integrated transaction may not be considered separately or independently of the overall transaction. As the Supreme Court stated, "[a] given result at the end of a straight path is not made a different result because reached by following a devious path."[143] On another occasion, the Court wrote that the doctrine is necessary because to allow sham transactions to escape tax liability would "exalt artifice above reality."[144] The Court also observed that the doctrine is applied to facilitate a "commonsense understanding of the economic substance of the transaction" by "examining the effect of the transaction as a whole."[145]

The courts have developed three tests to determine whether transactions should be "stepped" together and considered not as isolated incidents but as components in an overall plan.

The narrowest and most seldom applied test is the *binding commitment* test. This approach provides that a transaction will be stepped together if, at the first step of the transaction, a binding commitment was entered into to undertake later steps.[146] This test is of limited applicability because it appears to have been formulated to address a transaction that spanned several tax years.

The *interdependence* test focuses on whether the steps in the transaction are so interdependent that the "legal relations created by one transaction would have been fruitless without a completion of the series."[147] This test concentrates on the relationship between all of the steps. In applying this test, courts must look at whether each individual step had some "independent significance or whether they had meaning only as part of the larger transaction."[148]

The *end result* test amalgamates purportedly separate transactions when it appears they actually were prearranged parts of a "single transaction intended from the outset to be taken for the purpose of reaching the ultimate result."[149] This test is based on the initial intent of the parties. What is more, even though the initial arrangement between the parties need not be legally binding, there must be some "showing of an informal agreement or understanding."[150]

The step transaction doctrine applies in the charitable giving setting, primarily in the context of gifts of highly appreciated capital gain property. Generally, a gift of property of that nature to a public charity (Q 2:1) is deductible on the basis of the fair market value of the property (Q 4:5) and the capital gain in the property is not taxed. If, however, the donee was obligated to sell the gift property to a purchaser that was prearranged by the donor, the donor will have to recognize, for tax purposes, the capital gain element.[151] The charity cannot simply be used as the medium by which capital gain taxation is avoided, even though there otherwise is a bona fide gift (Q 1:13).

COMMENT: The key to avoiding this tax-adverse (to the donor) outcome is to be certain that the charity is not legally bound at the time of the gift to sell the property to a prospective purchaser. As one court noted, a "gift of appreciated property does not result in income to the donor so long as he gives the property away absolutely and parts with title thereto before the property gives rise to income by way of a sale."[152]

Of course, not every carefully planned transaction—in the charitable gift setting or otherwise—triggers the step transaction doctrine. In one instance, the IRS argued that a series of gifts of closely held stock to a university over a 10-year period was designed to mask taxable constructive dividends as nontaxable stock redemption (by the university) proceeds. The IRS wanted the court to "infer from the systematic nature of the gift-redemption cycle" that the donor and donee had "reached a mutually beneficial understanding."[153] But the court declined to find any informal agreement between the parties; it also refused to base tax liability on a "fictional" basis created by the IRS. This was the case even though the donor was the majority shareholder of the corporation, so that his vote alone was sufficient to ensure redemption of the university's shares. The court wrote that "foresight and planning do not transform a non-taxable event into one that is taxable."[154]

NOTE: The step transaction doctrine is being invoked as one of the principles of law used to defeat gift deductibility in the context of charitable split-interest insurance plans (Q 5:35).

Q 1:28   How much law should a professional fund-raiser know?

This question is inherently impossible to answer. On the assumption that knowledge is beneficial, an understanding of all law by a professional fund-raiser (or anyone else) would be the ideal. But that, too, is impossible; no one, not even a lawyer, can know all of the law. In any event, the function of a professional fund-raiser is to solicit and generate gifts, not to substitute for a lawyer. Indeed, in the optimum circumstances, the professional fund-raiser works closely with and complements the services of the lawyer (Q 1:29).

Thus, despite the inability to definitively answer this question, the attempt to do so must rest on the realization that there is a great amount of federal and state law that is directly applicable to the professional fund-raiser and the charitable organizations that he or she serves. It would not, therefore, be appropriate for the fund-raiser to be completely ignorant of this law (although some strive mightily to this end). Rather, the professional fund-raiser should have a grasp on the fundamentals of pertinent law and a sense of when to seek professional legal advice.

For example, if the professional fund-raiser is president of a foundation that is the development vehicle for a charitable organization, the fund-raiser should at least know the public charity status of the foundation (Chapter 2), the basics of the charitable giving rules (Chapter 4), and some understanding of the applicable state charitable solicitation acts (Chapter 9) and the federal tax law substantiation rules.

Likewise, if the professional fund-raiser is developing planned gifts (Chapter 5), he or she certainly needs to know the basics of the law as to each of the planned gift vehicles and the principal factors to take into consideration in deciding which vehicle or vehicles to use.

The professional fund-raiser should not (unless also a lawyer) prepare legal documents, such as trust agreements and wills, for their execution. The potential liability is too great and there is this matter of the unauthorized practice of law.

One of the difficulties here is that often the professional fund-raiser knows far more about elements of the law in his or her field (such as that concerning the appraisal rules (Q 4:39), the gift substantiation rules (Q 4:37), and/or planned giving (Chapter 5)) than the lawyer representing a potential donor. A task then befalling the fund-raiser is to—

diplomatically (so as not to induce the lawyer to thwart the gift)—communicate some of this knowledge to the lawyer. This can be done by means of documents, such as generic descriptive material and prototype trust forms. That is not practicing law, yet the receipt of material like this can assist the lawyer in avoiding being embarrassed in front of his or her client.

NOTE: A not uncommon story: A donor of valuable property to a charity is advised by her lawyer that she can base her charitable deduction on an appraisal of the property that is one year old. A fund-raising professional working for the charity learns of this and gently informs the lawyer that the appraisal cannot be more than 60 days of age.[155] Were it not for the intervention of the fund-raiser, the donor would not have been entitled to any charitable deduction for her gift.[156]

Perhaps the ultimate answer to this question is this: the professional fund-raiser should at least understand the elements of the law as presented in this book. Much beyond that, the services of a lawyer may be required.

Q 1:29   What should the relationship between a professional fund-raiser and the charitable organization's lawyer be?

At a minimum, it should be cordial. The relationship should be that of a two-person team (although others may be part of the team as well, such as those in management and finance). Each of these individuals has unique capabilities, and the ideal is to blend that expertise and experience for the benefit of the charitable organization involved. (This is the case irrespective of whether either or both of these individuals are functioning in-house or as an independent contractor.)

The task of the professional fund-raiser is to solicit contributions and consummate gifts. The role of the lawyer in this context basically is to aid in the gift planning stage and to prepare the documents needed to effectuate the gift. (In some instances, these roles are necessarily played by the same individual.)

Q 1:30   When does a professional fund-raiser need a lawyer?

The need of a professional fund-raiser for a lawyer is basically dependent on whether the fund-raiser is an employee of a charitable organization or is an independent contractor with respect to the organization.

NOTE: This concerns the need of a professional fund-raiser for a lawyer for professional, not personal, reasons. The fund-raiser must look elsewhere for tips as to the use of a lawyer when selling a home, divorcing a spouse, or being prosecuted for criminal conduct.

While the distinctions can be complex, essentially an individual is an employee of an organization where the hours of work are set by the organization, the services are provided on the premises of the organization using its equipment and other resources, and the compensation is a fixed amount, regularly paid (in the nature of a salary or wage). An individual is an independent contractor—basically a consultant—where that individual sets his or her work hours, has a base of operations (with its own equipment, supplies, and the like) that is separate from that of the organization, and bills the organization for services rendered, such as on the basis of an hourly rate or against a flat fee, all preferably set forth in a contract.

If the professional fund-raiser is an employee of the charitable organization, the only likely need for a lawyer is preparation of an employment agreement. The fund-raiser's duties may be described in the employer's bylaws or other document, and these may need to be reviewed by legal counsel. There are, of course, many realms of federal and state law potentially affecting the employed fund-raiser, including antitrust, employee benefits, labor, sexual harassment, and taxation. Absent litigation or some other legal proceeding where the fund-raiser is a party, however, the fund-raiser is unlikely to need separate legal counsel as to these areas.

NOTE: An example to the contrary could involve the intermediate sanctions rules. If a professional fund-raiser is facing charges of excessive compensation, the lawyer representing the charity can only take the matter so far. At some point, the fund-raiser may well be compelled to obtain separate legal counsel.

If the professional fund-raiser is an independent contractor, matters become more complex. If the fund-raiser is rendering services to one or more charitable organizations as an individual, he or she should have a lawyer who at least advises on the terms of a contract (Q 7:13–Q 7:15), income tax reporting (although for that a competent accountant will suffice), compliance with state law regulation (Chapter 9), and perhaps form of business entity.

If the professional fund-raiser is an independent contractor and practicing as part of an entity, a lawyer should provide advice as to the appropriate type of organization. Here, the organizational forms are the regular (C) corporation (Q 1:20), the small business (S) corporation (Q 1:21), the limited liability company (Q 1:26), or the partnership (Q 1:24) (or other form of joint venture). Again, tax considerations and state law compliance are areas where legal advice is essential.

CHAPTER 2

Public Charity Status

The federal tax law separates charitable organizations into two categories: public and private. The latter are termed private foundations. Although the law presumes that all charitable organizations are private foundations, nearly all charities are public charities. There are three basic classifications of public charities, but there are many types within each classification. Because the body of federal tax law concerning private foundations is so onerous, it is important for a charitable organization to achieve public charity status if it can.

Public charity status is critical to successful fund-raising. This is because the federal charitable giving rules favor public charities and most private foundations confine their grant making to these charities. It is, thus, essential that the professional fund-raiser understand these distinctions—and know the public charity status of each charity for which he or she provides services.

Here are the questions most frequently asked by professional fund-raisers (or that should be asked by them) about the difference between public charities and private foundations, how to acquire and maintain public charity status, and the oft-misunderstood supporting organization—and the answers to them.

Q 2:1   What is a *public charity*?

A tax-exempt charitable organization is either a *public charity* or a *private foundation*. Every exempt charitable organization, domestic or foreign, is presumed to be a private foundation; this presumption can be rebutted by demonstrating to the IRS that the organization is a public charity.[1] There are three basic classifications of public charities, but there are many types of them (Q 2:3).

Q 2:2   What is a *private foundation*?

There is no true definition of a private foundation; there is only a "virtually real" definition of that term. This definition describes charitable organizations that are not public charities.[2] Nonetheless, the basic attributes of a typical private foundation are well known.

Generically, a private foundation has three characteristics:

1. It is a charitable organization that was initially funded by one source (usually an individual, a family, or a business).
2. Its ongoing revenue income comes from investments (in the nature of an endowment fund).
3. It makes grants to other charitable organizations rather than operate its own program.

The nature of its funding and, sometimes, the nature of its governance (such as a closed, family-oriented board of trustees), are the characteristics that make this type of charitable organization *private*.

TIP: The federal tax rules applicable to private foundations are onerous and, because of various penalty excise taxes, can be costly.[3] One of the most important services a lawyer for a charitable organization can provide is advice on the organization's basis for avoidance of the private foundation rules.

Q 2:3   What are the categories of public charities?

There are three basic categories of public charities: (1) institutions, (2) publicly supported organizations, and (3) supporting organizations.

Institutions are charitable organizations that are clearly not private foundations, simply by virtue of their programs and structure.[4] These entities are churches, associations and conventions of churches, integrated auxiliaries of churches, colleges, universities, schools, hospitals, certain other health care providers, medical research organizations, certain supporting foundations for governmental colleges and universities, and a variety of governmental units.

Because they have a broad base of contributions from the general public, publicly supported charities generally are the antithesis of private foundations. Publicly supported organizations and supporting organizations are discussed below (Q 2:7–Q 2:29).

Q 2:4   How does an organization acquire public charity status?

Most commonly, an organization acquires public charity status at the same time it acquires recognition of tax-exempt status as a charitable organization (Chapter 3). As part of the organization's filing of an application for recognition of exemption, it selects the category of public charity that it wants.[5] If the IRS agrees that the organization qualifies as a type of public charity, it includes that classification in the determination letter or ruling that it issues. (This is the process by which a charitable organization rebuts the presumption that it is a private foundation (Q 2:1).) Depending on the category of public charity, the organization will receive either an advance ruling (Q 2:9) or a definitive ruling (Q 2:11).

Q 2:5   How does an organization maintain its public charity status?

The manner in which an organization maintains its public charity status depends in large part on the type of public charity that it is. If it is an institution (Q 2:3) or a supporting organization (Q 2:15–Q 2:29), it remains a public charity as long as it continues to satisfy the programmatic or structural criteria that originally gave rise to the classification. If it is a publicly supported organization (Q 2:7–Q 2:14), it must provide its public support information to the IRS each year. This is done as part of the annual information return; there is a schedule by which both donative publicly supported charitable organizations and service provider publicly supported organizations display support information for a four-year measuring period.[6] An organization must only demonstrate that it qualifies under one of the categories each year, irrespective of the category that is reflected on its ruling.

Q 2:6   Why is it so important to be classified as a public charity and avoid private foundation status?

There are no disadvantages to public charity status; all of the disadvantages lie in classification as a private foundation. The disadvantages vary according to the nature of the organization; for some organizations, all of the disadvantages are important.

One of the principal disadvantages to private foundation status is the fact that, as a practical matter, private foundations will not make grants to other private foundations. A private foundation grantor must exercise *expenditure responsibility* as part of this type of grant,[7] and most private foundations do not have the resources to undertake, and do not want the risk of, expenditure responsibility grants. Also, in some instances, this type of grant will not qualify under the mandatory payout requirements.[8] Any charitable organization that is structured as a private foundation has basically denied itself access to funding by private foundation grants.

Another disadvantage to private foundation status is that contributions to private foundations may be less deductible than those to public charities.[9] For example, in a single tax year, an individual may make deductible gifts of money to public charities in amounts up to 50 percent of his or her adjusted gross income, whereas gifts of money to private foundations are subject to a 30 percent limitation. Similarly, gifts of appreciated property to public charities are deductible up to a 30 percent limitation, but the limitation generally is 20 percent in the case of private foundations (Q 4:4, Q 4:7).

Other disadvantages to private foundation status include

1. Compliance with the massive federal tax rules regulating the operations of private foundations.[10]
2. Payment of a 2 percent tax on net investment income, including capital gain.[11]
3. The requirement of filing a more complex annual information return.[12]
4. The need to publish a newspaper advertisement as to the availability of the annual return.[13]

CAUTION: On occasion, a charitable organization—not understanding the rules in this area—indicates on the application for recognition of exemption (see Chapter 3) that it is a private foundation, when in fact it will clearly be qualifying as a publicly supported charity. The IRS is unnecessarily harsh on the point, rarely permitting the organization to amend the application and instead forcing it to formally terminate its private foundation status, including "starting over" with an advance ruling (Q 2:9). This can cause enormous funding problems in the early years when reliance is placed on private foundation grants (Q 2:6). Thus, a charitable organization should be certain, when selecting foundation status, that that is the correct classification.

Q 2:7   What is a *donative publicly supported* charitable organization?

A *donative* publicly supported charitable organization is an organization that receives a substantial amount of its support in the form of gifts and grants from the general public or from the U.S. government, a state, or a political subdivision.[14] In this setting, *substantial* generally means at least one-third. The denominator of this support ratio includes investment income; fee-for-service revenue is not included in either the numerator or denominator. These calculations are made on the basis of a four-year moving average. (Generally, the source of the balance of the support is irrelevant.)

Support from any one source is public support to the extent that the amount does not exceed an amount equal to 2 percent of the support fraction denominator. For example, if an organization received $400,000 over its most recent four years, its public support would be the contributed amounts that did not exceed $8,000 per source (.02 × $400,000). If the organization is able to show that at least $133,334 of the $400,000 came from public support, it can be considered a donative publicly supported organization for the two years immediately succeeding the four measuring years. Unusual grants are excluded from the computation.

TIP: If an organization receives a substantial part of its support in the form of fee-for-service revenue, it cannot qualify as a donative publicly supported organization, even if it meets the support test for the small amount of contributions it receives.

Some additional rules apply to the computation of support for donative publicly supported organizations:

1. Amounts from other donative publicly supported organizations constitute public support in full (that is, they are not limited by the 2 percent rule).
2. Gifts and grants that exceed the 2 percent limitation constitute public support to the extent of the 2 percent limitation amount.
3. There are attribution rules in determining sources of support (for example, gifts from a husband and wife are considered as coming from one source).

To illustrate the second additional rule, if the organization in the above example received a $10,000 contribution from one source, $8,000 of it would be public support.

Two other categories of publicly supported organizations are recognized: (1) those that are public charities by virtue of the *facts-and-circumstances-test*[15] or (2) community foundations.[16] Organizations in the former category have at least 10 percent of public support and have characteristics that demonstrate public involvement with the organization (such as public use of facilities, public involvement in the programs, or a board of directors reflective of the community). A community foundation is a charitable organization that receives funding from and makes grants within a discrete community (such as a city).

Q 2:8   What is a *service provider publicly supported* charitable organization?

A *service provider* publicly supported organization is the other basic type of publicly supported charity.[17] This type of an organization normally receives at least one-third of its support in the form of gifts, grants, and exempt function revenue from the general public. The ratio calculation is made on the basis of a four-year moving average. The denominator of the ratio consists of the various forms of public support, net unrelated business income, investment income, tax revenues levied for the benefit of the organization, and the value of certain services or facilities furnished by a governmental unit.[18] Gift and grant support from any one source is public support to the extent that the amount derived did not come from a *disqualified person*.[19] Unusual grants are excluded from the computation.

The term *disqualified person* includes an organization's directors, trustees, officers, key employees having responsibilities similar to those of officers, substantial contributors, family members of these individuals, and certain entities related to or affiliated with these persons.[20] A *substantial contributor* is a person who contributed or granted more than $5,000 to the charitable organization, where that amount was more than 2 percent of the gifts and grants to the organization during the period of its existence.[21] In almost all cases, once a person is classified as a substantial contributor, that classification remains irrespective of the financial growth of the charity.

Public support can include *exempt function revenue*.[22] This is revenue in the form of gross receipts from admissions, sales of merchandise, performance of services, or furnishing of facilities, in an activity that is not an unrelated business. Revenue of this nature, however, is not public support to the extent that the receipts from any person or from any bureau or similar agency of a governmental unit in any tax year exceed the greater of $5,000 or 1 percent of the organization's support in that year. Also, this type of support from disqualified persons is not public support.

Using the figures of the above example, an organization attempting to qualify as a service provider publicly supported charity would also have to receive at least $133,334 in public support during the four-year measuring period. This support could be in the form of gifts, grants, and/or exempt function revenue. None of this support, however, could be from substantial contributors, board members, or other disqualified persons.

A service provider publicly supported organization cannot normally receive more than one-third of its support from gross investment income.[23]

NOTE: A service provider publicly supported organization that utilizes a supporting organization (2:15) must be cautious: funds transferred from the supporting organization may, in whole or in part, retain their character as investment income.

Q 2:9   What is an *advance ruling?*

An *advance ruling* is a ruling issued by the IRS to a new charitable organization that is expecting to qualify as a publicly supported organization (in either category, donative (2:7) or service provider (Q 2:8)). This ruling is part of the basic ruling recognizing tax-exempt status and charitable donee status (Q 1:8). Being new, the organization does not have a financial history on which to base a determination as to whether it is publicly supported. Consequently, the IRS makes this initial determination of the organization's publicly supported charity status on the basis of a budget provided by the organization; where that information appears credible, the IRS will rule that the organization is reasonably expected to constitute a publicly supported organization. The term *advance* is used because the ruling is issued before actual development of the necessary financial data that will indicate whether the organization is in fact publicly supported. In this sense, the ruling is a probationary or tentative ruling as to publicly supported charity status.

NOTE: The concept of an advance ruling does not apply to recognition of tax exemption or charitable donee status. Advance rulings are issued to both putative donative publicly supported organizations and service provider publicly supported organizations.

If a new charitable organization wishes to be regarded by the IRS as a publicly supported charity, it must receive an advance ruling where it is in existence for only one year. (That "year" must be less than eight months.[24]) Where the organization has a financial history that is longer, it is entitled to, but need not pursue, a definitive ruling (Q 2:11).

TIP: This area of the law can be confusing, because of the source of it. The IRS does not follow the existing regulations on the subject. Instead, it uses different rules that can be found only in the instructions accompanying the application for recognition of tax exemption.

The period of time the advance ruling is in effect is the *advance ruling period*—the organization's first five years.

NOTE: This use of the term *year* can be tricky. For purposes of being able to gain a definitive ruling with only one year of existence, the "year" must be a period of at least eight months (Q 2:11). However, when *measuring* an entity's advance ruling period, the first year can be a period of any length—months, weeks, or some number of days. This may mitigate against forming, late in a year, a charitable entity that is intended to be publicly supported.

Once the advance ruling period has expired (at the close of the appropriate year) and if the organization has satisfied one of the public support tests, the advance ruling will ripen into a definitive ruling. The organization is expected to apply for a definitive ruling within 90 days after the close of the advance ruling period. The requisite financial information should be provided on an IRS form.[25]

Q 2:10   At the end of the advance ruling period, will the IRS automatically request more information regarding the organization's public support or does the organization need to initiate contact with the IRS?

The responsibility to apply to the IRS for a definitive ruling within 90 days following the close of the advance ruling period lies with the organization. The IRS will not initiate contact with the charitable organization on this point at this time, beyond sometimes sending a copy of the requisite form (Q 2:9). Although it is not specifically required, the IRS prefers that the necessary information be tendered on that form.

Once the information is submitted, it is very rare for the IRS to request additional information; that is, the IRS will normally accept the public support information on its face. If the information reflects sufficient public support, the IRS will issue a definitive ruling. If the information shows that the organization did not receive adequate public support during the advance ruling period, the IRS—without inquiry—is likely to classify the organization as a private foundation.

It is important for an organization in this position to accompany the form with a cover letter explaining why the organization meets the public support test (assuming it does) and to include the precise public support ratio. On occasion, if an organization has not met a public support test during the advance ruling period but seems clearly on the way to doing so in the succeeding year, the IRS will issue a favorable definitive ruling.

Q 2:11   What is a *definitive ruling?*

A *definitive ruling* is a ruling issued by the IRS to a charitable organization that qualifies as a publicly supported organization. This ruling is part of the basic declaration that recognizes tax-exempt status and charitable donee status. Definitive rulings are issued to both donative publicly supported organizations and service provider publicly supported organizations.

An eligible charitable organization is entitled to a definitive ruling if it has completed at least one tax year (consisting of at least eight months) and meets the requirements for one of the categories of publicly supported organization. A charitable organization, however, that has been in existence for a period of that duration and has not yet achieved the necessary level of public support to qualify as a publicly supported organization, yet expects to qualify as a publicly supported organization, can obtain an advance ruling that it is reasonably expected to be a publicly supported organization.[26]

Q 2:12   Does it matter which category of publicly supported charity an organization uses?

Once a charitable organization meets the criteria of either type of publicly supported organization (donative or service provider), the IRS does not care which category the organization is in at any point in time. For example, an organization may receive an advance ruling that it is a donative publicly supported organization and subsequently be able to qualify only as a service provider publicly supported organization. Or, once a definitive ruling as to one of the classifications is received, the organization may annually shift from one category of publicly supported charity to the other.

In general, it is preferable, if possible, for a charitable organization to be classified as a donative publicly supported organization. Policy makers and regulators tend to look more favorably on charitable organizations that are supported primarily by gifts and grants. Charitable organizations that receive significant amounts of fee-for-service revenue are far more susceptible to allegations that they are operating in a commercial manner.

Whatever its actual category, a charitable organization may prefer to be regarded as a donative publicly supported organization rather than a service provider publicly supported organization. (There is no advantage to classification as a service provider publicly supported organization instead of a donative publicly supported organization.) Only a donative publicly supported organization is eligible to maintain a pooled income fund.[27] This eligibility extends, however, to organizations *described in* the rules pertaining to donative publicly supported organizations.[28] if a charitable organization has received a definitive ruling that it is a service provider publicly supported organization, but it meets the support requirements for a donative publicly supported organization, it may maintain a pooled income fund (Q 5:17).

TIP: The IRS prefers to classify publicly supported organizations as donative. On occasion, an organization that has applied for service provider status will find that the IRS wants to accord it donative status. Unless it is clear that the organization will not meet the donative entity rules or there is a specific reason for wanting the service provider category, it is best to go along with the IRS on this point.

Q 2:13   What happens when an organization ceases to be a publicly supported charity?

If a charitable organization ceases to qualify as a publicly supported entity, the technical rule is that it automatically becomes a private foundation. This can happen in one of two ways:

1. The organization may reach the end of its advance ruling period (Q 2:9) and not have the requisite public support.

2. The organization may have a definitive ruling that it has publicly supported charity status (Q 2:11) but, at a point in time, fail to continue to qualify under either category of publicly supported charity.

In either circumstance, the organization will become a private foundation unless some other category of public charity status is available. One possibility is that the organization can (temporarily or otherwise) qualify as a publicly supported organization by reason of the facts-and-circumstances test (Q 2:7). Another is that the organization can be restructured as a supporting organization (Q 2:15–Q 2:29). Still another is that the organization can become one of the institutions (such as an educational organization structured as a school) (Q 2:3).

If a charitable organization in this circumstance cannot avoid private foundation status, it is hardly the "end of the world" for the entity. It may be possible for the organization to become a hybrid entity (a blend of public charity and private foundation), usually a private operating foundation[29] or an exempt operating foundation.[30] A charitable organization that is classified as a private foundation can at any time demonstrate compliance with one of the bases for public charity status, terminate its private foundation status, and proceed on a definitive ruling or advance ruling basis.

Q 2:14   What should an organization do when it realizes, during the advance ruling period, that it will not qualify as a publicly supported organization as of the close of that period?

There is no law on this point. In practice, a charitable organization that has an advance ruling, and realizes along the course of its advance ruling period that it cannot qualify as a publicly supported organization, can convert to a supporting organization (Q 2:15–Q 2:28) or, as a less likely choice, an institution, such as a school (Q 2:3). If the organization qualifies for the alternative status, the IRS will issue a ruling to that effect and will not attempt to assess tax on the organization's investment income (Q 2:6) for the early years. The fact that the organization did not meet a public support test during the initial months of the advance ruling period is ignored.

One aspect of this matter is clear: the organization should not simply allow the advance ruling period to expire without taking action. Occasionally, where the organization meets a public support test by taking into account the year following the advance ruling period but has not timely filed the support information (Q 2:9), the IRS will still issue a definitive ruling. But this action is wholly within the discretion of the IRS personnel and that outcome should not be assumed.

TIP: A charitable organization that expects to meet a public support test as of the close of its advance ruling period, but then does not, is likely to not have the requisite private foundation provisions in its articles of organization. Unless this matter is remedied by state law, the organization will lose its tax-exempt status. It is imperative to place the private foundation provisions in the governing instrument as a fall-back position where the state does not impose the rules as a matter of law. On occasion, the IRS will elongate the advance ruling period where the test is met using the support in the year following the advance ruling period, but, as noted, that type of administrative relief cannot be assumed.

Q 2:15   What is a *supporting organization*?

A *supporting organization* is a charitable organization that would be a private foundation but for its structural or operational relationship with one or more charitable organizations that are either public institutions (Q 2:3) or publicly supported organizations (Q 2:7, Q 2:8).[31] This type of organization must be organized, and at all times thereafter operated, exclusively for the benefit of, to perform the functions of, or to carry out the purposes of at least one of these public charities, which are *supported organizations*. Also, it must be operated, supervised, or controlled by or in connection with one or more supported organizations. A supporting organization may not be controlled directly or indirectly by one or more disqualified persons (Q 2:23), other than foundation managers and one or more supported organizations.

The supporting organization must meet an *organizational test*, which basically requires that its articles of organization must limit its purposes to those of a supporting entity and not empower the organization to support or benefit any other organizations.[32] The supported organization(s) must be specified in the articles, although the manner of the specification depends on the nature of the relationship with the supported organization(s) (Q 2:16). Also, the supporting organization must adhere to an *operational test*: it must engage solely in activities that support or benefit one or more supported organizations (Q 2:17).[33]

Q 2:16   What are the requisite relationships between a supporting organization and a supported organization?

There are three of these relationships, defined as

1. *Operated, supervised, or controlled by.*
2. *Supervised or controlled in connection with.*
3. *Operated in connection with.*

Irrespective of the relationship, the supporting organization must always be responsive to the needs or demands of one or more supported organizations and constitute an integral part of or maintain a significant involvement in the operations of one or more supported organizations.[34]

The relationship encompassed by the phrase *operated, supervised, or controlled by* contemplates the presence of a substantial degree of direction by one or more supported organizations over the policies, programs, and activities of the supporting organization.[35] This relationship, which is basically that of parent and subsidiary, is normally established by causing at least a majority of the directors or officers of the supporting organization to be composed of representatives of the supported organization or to be appointed or elected by the governing body, officers, or membership of the supported organization.

TIP: This is the most common relationship of the three. It is the easiest and most direct control relationship to construct, and it assures the supported organization that the benefits it expects from the supporting entity will be received.

The relationship manifested by the phrase *supervised or controlled in connection with* contemplates the presence of common supervision or control by persons supervising or controlling both entities to ensure that the supporting organization will be responsive to the needs and requirements of the supported organization(s).[36] This relationship—one of "brother and sister" entities—requires that the control or management of the supporting organization be vested in the same persons who control or manage the supported organization(s).

The relationship envisioned by the phrase *operated in connection with* contemplates that the supporting organization is responsive to and significantly involved in the operations of the supported organization(s).[37] Generally, the supporting organization must meet both a *responsiveness test* and an *integral part test*.

The responsiveness test is satisfied where the supporting organization is responsive to the needs or demands of one or more supported organizations.[38] The test can be satisfied where the supporting organization and the supported organization(s) are in close operational conjunction. There are several ways to show this. They include: (1) having one or more of the officers or directors of the supporting organization elected or appointed by the officers or directors of the supported organization(s) or (2) demonstrating that the officers or directors of the supporting organization maintain a close and continuous working relationship with the officers and directors of the supported organization(s). The officers and directors of the supported organization(s) must have a significant voice in the investment policies of the supporting organization, the timing of and manner of making grants, the selection of grant recipients by the supporting organization, and the direction of the use of the income or assets of the supporting organization.

The responsiveness test may also be met where (1) the supporting organization is a charitable trust under state law, (2) each specified supported organization is a named beneficiary under the trust's governing instrument, and (3) each supported organization has the power, under state law, to enforce the trust and compel an accounting.

A supporting organization satisfies the integral part test where it maintains a significant involvement in the operations of one or more supported organizations and the beneficiary organization(s) are dependent on the supporting organization for the type of support it provides.[39] This test is met where the activities engaged in by the supporting organization for or on behalf of the supported organization(s) are activities to perform the functions of, or to carry out the purposes of, the supported organization(s) and, but for the involvement of the supporting organization, would normally be engaged in by the supported organization(s).

There is a second way to meet the integral part test.

TIP: Although these requirements are considerably complex, these rules represent the furthest reaches under which a charitable organization can avoid private foundation status.

Under this approach, the supporting organization makes payments of substantially all of its income to or for the use of one or more supported organizations, and the amount of support received by one or more of the supported organizations is sufficient to ensure the attentiveness of the organization(s) to the operations of the supporting organization. The phrase *substantially all* means at least 85 percent.[40] A substantial amount of the total support from the supporting organization must go to those supported organizations that meet an attentiveness requirement with respect to the supporting organization.

In general, the amount of support received by a supported organization must represent a sufficient part of its total support so as to ensure the requisite attentiveness. If the supporting organization makes payments to or for the use of a department or school of a university, hospital, or church, the total support of the department or school is the measuring base, rather than the total support of the beneficiary institution.

Even where the amount of support received by a supported organization does not represent a sufficient part of its total support, the amount of support from a supporting organization may be sufficient to meet the requirements of the integral part test if it can be demonstrated that, in order to avoid the interruption of the conduct of a particular function or activity, the beneficiary organization will be sufficiently attentive to the operations of the supporting organization. This may be the case where either the supporting organization or the beneficiary organization earmarks the support received from the supporting organization for a particular program or activity, even if the program or activity is not the beneficiary organization's primary program or activity, so long as the program or activity is a substantial one.

All pertinent factors—including the number of the supporting organizations (Q 2:19), the length and nature of the relationship between the beneficiary organization and the supporting organization, and the purpose to which the funds are put (Q 2:17)—are considered in determining whether the amount of support received by a beneficiary organization is sufficient to ensure its attentiveness to the operations of the supporting organization. Inasmuch as, in the view of the IRS, the attentiveness of a supported organization is motivated by reason of the amount of funds received from the supporting organization, the more substantial the amount involved (in terms of a percentage of the total support of the supported organization), the greater the likelihood that the required degree of attentiveness will be present. Other evidence of actual attentiveness by the supported organization is, however, of almost equal importance. The mere making of reports to each of the supported organizations does not alone satisfy the attentiveness requirement of the integral part test.

Where none of the supported organizations is dependent on the supporting organization for a sufficient amount of the beneficiary organization's support, the integral part test cannot be satisfied, even though the supported organizations have enforceable rights against the supporting organization under state law.

Q 2:17   What are the functions of a supporting organization?

With the emphasis on *support*, the most common function of a supporting organization is as a funding mechanism for the supported organization(s).[41] In some instances, the supporting organization is the endowment fund for one or more beneficiary organizations. Endowments can be established by a public charity's transfer of some or all of its investment assets to a newly created supporting entity.

TIP: There seems to be a widespread belief that a public charity cannot spawn a supporting organization. This is not the case. For example, in the endowment fund setting, there may be considerable merit in having the fund in a separate entity (1) for liability purposes and (2) to place the assets in the hands of trustees who are more concerned with long-term operations than immediate budgetary pressures.[42] Health care providers and other public charities use the supporting organization vehicle to establish "holding companies" for more effective management.[43]

The law in this area speaks also of providing a *benefit* to a supported organization (Q 2:15). Aside from providing the supported organization with money, an organization can support or benefit another organization by carrying on its own programs or activities to support or benefit a supported organization. For example, a supporting organization supported a medical school at a university by operating teaching, research, and services programs as a faculty practice plan.[44] As another illustration, as part of its relationship with a public charity that provided residential placement services for mentally and physically handicapped adults, a supporting organization established and operated an employment facility for the handicapped and an information center about various handicapping conditions.[45]

> **COMMENT:** A contemporary use of a supporting organization was presented in the case of a hospital that wanted a temporary residential facility for patients awaiting surgery, and their family and friends. The hospital created a supporting organization, which in turn acquired a motel and converted it into the facility. The purpose of the supporting organization, then, is to operate the facility; that alone, the IRS ruled, is the requisite support and benefit for the hospital.[46]

A supporting organization may engage in fund-raising activities, such as charitable gift solicitations, special events (such as dinners and theater outings), and unrelated business activities, and grant the funds to the supported organization(s) or to other permissible beneficiaries.

Q 2:18   Does the supported organization have to be identified in the organizational document of the supporting organization?

Usually, but not always. Generally, it is expected that the articles of organization of the supporting organization will designate the (or each of the) supported organization(s) by name. The manner of the specification depends on the nature of the relationship between the supported and supporting organizations (Q 2:16).[47]

If the relationship is one of *operated, supervised, or controlled by* or *supervised or controlled in connection with*, designation of a supported organization by name is not required as long as two rules are followed:

1. The articles of organization of the supporting organization must require that it be operated to support or benefit one or more supported organizations that are designated by class or purpose.

2. The class or purpose must include one or more supported organizations to which one of the two relationships pertains, or organizations that are closely related in purpose or function to the supported organizations to which one of the relationships pertains.

If the relationship is one of *operated in connection with*, generally the supporting organization's articles must designate the specified supported organization by name.

TIP: Irrespective of the relationship, it is usually preferable—from the standpoint of all organizations involved—for the supported organization(s) to be designated by name in the supporting organization's articles.

Where the relationship between the organizations is other than *operated in connection with*, the articles of organization of a supporting organization may (1) permit the substitution of an eligible organization within a class for another organization either in the same class or in a different class designated in the articles, (2) permit the supporting organization to operate for the benefit of new or additional organizations in the same class or in a different class designated in the articles, or (3) permit the supporting organization to vary the amount of its support among different eligible organizations within the class or classes of organizations designated by the articles.

An organization that is *operated in connection with* one or more supported organizations can satisfy this specification requirement even if its articles permit an organization that is designated by class or purpose to be substituted for an organization designated in its articles, but only where the substitution is "conditioned upon the occurrence of an event which is beyond the control of the supporting organization." This type of an event would be loss of tax exemption, substantial failure or abandonment of operations, or dissolution of the supported organization(s) designated in the articles. In one instance, a charitable entity failed to qualify as a supporting organization because its articles permitted substitution too freely: whenever, in the discretion of its trustee, the charitable undertakings of the supported organizations become "unnecessary, undesirable, impracticable, impossible or no longer adapted to the needs of the public," substitution was permitted.[48]

Q 2:19 How many supported organizations can a supporting organization support?

The law does not place any specific limitation on the number of supported organizations that can be served by a supporting organization. Whatever the number, there must be a requisite relationship between the supporting organization and each of the supported organizations (Q 2:16). As a practical matter, this relationship requirement serves as somewhat of a limitation on the number of supported organizations that can be clustered around a supporting organization. Yet, there is a supporting organization that serves over 300 public charitable entities.

Q 2:20 Can a supporting organization support or benefit a charitable organization or other person, in addition to one or more supported organizations?

Yes, although the opportunities for doing this are limited. The constraint comes from the fact that the law requires that a supporting organization be operated *exclusively* to support or benefit one or more qualified public entities (Q 2:15). The limitation also stems from the requirement of the requisite relationship and the specification rules (Q 2:16, Q 2:18). In general, a supporting organization must engage *solely* in activities that support or benefit one or more supported organizations.

A supporting organization may make payments to or for the use of, or provide services or facilities for, individual members of the charitable class that is benefited by a specified supported organization. Also, a supporting organization may make a payment through another, unrelated organization to a member of a charitable class benefited by a specified supported organization, but only where the payment constitutes a grant to an individual rather than a grant to an organization. At the same time, a supporting organization can support or benefit a charitable organization (other than a private foundation) if it is operated, supervised, or controlled directly by or in connection with a supported organization.[49] A supporting organization will, however, lose its status as such if it pursues a purpose other than supporting or benefiting one or more supported organizations.

A supporting organization can carry on an independent activity as part of its support function (Q 2:17). This type of support must be limited to permissible beneficiaries, as described above.

In practice, however, it is quite common for supporting organizations to make payments to noncharitable entities as part of their support activities. For example, a supporting organization can procure and pay for services that are rendered to or for the benefit of a supported organization. The supporting organization can also engage in fund-raising activities, such as special events, for the benefit of a supported organization. In that capacity, the supporting organization can contract with and pay for services such as advertising, catering, decorating, and entertainment.

Q 2:21   Can a supporting organization support another supporting organization?

Although the law is not clear on the point, the answer probably is no. The law requires that a supporting organization operate for the benefit of, to perform the functions of, or to carry out the purposes of one or more public institutions or publicly supporting organizations.[50] A superficial reading of this law could lead one to the conclusion that a supporting organization may not be supported in this manner because it is not a public institution or publicly supported organization.

It is quite possible, however, that by supporting a supporting organization, a supporting organization could simultaneously benefit or carry out the purposes of a public institution or publicly supported organization. In fact, the regulations state that any charitable organization (other than a private foundation) can be a beneficiary of a supporting organization where the recipient organization is operated or controlled by a qualified supported organization.[51] The IRS is of the view, however, that this regulation was not intended to allow one supporting organization to support another under any circumstances. Thus, it would not be advisable to structure this type of an arrangement without first obtaining a ruling from the IRS.

NOTE: To date, the IRS has not issued a ruling on the point. This is either because the IRS has not received a ruling request or because any such request was withdrawn in the face of an adverse position by the IRS.

Q 2:22   Can a charitable organization be a supporting organization with respect to a tax-exempt organization that is not a charitable one?

Yes. A charitable organization can support or benefit an exempt organization other than a charitable entity where the supported organization is a tax-exempt social welfare organization (Q 1:18), a tax-exempt labor organization,[52] or a tax-exempt association that is a business league (Q 1:19). For this arrangement to be successful, however, the supported organization must meet the public support test applied to service provider publicly supported charitable organizations (Q 2:8). This rule is largely designed to establish nonprivate foundation status for "foundations" and other funds that are affiliated with and operated for the benefit of these eligible noncharitable exempt organizations.

Q 2:23 Are any limitations placed on the composition of the board of directors of a supporting organization?

Yes. The general concept is that a supporting organization will be controlled, through a structural or programmatic relationship, by one or more eligible public organizations. Thus, a supporting organization may not be controlled, directly or indirectly, by one or more disqualified persons (Q 2:15)—other than, of course, foundation managers and one or more supported organizations.[53] A supporting organization is controlled by one or more disqualified persons if, by aggregating their votes or positions of authority, they may require the organization to perform any act that significantly affects its operations or may prevent the supporting organization from performing the act. Generally, a supporting organization is considered to be controlled in this manner if the voting power of disqualified persons is 50 percent or more of the total voting power of the organization's governing board or if one or more disqualified persons have the right to exercise veto power over the actions of the organization. All pertinent facts and circumstances are taken into consideration in determining whether a disqualified person indirectly controls an organization.

An individual who is a disqualified person with respect to a supporting organization (such as being a substantial contributor (Q 2:8)) does not lose that status because a supported organization appointed or otherwise designated him or her a foundation manager of the supporting organization as the representative of the supported organization.

In one instance, the IRS concluded that the board of directors of a supporting organization was indirectly controlled by a disqualified person.[54] The organization's board of directors was composed of a substantial contributor to it, two employees of a business corporation of which more than 35 percent of the voting power was owned by the substantial contributor (making the corporation itself a disqualified person (Q 2:8)), and one individual selected by the supported organization. None of the directors had any veto power over the organization's actions. While conceding that the supporting organization was not directly controlled by the disqualified person, the IRS said that "one circumstance to be considered is whether a disqualified person is in a position to influence the decisions of members of the organization's governing body who are not themselves disqualified persons." The IRS concluded that the two individuals who were employees of the disqualified person corporation should be considered disqualified persons for purposes of applying the 50 percent control rule. This led to a ruling that the organization was indirectly controlled by disqualified persons and therefore could not qualify as a supporting organization.

TIP: This matter of indirect control by disqualified persons is very much a facts-and-circumstances test. The IRS is particularly sensitive to the possibility that creative structuring is being used to mask control of a supporting organization by one or more disqualified persons. The IRS tends to be rather strict on this point.

This control element can be the difference between the qualification of an organization as a supporting organization or as a common fund private foundation. The right of the donors to designate the recipients of the organization's grants can constitute control of the organization by them; supporting organization classification is precluded where this control element rests with substantial contributors.[55]

Q 2:24   Should a supporting organization be separately incorporated?

The law does not require that a supporting organization be incorporated. In most instances, however, supporting organizations are incorporated, for the same reasons most nonprofit corporations use the corporate form—avoidance of personal liability for directors and officers.[56] One context in which the trust form may be advisable is where it may be needed as a way to satisfy the responsiveness test (Q 2:16).

Q 2.25   Should a supporting organization have bylaws?

This answer depends on the type of organization that the supporting organization is. If it is a corporation (Q 2:24) or an unincorporated association, it should have bylaws. Charitable trusts do not usually have bylaws, although when the trust form is used for a supporting organization, a set of bylaws or a document akin to bylaws is advisable.

NOTE: There is a specific organizational test in this setting (Q 2:15). The requisite language, however, must be contained in the articles of organization; inclusion only in the bylaws is inadequate.

Q 2:26   Who elects or appoints the directors of a supporting organization?

Selection of directors depends on the type of supporting organization, that is, on the nature of the relationship between the supporting entity and the supported organization(s) (Q 2:16). If the relationship is that of *operated, supervised, or controlled by*, at least a majority of the board of the supporting organization would be elected or appointed by the supported organization. The entirety of the supporting organization's board can be selected in this manner, or the minority members can be selected by the majority members.

If the relationship is that of *supervised or controlled in connection with*, the boards of directors of the two organizations will be the same. Thus, the organizational documents of the supporting organization would state that its governing board is the same group that comprises the board of the supported entity.

Where the relationship is embraced by the phrase *operated in connection with*, the board of directors of the supporting organization can possibly be wholly independent of the supported organization from the standpoint of its governance. Thus, the board can be structured in any way that is deemed appropriate by the parties involved.

NOTE: The board of directors of the supporting organization cannot be controlled by disqualified persons with respect to it (Q 2:23).

It may be necessary to have one or more of the directors of the supporting organization elected or appointed by the directors of the supported organization, to facilitate compliance with the responsiveness test (Q 2:16).

Q 2:27   Can a supporting organization maintain its own financial affairs (such as by means of a separate bank account and separate investments)?

The supporting organization not only can maintain its own financial affairs but it should. This type of entity is a separate organization, and its legal status (including tax exemption) is predicated on that fact. Thus, separate financial resources are (or should be) always the case. This is particularly true with respect to supporting organizations that support or benefit noncharitable entities (Q 2:22).

One of the overarching requirements often is that the supported organization have a significant involvement in the operations of the supporting organization (Q 2:16). This is likely to mean that the board of the supported organization has direction over the investment policies of the supporting organization. For example, for purposes of meeting the responsiveness test, the officers and directors of the supported organization(s) may have to have a significant voice in the investment policies of the supporting organization, the timing of grants, the manner of making them, and the selection of recipients by the supporting organization, and in otherwise directing the use of the income or assets of the supporting organization (Q 2:16).

Q 2:28   What financial reports and disclosure should a supporting organization make to the supported organization?

The law on this point is next to nonexistent. For the most part, this is a management matter rather than a legal one. State law may apply, particularly if the supporting entity is a charitable trust.

To the extent the federal rules address the point, it is a function of the relationship between the supported organization and the supporting organization. In general, the supporting organization must be responsive to the demands of the supported organization (Q 2:16). Thus, the law generally requires that the supporting organization provide whatever financial information about itself that the board of the supported organization "demands." Where the relationship is one of *operated, supervised, or controlled by* or *supervised or controlled in connection with*, the board of the supported organization is in the position of receiving any information about the supporting organization—financial or otherwise—that it wants.

Financial disclosure to the supported organization becomes most problematic when the relationship is evidenced by the phrase *operated in connection with*. In this situation, the board composition of the supporting organization may be such that financial information is not readily available to the board of the supported organization. A problem may arise in the context of meeting the attentiveness requirement of the integral part test. However, the mere making of reports to a supported organization does not alone enable the supporting organization to meet this requirement (Q 2:16). Thus, where the *operated in connection with* relationship is involved, the sharing of financial information may be largely political, that is, whatever the parties can work out.

Q 2:29   What oversight should the supported organization perform?

No oversight requirement is imposed by law on the supported organization (other than the supervision that may flow out of fiduciary responsibility duties[57]). The relationship responsibilities all fall on the supporting organization, as part of its justification for nonprivate-foundation status. The supporting organization must always be responsive to the needs or demands of one or more supported organizations and must constitute an integral part of or maintain a significant involvement in the operations of one or more supported organizations (Q 2:16).

Good management practice would dictate that the supported organization be concerned with, and do what it can to conserve, the state and nature of the resources held by the supporting organization. Where the relationship is one of *operated, supervised, or controlled by* or *supervised or controlled in connection with*, any management oversight duties that the supported organization may wish to undertake are readily available (Q 2:28).

Q 2:30   Isn't there some current controversy concerning the use of supporting organizations?

Yes, unfortunately, there is. The IRS is unhappy with some contemporary developments concerning supporting organizations, to the extent that the IRS has classified, as an "aggressive tax avoidance scheme," certain "inappropriate uses" of supporting organizations.[58] The principal difficulty here, as with donor-advised funds (4:36), is the matter of ongoing donor control. As discussed, disqualified persons are not permitted to control supporting organizations (Q 2:23).

Yet, stimulated in part by a high-profile article in 1998 in *The Wall Street Journal*,[59] the IRS is concerned that there is a growing use of "this technique [the operation of supporting organizations] to allow wealthy persons to obtain substantial charitable tax deductions while maintaining control of the property." This control is achieved "by virtue of the donor's position or influence on or over the Board of Directors of the exempt supporting organization."[60]

The IRS is—quite understandably—vexed because of a promotion, which terms the supporting organization a "private credit facility" and an "intergenerational private lending institution."[61] This promotion observes that family members can borrow money from the supporting organization at a low interest rate, then invest the money at a higher interest rate, artfully stating that they can "pocket the difference."

Needless to say, the IRS finds fault with this planning technique. One, this arrangement probably violates the control test. The IRS noted that disqualified persons may not control the supporting organization indirectly, such as by employees or business agents. Two, the IRS warned that transactions of this nature can jeopardize the tax-exempt status of the organization, either because of excessive private benefit (Q 1:11) or private inurement (Q 1:10). Three, this transaction is likely to be an excess benefit transaction under the intermediate sanctions rules. Fourth, promotions of this type may result in imposition of the abusive tax shelter and aiding and abetting penalties.[62]

The IRS went out of its way to comment that the "official" board of directors of a supporting organization that never or seldom meets "is likely to be found suspect." That is, it probably is failing the control test.

It is not clear as to where all of this is leading. It may be anticipated that the IRS will more closely scrutinize board composition and relationships during the application process (see Chapter 3) and on audit. There may be some legislative activity in this area, although existing law is clear on the matter of control by disqualified persons.

CHAPTER 3

Tax Exemption Application

Under the federal income tax system, every element of gross income received by a person—whether a corporate entity or a human being—is subject to taxation, unless there is an express statutory provision that exempts from tax either that form of income or that type of person.

Many types of nonprofit organizations are eligible for exemption from the federal income tax. But the exemption is not forthcoming merely because an organization is not organized and operated for profit. Organizations are tax-exempt where they meet the requirements of the particular statutory provision that authorizes the tax-exempt status.

A great myth is that the IRS grants tax-exempt status. This is not the case—and the correct concept, concerning recognition of exempt status, is frequently puzzling. The government's forms in this setting can appear daunting. Various and additional rules for charitable organizations can add to the perplexity. There is much in the application for recognition of tax-exempt status for charitable organizations that relates to their fund-raising program.

Here are the questions most frequently asked by professional fund-raisers (or that should be asked by them) about the exemption application process—and the answers to them.

Q 3:1   Are all nonprofit organizations tax-exempt organizations?

No. As discussed (Q 1:6), a nonprofit organization basically is a creature of state law (such as a nonprofit corporation or charitable trust) and is an entity that may not engage in forms of private inurement. While nearly every tax-exempt organization is a nonprofit entity, it is not enough simply to achieve tax-exempt status to be a nonprofit organization.

Q 3:2   How does a *nonprofit* organization become a *tax-exempt* organization?

To qualify for tax-exempt status under the federal tax law, a nonprofit organization must meet the criteria of at least one provision of the Internal Revenue Code describing tax-exempt organizations. That is, in general, an organization that meets the appropriate statutory criteria qualifies—for that reason alone—as a tax-exempt organization.

NOTE: Most tax-exempt organizations under the federal tax law are those that are described in section 501(c)(1)-(27) of the Code. Other Code provisions that provide for income tax exemption are sections 521 and 526–529. Depending on how these provisions are parsed and the breadth of the term *tax-exempt organization* used, there are at least 63 categories of tax-exempt organizations provided for in the federal income tax law.[1] The professional fund-raiser is primarily concerned with organizations referenced in Code section 501(c)(3) (Q 1:8).

Q 3:3   Concerning tax exemption, what taxes are involved?

For the most part, a reference to a tax-exempt organization is to an entity that is exempt from the federal income tax (Q 1:7). There are other federal taxes from which nonprofit organizations are exempt, but the federal income tax exemption is certainly the principal one. There are state tax exemptions as well, including state income tax exemptions.

State law, moreover, provides exemptions from sales, use, tangible personal property, intangible personal property, real property, and other taxes.

Frequently, the law providing exemption for nonprofit organizations from state income tax tracks the rules for exemption from federal income tax. (The criteria for exemption tend to become more rigorous when a property tax exemption is involved, particularly the real property tax exemption.) Therefore, the federal rules usually are the place to start.

Q 3:4   Is a nonprofit organization required to apply to the IRS for tax-exempt status?

A very literal answer to this question is no. This is because the IRS does not grant tax-exempt status. Tax exemption is a feature of an organization that is available to it by operation of law.

What the IRS does is grant *recognition* of tax-exempt status. This role of the IRS in recognizing the exempt status of organizations is part of its overall responsibility for evaluating the tax status of organizations.[2]

Q 3:5   What does *recognition* of tax exemption mean?

Whether a nonprofit organization is entitled to tax exemption, on an initial or continuing basis, is a matter of law. The U.S. Congress—not the IRS—defines the categories of organizations that are eligible for tax exemption, and it is up to Congress to determine whether a category of exemption from tax should be continued, in whole or in part. Except for state and local governmental entities, there is no constitutional right to a tax exemption.

Despite what is often thought, the IRS does not *grant* tax-exempt status. Congress, by means of sections of the Internal Revenue Code that it has enacted, performs that role. Rather, the function of the IRS in this regard is to *recognize* tax exemptions that Congress has created.

Consequently, when an organization makes application to the IRS for a ruling or determination as to tax-exempt status, it is requesting the IRS to recognize a tax exemption that already exists (assuming the organization qualifies). Similarly, the IRS may determine that an organization is no longer entitled to tax-exempt status and act to revoke its prior recognition of exempt status.

For many nonprofit organizations that are eligible for a tax exemption, it is not required that the exemption be recognized by the IRS. Whether a nonprofit organization seeks an IRS determination on the point is a management decision, which usually takes into account the degree of confidence the individuals involved have in the eligibility for the exemption, and the costs associated with the application process. Most organizations in this position elect to pursue recognition of tax-exempt status.

Q 3:6   Must an organization, desiring to be a charitable one, seek recognition of tax-exempt status?

With a few exceptions (Q 3:10), charitable organizations must, to be tax-exempt and to be charitable donees, (successfully) seek recognition of the exemption from the IRS.[3] Thus, by contrast, entities such as social welfare organizations (Q 1:18), labor organizations,[4] trade and professional associations (Q 1:19), social clubs,[5] and veterans' organizations[6] need not (but may) pursue recognition of tax-exempt status.[7]

Q 3:7   How is this recognition of tax exemption initiated?

Unlike most requests for a ruling from the IRS (which are commenced by a letter to the IRS), a request for recognition of tax exemption is initiated by filing a form, entitled "Application for Recognition of Exemption." Charitable organizations file Form 1023; most other organizations file Form 1024.

Q 3:8   How does an organization remain tax-exempt?

Subject only to the authority in the IRS to revoke recognition of exemption for good cause (such as a change in the law), an organization that has been recognized by the IRS as being tax-exempt can rely on the determination as long as there are no substantial changes in its character, purposes, or methods of operation.[8] Should material changes occur, the organization should notify the IRS and may have to obtain a reevaluation of its exempt status.

Q 3:9   What is the recognition application procedure?

The IRS has promulgated specific rules by which a ruling or determination letter may be issued to an organization in response to the filing of an application for recognition of its tax-exempt status.

NOTE: A recognition of exemption by the IRS from an office outside Washington, D.C., is termed a *determination letter*.[9] This type of recognition from the IRS's National Office in Washington, D.C., is termed a *ruling*.[10] In practice, both of these types of determinations are often generically referred to as *rulings*.

An organization seeking recognition of exemption must file an application with the IRS Service Center in Cincinnati, Ohio.

This application process requires the organization to reveal some information about its fund-raising program.

A ruling or determination will be issued to an organization, as long as the application and supporting documents establish that it meets the particular statutory requirements. The application must include a statement describing the organization's purposes, copies of its governing instruments (such as, in the case of a corporation, its articles of incorporation and bylaws), and either a financial statement or a proposed multiyear budget.

The application filed by a charitable organization must also include a summary of the sources of its financial support, its fund-raising program, the composition of its governing body (usually board of directors), its relationship with other organizations (if any), the nature of its services or products and the basis for any charges for them, and its membership (if any).

An application for recognition of exemption should be regarded as an important legal document and prepared accordingly. Throughout an organization's existence, it will likely be called on to provide its application for recognition of exemption to others for review. Indeed, a nonprofit organization is required by federal law to provide a copy of this application to anyone who requests it.[11]

Q 3:10   What information must be provided by means of the application for recognition of exemption?

The application for recognition of tax exemption filed by charitable organizations (Form 1023) comes in a packet.

NOTE: This analysis of the application for recognition of tax exemption is based on the Form 1023 dated September 1998. The reader may wish to obtain a copy of this form and have it available for purposes of this discussion.

This packet includes instructions for preparation of the form, the form itself (in duplicate), and the Form 872-C. (Form 874-C is used to extend the statute of limitations in case there is a need to assess the tax on the net income of private foundations.) Only one copy of Form 1023 need be filed with the IRS; the other copy may be used in drafting the application.

PART I

Part I of Form 1023 requests certain basic information about the applicant organization, such as its name, address, and date of formation. Every nonprofit organization must have an *employer identification number* (even if there are no employees); this is obtained by filing a Form SS-4. The Form SS-4 may be filed as soon as the organization is formed and organized, or it may be filed with the Form 1023.

The contact person (question 3) may be either someone directly involved with the organization, such as an officer or director, or an independent representative of the organization, such as a lawyer or accountant. If this type of a representative is being used, he or she must be granted a power of attorney, which is filed with the application, on Form 2848.

The organization must state the month in which its annual accounting period ends (question 4). The determination of a fiscal year should be given some thought; most organizations use the calendar year (in which case the answer is "December"). Whatever period is selected, the organization should be certain that the same period is stated on Form SS-4 and used when compiling its multiyear budget (see below).

The date of formation is to be provided (question 5). If incorporated, for example, this date will be the date the state agency received the articles of incorporation. This date is significant in relation to the *15-month rule* (see below).

Question 11 of Form 1023 requires an applicant organization to identify its "type." Generally, the organization must be one of three types: nonprofit corporation, trust, or unincorporated association.

If a corporation, the attachments will be the articles of incorporation and bylaws, any amendments to these documents, and the certificates of incorporation and amendment (if any) issued by the state. If a trust, the attachments will be the trust document(s). If an unincorporated association, the attachments will be the constitution and bylaws.

PART II

The applicant charitable organization must identify, in order of size, its sources of financial support (question 2). Typical answers are contributions from the general public, other contributions, grants, dues, other exempt function (fee-for-service) revenue, and/or investment income. Whatever sources of support are identified here, the organization should be careful to be consistent when preparing the multiyear budget and selecting the nonprivate foundation status, if any (see below).

The organization must describe its actual and planned fund-raising program (question 3). The organization should summarize its use of, or plans to use, selective mailings, fund-raising committees, volunteers, professional fund-raisers, and the like. Again, the organization should be certain to conform its discussion of financial support with that of its fund-raising plans. The organization can describe a very detailed fund-raising program or it can state that it has yet to develop a semblance of a fund-raising program.

The organization must provide a narrative of its activities (question 1). Usually, this is an essay that is descriptive of the organization's programs and should be carefully written. Good practice is to open with a description of the organization's purposes, followed by one or more paragraphs summarizing its program activities. This response should be as full as is reasonable and may well occupy more space than is provided, in which case the response can be in the form of a separate exhibit.

The names and addresses of the organization's officers and directors must be provided, along with the amount (if any) of their annual compensation (question 4). As to compensation, this includes all compensation, not just that for serving as an officer or director (or trustee).

Question 5, concerning relationships with other organizations, can be very important for some organizations. As a general rule, it does not matter whether the charitable organization has a special relationship with, or is controlled by, another organization. For example, some charitable organizations are controlled by other types of tax-exempt organizations, such as social welfare organizations (Q 1:18) or trade associations (Q 1:19), or are controlled by for-profit corporations (such as corporation-related foundations).

Question 11, concerning membership groups, is basically self-explanatory. It relates to organizations that have a true membership, however, not merely arrangements where the concept of a "membership" is used as a fund-raising technique.

PART III

Question 5 of Part I, concerning the date of formation of an organization, can be of no particular importance or it can be of extreme importance, depending on the circumstances. The basic rule, reflected in question 1, is that the recognition of exemption will be retroactive to the date of formation of the charitable organization where the application is filed with the IRS within 15 months from the end of the month in which the organization was established.[12] For example, if the organization is created on January 15, 2000, and the application for recognition of exemption is filed on or before April 30, 2001, the recognition of exemption (if granted) will be retroactive to January 15, 2000, irrespective of when the determination is made by the IRS. To continue with this example, however, if the application is filed on or after May 1, 2001, the recognition of exemption generally would, under the 15-month rule, be effective only as of the date the application was received by the IRS. (Nonetheless, as discussed below, the emergence of a 27-month rule has alleviated the time pressures in this context.)

As to the matter of tax-exempt status, the 15-month rule may not be of any particular importance, in that the charitable organization can qualify as a tax-exempt social welfare organization (Q 1:18) (which does not require recognition of tax-exempt status) until the date of its classification as a charitable organization.[13] This alleviation of the tax-exemption problem, however, as reflected in question 7, is of no assistance with respect to the posture of the organization as a charitable donee or as a nonprivate foundation (if the latter is applicable). Donors making gifts during the interim period will, upon audit, find their charitable deductions disallowed. Private foundations making grants during the interim period may be subject to taxation for failure to exercise *expenditure responsibility*. Thus, it is imperative that an organization desiring to be recognized as a charitable organization from its date of formation file a completed application for recognition of tax exemption prior to the expiration of the 15-month period.

There are, nonetheless, some exceptions to the 15-month rule. One is an automatic 12-month extension of time within which to file the application (question 3);[14] this has essentially converted the standard to a 27-month rule. In some instances, the IRS can accord relief in this area (question 5). Certain small organizations, churches, conventions or associations of churches, integrated auxiliaries of churches, and other organizations are exempted from this application requirement (question 2).[15]

Questions 8 through 10 can be of very large consequence. This is where the public charity/private foundation rules come into play (Chapter 2). If the applicant charitable organization is a private foundation, the answer to question 8 is yes. If the organization is seeking classification as a private operating foundation, it should so indicate in response to question 9 and complete Part IV.

If the organization, however, believes it can avoid private foundation status by reason of being one of the entities listed in question 10, it must select either a *definitive* ruling (Q 2:11) or an *advance* ruling (Q 2:9). For new charitable organizations (that is, those with a tax year of less than eight months) that are seeking to be classified as publicly supported entities, an advance ruling (selected by responding to question 11) is the correct choice. This is because they lack the financial history to demonstrate actual public support, which is required before a publicly supported organization can receive a definitive ruling. If the applicant believes it will be supported principally by gifts and grants (Q 2:7), it should check the box correlating with question 10(h). The box of question 10(i) is for organizations that are expecting support in the form of a blend of gifts, grants, and exempt function income (Q 2:8).

Either type of putative publicly supported organization must demonstrate its initial qualification for nonprivate foundation status by convincing the IRS that it will receive the requisite extent of public support. This is done by submitting a proposed budget. This budget summarizes contemplated types of revenue (such as gifts, grants, exempt function revenue, and investment income) and types of expenses (such as expenditures for program, compensation, occupancy, telephone, travel, postage, and fund-raising) for each of five years. For this purpose, a year is a period consisting of at least eight months. (For new organizations, this budget is submitted in lieu of the financial statements reflected in Part IV of Form 1023.) The five-year period is the *advance ruling* period. Thus, as question 11 reflects, an organization with a tax year of at least eight months, but that has a period of existence of less than five years can obtain either an advance or definitive ruling.

In designing the budget, the five years involved are the fiscal years of the organization. The applicant organization should be certain that the fiscal year used to develop the budget is the same period referenced in the response to question 4 of Part I. Also in this process, the organization should be certain that the types of revenue stated in the budget correspond to the types of revenue summarized in the response to question 2 of Part III.

The advance ruling pertains only to the applicant organization's status as a publicly supported entity. That is, it is not an advance ruling as to tax-exempt status or charitable donee status. Thus, the advance ruling period is a probationary or conditional ruling, as to "public" status. Once the advance ruling period expires and the organization has in fact received adequate public support during the five-year period, that fact will be reported to the IRS, which will in turn issue a definitive ruling that it is a publicly supported charity. Just as the advance ruling is conditional, the definitive ruling is permanent (unless upset by a subsequent loss of qualification for exemption or change in the law).

The publicly supported charitable organization must, during and after the expiration of the advance ruling period, continue on an ongoing basis to show that it qualifies as a publicly supported charity, assuming it wants to retain that status. This is done by reporting the financial support information as part of the annual information return (Chapter 8).

It does not matter which type of publicly supported organization the charitable entity is at any point in its existence; the principal objective is to qualify, at any one time, under one category or another. Thus, an organization can shift from one classification of publicly supported organization to another throughout its duration. Likewise, a charitable organization can, without concern, select one category of publicly supported organization when it completes Part III and only satisfy the requirements of the other category as of the close of the advance ruling period.

If an organization selects a category of publicly supported charitable organization when it prepares Part III, and finds at the close of the advance ruling period that it did not meet either set of requirements for publicly supported status, it will be categorized as a private foundation, unless it can demonstrate eligibility for otherwise avoiding private foundation status. This can be done if the organization qualifies as an entity such as a church, school, hospital, or supporting organization (see below).

If the organization is classified as a private foundation following the close of its advance ruling period, it will have to pay the excise tax on its net investment income[16] for each of the years in the advance ruling period (and thereafter). For the IRS to be able to assess the tax retroactively, the taxpayer must agree to waive the running of the statute of limitations, which otherwise would preclude the IRS from reaching that far back. The waiver is granted by the execution of Form 872-C (in duplicate), which, as noted, is part of the Form 1023 package.

An applicant organization that qualifies as a church, school, hospital, supporting organization, or the like is eligible to receive a definitive ruling at the outset. This is because its financial support is not the factor used in classifying it as a public entity. Instead, its public status derives from what it does programmatically.

An organization can receive a definitive ruling that it is publicly supported if it has been in existence for, as noted, a tax year of at least eight months and received the requisite public support during that period. The organization in this situation would submit a completed Part IV for each of these years.

Every organization that is requesting a definitive ruling must evidence its selection of nonprivate foundation status by answering questions 12 through 15 of Part III. Questions 12 and 15 are to be answered by organizations seeking an advance ruling. Certain organizations are required to submit a schedule (question 15); these organizations include churches (Schedule A), schools (Schedule B), supporting organizations (Schedule D), scholarship-granting organizations (Schedule H), and successors to for-profit entities (Schedule I).

SUMMARY

This application for recognition of tax exemption as a charitable organization, if properly completed, amounts to a rather complete portrait of the programs, fund-raising plans, and other aspects of the applicant organization. That is why it is important to devote some time and thinking to the preparation of the form. It is, as noted, a public document and, during the course of the organization's existence, the organization may well be called on to supply a copy of the application. Since those who request the document are likely to be prospective donors or grantors, or representatives of the media, it is particularly important that it be properly prepared.

If a fund-raising professional—either in-house executive or consultant—is serving an applicant organization at this stage, he or she should participate in the preparation of this application. Too frequently, however, that is not the case, which can cause the portions of the application that pertain to fund-raising to be incomplete or inaccurate.

CHAPTER 4

Charitable Contribution Deduction Rules

No aspect of the law is more important to the professional fund-raiser than the charitable contribution deduction rules. Donors usually give with donative intent being the primary motive but the stimulus of the charitable deduction cannot be minimized. This deduction often shapes the form and timing of gifts, and enables donors to give more generously than would otherwise be the case.

Thus, the fund-raiser should have at least a grasp of the basics of this body of law. This area of the law, being fluid, is constantly undergoing change and the fund-raiser should check with legal counsel from time to time when making decisions, or when prospective donors are making decisions, based on what is thought to be the state of the law. Nonetheless, the fund-raiser should have a basic grounding in the tax law surrounding the charitable deduction—and the purpose of this chapter is to provide that framework.

Here are the questions most frequently asked by professional fund-raisers (or that should be asked by them) about the charitable contribution deduction rules—and the answers to them.

Q 4:1   What are the charitable contribution deductions?

The federal tax law provides three sets of charitable contribution deductions. Most state laws make available one or more of these deductions as well.

The federal charitable contribution deduction that attracts the most attention is the income tax charitable deduction. There are, however, two other charitable contribution deductions: one that is part of the federal gift tax law and one that is part of the federal estate tax law. The discussion that follows is confined to the federal income tax charitable contribution deduction.

Q 4:2   Are all tax-exempt organizations eligible to receive tax-deductible contributions?

No. The categories of organizations that are eligible for *exemption* from the federal income tax are considerably more extensive than the categories of organizations that are eligible to receive contributions that are *deductible* under the federal income tax as charitable gifts.

There are only five classifications of entities that are charitable donees for this purpose:

1. Charitable organizations that are such for tax exemption purposes, including educational, religious, and scientific entities.

   NOTE: The range of charitable organizations for deductible charitable giving purposes is almost the same as that for income tax exemption purposes. There is one minor exception: organizations that *test for public safety* are charitable, but only for exemption purposes.[1]

   ---

2. Governments, namely, a state, a possession of the federal government, a political subdivision of either, the federal government itself, and the District of Columbia, as long as the gift is made for a public purpose.
3. An organization of war veterans, and an auxiliary unit of or foundation for a veterans' organization.
4. Many fraternal societies that operate under the lodge system, as long as the gift is to be used for charitable purposes.
5. Membership cemetery companies and corporations chartered for burial purposes as cemetery corporations.[2]

CAUTION: On occasion, a gift is made to a nonprofit organization where the donor understands that there is no income tax charitable contribution deduction. Nonetheless, the donor (and sometimes his or her tax advisor) may overlook the fact that there may be a gift tax obligation.

Generally, contributions to other types of tax-exempt organizations are not deductible.

TIP: Although contributions to exempt organizations other than those in these five categories generally are not deductible, this limitation is rather easily sidestepped by the creation of a related charitable entity, often loosely termed a *foundation*. Tax-exempt organizations that effectively use related foundations for purposes of attracting deductible charitable gifts include trade, business, and professional associations (Q 1:19), and social welfare organizations (Q 1:18). In some instances, an otherwise nonqualifying organization is allowed to receive a contribution that is deductible where the gift money or property is devoted to charitable purposes.

COMMENT: It is common for a charitable organization—one that itself is eligible to receive deductible gifts—to utilize a related foundation. This is done for management, not tax, purposes. Organizations that follow this approach include hospitals and other health care providers, colleges, universities, schools, and various religious organizations.

Q 4:3   What are the federal income tax rules for deductibility of a contribution of money to a public charity by an individual?

A charitable contribution is, of course, often made with money. Some prefer the word *cash*. (Some don't care about the terminology as long as they obtain the currency.) While this type of gift is usually deductible, there are limitations on the extent of deductibility in any one tax year.

NOTE: For a charitable contribution of money to be deductible by an individual under the federal income tax law, he or she must itemize deductions.

The limitations in this area are based in part on the concept of the *contribution base*. An individual's contribution base essentially is the same as the amount of his or her *adjusted gross income*.[3] Technically, an individual's *contribution base* is his or her adjusted gross income, computed without regard to any net operating loss carryback to the taxable year.[4]

NOTE: Throughout, reference will be made to *adjusted gross income* rather than the more technical term *contribution base*.

In the case of an individual, where a charitable gift is made with money and the charitable donee is a public charity (Q 2:1) or a select type of private foundation, usually a private operating foundation (Q 2:13), the extent of the charitable contribution deduction under the federal income tax law, for the year of the gift, cannot exceed 50 percent of the donor's adjusted gross income.[5] Any excess portion can be carried forward and deducted over a period of up to five subsequent years.[6]

Thus, for example, if an individual had adjusted gross income in the amount of $100,000 for 2000 and made gifts of money to one or more public charities in that year totaling $40,000, the gifts would be fully deductible (assuming no other gifts and no application of any other limitations) for 2000. If this donor were more generous and contributed $60,000 in 2000, the charitable deduction for 2000 would generally be $50,000 (50% of $100,000) and the excess amount of $10,000 would be carried forward, to be potentially deductible for 2001.

The charitable contribution deduction for individuals is subject to the 3 percent limitation on overall itemized deductions.[7] A gift of money may have to be *substantiated* (Q 4:37) and/or may be a *quid pro quo contribution* (Q 4:38). A planned gift can be made in whole or in part with money (Chapter 5).

Q 4:4 What are the federal income tax rules for deductibility of a contribution of money to a charitable organization, other than a public charity, by an individual?

In the case of an individual, where a charitable gift is made with money and the charitable donee is a charitable organization other than a public charity, such as a private foundation (Q 2:2), the extent of the charitable contribution deduction under the federal income tax law, for the year of the gift, cannot exceed 30 percent of the donor's adjusted gross income.[8] Any excess portion can be carried forward and deducted over a period of up to five subsequent years.[9]

Thus, for example, if an individual had adjusted gross income in the amount of $100,000 for 2000 and made a gift of money to a private foundation in that year in the amount of $20,000, the gift would be fully deductible (assuming no other gifts and no application of any other limitations) for 2000. If this gift were instead $40,000 in 2000, the charitable deduction for 2000 would generally be $30,000 (30% of $100,000) and the excess amount of $10,000 would be carried forward, to be potentially deductible for 2001.

COMMENT: An individual may, in any one year, make charitable gifts to a number of charitable organizations, some public and some not.

Each gift deduction must be separately calculated using the appropriate limitation. No matter the combination, the total amount of deductible giving in a year cannot exceed the 50 percent maximum.[10]

Q 4:5 What are the federal income tax rules for deductibility of a contribution of property to a public charity by an individual?

The rules pertaining to charitable contributions by individuals of property are more complex than those involving gifts of money (Q 4:3, Q 4:4). This type of gift is usually deductible, but there are several limitations on the extent of deductibility in any tax year.

The primary set of these limitations imposes percentage maximums, applied in the same fashion as is the case with respect to gifts of money (Q 4:3). Thus, for individuals, where a charitable gift consists of property and the charitable donee is a public charity (Q 2:1) or a select type of private foundation (Q 2:13), the extent of the charitable deduction under the federal income tax law generally cannot exceed 30 percent of the donor's adjusted gross income.[11] Any excess portion can be carried forward and deducted over a period of up to five subsequent years.[12]

Thus, for example, if an individual had adjusted gross income in the amount of $100,000 for 2000 and made gifts of property to one or more public charities in that year totaling $20,000, the gifts would be fully deductible (assuming no other gifts and no application of any other limitations) for 2000. If this donor instead made gifts of this nature in the amount of $40,000 in 2000, the charitable deduction for 2000 would generally be $30,000 (30% of $100,000) and the excess amount of $10,000 would be carried forward, to be potentially deductible for 2001.

One of the most appealing features of the federal income tax law in this context is that a charitable contribution of property that has appreciated in value often is deductible based on the full fair market value of the property.[13] The capital gain inherent in the appreciated property, which would be taxable had the property instead been sold or otherwise disposed of, goes untaxed.

NOTE: For this benefit to be available, the property must be *capital gain property* rather than *ordinary income property*. As a generalization, this distinction is based on the tax treatment of the revenue that would result if the property were sold. That is, the revenue would either be *long-term capital gain*, or *ordinary income* or *short-term capital gain*. (Generally, long-term capital gain property is a capital asset held for at least 12 months.[14]) Where the property is ordinary income property, the charitable contribution deduction must be reduced by the amount of gain that would either be ordinary income or short-term capital gain; in other words, the deduction is confined to the donor's basis in the property.[15]

As an illustration, an individual purchased an item of (capital gain) property for $20,000 and it is now worth $40,000. He or she contributes this property to a public charity in 2000 and receives a potential charitable contribution deduction of $40,000. The capital gain of $20,000 that would have been triggered had the property been sold escapes taxation.

The charitable deduction is a *potential* one because the actual deduction is determined by application of the appropriate percentage limitation. If this donor's adjusted gross income for 2000 was $100,000, the charitable deduction would be $30,000 and the excess of $10,000 would be carried forward to 2001 (still subject to the 30% limitation).

TIP: This rule pertaining to the favorable tax treatment for gifts of appreciated property is equally applicable in the planned giving setting (Chapter 5). In many situations (but not all), the deductible remainder interest is based on the full fair market value of the contributed property and the appreciation element (gain) is not taxed.

Again, a gift of property may have to be *substantiated* (Q 4:37), may be a *quid pro quo contribution* (Q 4:38), and/or may be subject to appraisal requirements (Q 4:39). A planned gift is often made, in whole or in part, with (appreciated) property (Q 5:1).

Q 4:6   Are there any exceptions to this rule?

Yes. The federal tax law provides an opportunity for an individual donor to elect application of the 50 percent limitation (Q 4:3) where the 30 percent limitation (Q 4:5) would otherwise apply. That is, an individual may elect for a tax year to reduce his or her potential federal income tax charitable contribution deduction, occasioned by the gift or gifts of capital gain property (Q 4:5) to charity made during that year, by the amount of what would have been long-term capital gain had the property been sold, in exchange for use of the 50 percent limitation.[16]

COMMENT: Of course, in deciding whether to make this election, the individual must determine whether the 50 percent limitation or the 30 percent limitation is most suitable for him or her (or both) under the

---

circumstances. A principal factor usually is the extent to which the property has appreciated in value; this election can be preferable where the property has not appreciated much in value.

Q 4:7   What are the federal income tax rules for deductibility of a contribution of property to a charitable organization, other than a public charity, by an individual?

In the case of an individual, where a charitable gift is made with property and the charitable donee is a charitable organization other than a public charity, such as a private foundation (Q 2:2), the extent of the charitable contribution deduction under the federal income tax law, for the year of the gift, generally cannot exceed 20 percent of the donor's adjusted gross income.[17] Any excess portion can be carried forward and deducted over a period of up to five subsequent years.[18]

Thus, for example, if an individual had adjusted gross income in the amount of $100,000 for 2000 and made a gift of property to a private foundation in that year in the amount of $15,000, the gift would be fully deductible (assuming no other gifts and no application of any other limitations) for 2000. If this gift were instead $30,000 in 2000, the charitable deduction for 2000 would generally be $20,000 (20% of $100,000) and the excess amount of $10,000 would be carried forward, to be potentially deductible for 2001 (still subject to the 20% limitation).

Q 4:8   What about a gift by an individual of property to a private foundation?

In the case of a gift by an individual of property to a private foundation, the percentage limitation of 20 percent applies (Q 4:7). Moreover, there is a *deduction reduction rule* which generally applies in this context. That rule is this: where property is contributed to a private foundation, the amount of the contribution deduction must be reduced by the amount of the long-term capital gain inherent in the property.[19]

There is, however, a significant exception to that rule. It concerns *qualified appreciated stock*, which essentially means publicly traded securities.[20] This type of stock can be contributed to a private foundation with the charitable deduction based on the full fair market value of the stock (as long as all of the inherent gain is long-term capital gain).

NOTE: This special rule has a fitful history. It would expire, leaving prospective donors to wonder whether it would be resuscitated. Then Congress would resurrect it, only to have it once again expire. Mercifully, in 1998, Congress made the rule permanent.

Q 4:9   What are the federal income tax rules as to timing of the deductibility of a contribution by an individual?

A federal income tax charitable contribution deduction for a gift made by an individual arises at the time of, and for the year in which, the deduction is made.

Q 4:10   What are the federal income tax rules for deductibility of a charitable contribution by a for-profit corporation?

The answer to this question depends on the type of for-profit corporation that is the donor. There are essentially two types of these corporations. The larger corporations are sometimes referred to as *regular* corporations or C corporations (Q 1:20).

The other type of corporation is the *small business* corporation. These entities are the subject of Subchapter S of the Code and thus are often termed *S corporations* (Q 1:21).

This answer, then, assumes the donor is a C corporation. The rules as to a gift by an S corporation are summarized elsewhere (Q 4:14).

A for-profit corporation may make a charitable gift of money. That contribution may not exceed, in any tax year, 10 percent of the corporation's pre-tax net income.[21] Carryover rules are available.[22] Generally, this set of rules applies in instances of charitable gifts of property.

There are, however, special rules limiting the deductibility of corporate gifts. In optimal circumstances, the allowable charitable contribution deduction is an amount equal to as much as twice the corporation's basis in the property. These special rules—providing what is termed an *augmented deduction*—pertain to gifts of the following types of property:

1. Inventory, with the deduction enhanced when the property is to be used for the care of the ill, the needy, or infants (Q 4:11).
2. Tangible personal property to be used for scientific research (a *qualified research contribution*) (Q 4:20).
3. Computer technology and equipment for elementary or secondary school purposes (Q 4:21).

NOTE: The third of these rules is inapplicable to a contribution made during a tax year beginning after December 31, 2000.[23]

Q 4:11   What are the federal income tax rules concerning corporate gifts of inventory?

Special federal tax rules govern charitable contributions of items of inventory of a corporation.

NOTE: The term *inventory* means property that is stock in trade of a business enterprise, held for sale to customers. When the property is sold, the resulting income is *ordinary income* (Q 4:5).

In general, the amount of the charitable deduction for contributions of property is measured by using the fair market value of the property. This is usually the case where the property is *capital gain property* (*id.*). By contrast, this is not the outcome where the property is *ordinary income property*; then the charitable deduction is limited to the donor's basis in the property.

NOTE: Another way to view this is that the amount that might otherwise be deductible (using fair market value) must be reduced by the amount of ordinary income that would have resulted had the item of property been sold.

Thus, when a corporation makes a charitable contribution of property out of its inventory, the gift deduction is generally confined to an amount which may not exceed the donor's cost basis in the property.[24]

Nevertheless, a special rule provides an augmented deduction under certain circumstances, pursuant to which the charitable deduction for contributions of inventory may be an amount equal to as much as twice the cost basis in the property.[25] These eligible gifts of inventory are known as *qualified contributions*.[26]

In the case of a gift of inventory, the charitable contribution deduction that might otherwise result generally must be reduced by an amount equal to one-half of the amount of gain that would not have been long-term capital gain if the property had been sold by the donor at fair market value at the date of the contribution.[27] If, after this reduction, the amount of the deduction would be more than twice the basis in the contributed property, the amount of the deduction must be further reduced to an amount equal to twice the cost basis in the property.[28]

CAUTION: In the popular literature, this rule is often misstated (other than in this book). For example, in an article in *The New York Times*,

---

the reporter, attempting to explain this rule, wrote that "American companies . . . are eligible for twice the normal tax deductions when they participate in a humanitarian effort."[29] (That would be generous.) The fact is that under the most optimum of circumstances, these gifts are deductible in amounts that cannot exceed twice the donors' *basis* in the donated properties.

This augmented deduction is available under the following circumstances:

1. The gift is of property that is

   - Stock in trade of the corporation or other property of a kind which would properly be included in the inventory of the corporation if on hand at the close of the tax year.[30]
   - Property held by the corporation primarily for sale to customers in the ordinary course of the trade or business.[31]
   - Property, used in a trade or business, of a character which is subject to the allowance for depreciation,[32] or
   - Real property used in a trade or business.[33]

2. The donor is a corporation.

   > **NOTE:** This requirement means the entity must be a regular (C) corporation, not a small business (S) corporation (Q 1:20, Q 1:21).

3. The donee is a charitable organization (Q 1:8).
4. The donee is not a private foundation (Q 2:2).

   > **NOTE:** The donee can, however, be a private operating foundation (Q 2:13).

5. The use of the property by the donee is related to its tax-exempt purposes (Q 6:1).

   > **NOTE:** This rule means that the gift property may not be used in connection with any activity that gives rise to unrelated business income.

6. The property is to be used by the donee solely for the care of the ill, the needy, or infants.

CAUTION: This is a core component of these requirements. No other individual may use the contributed property except as incidental to primary use in the care of the ill,
the needy, or infants. The tax regulations go into some detail in defining the pertinent terms, such as *ill, needy,* and
care of the needy. An *infant* is a "minor child."[34]

NOTE: The IRS is not particularly lenient in this area. In
one instance, gifts of books to prisoners in state correc-
tional facilities were found to not qualify under these rules.
The IRS reviewed general prison population statistics as to
those who are disabled and lacking a high school education—and concluded that their number was insufficient to
qualify the prisoners as needy.[35]

7. The property is not transferred by the donee in exchange for
money, other property, or services.

NOTE: This is not an absolute rule. For example, a contribution may qualify under these rules if the donee organization charges a fee to another organization in connection
with its transfer of the donated property if (1) the fee is nominal in relation to the value of the transferred property and is
not determined by that value, and (2) the fee is designed to
reimburse the donee organization for its administrative,
warehousing, or similar costs.

8. The donor receives from the donee a written statement representing that its use and disposition of the property will be in accordance with these rules.

NOTE: This written statement must be furnished within a
reasonable period after the contribution. In any event, it
must be furnished no later than the date (including exten-
sions) by which the donor is required to file its federal (corporate) income tax return for the year of the contribution.

COMMENT: The required books and records need not
trace the receipt and disposition of specific items of donated property if they disclose compliance with the requirements by reference to *aggregate quantities* of donated
property. The books and records are *adequate* if they reflect "total amounts received and distributed" (or used),
and outline the procedure used for determining that the ul-

timate recipient of the property is an ill or needy individual, or infant.

9. The property is in compliance with all applicable requirements of the Federal Food, Drug, and Cosmetic Act.

To reiterate, a contribution that satisfies these requirements is a *qualified contribution*.

COMMENT: This is a controversial tax law provision. Often, the charge is that the property contributed has no value at the time of the gift (e.g., pharmaceuticals whose shelf-life has expired) or lacks value in the particular circumstances. For example, an article in *The New York Times* in mid-1999 insinuated that corporations are deliberately making gifts of medicines for foreign charitable purposes that often are not useable. As much as one-half of the shipments were said to be "inappropriate and likely to gather dust in warehouses or be destroyed at government expense." The medicines were said to frequently be outdated and donated by drug companies to be rid of material that cannot be sold. Another practice: "Some companies turn up the pressure by insisting that charities take unwanted donations as a condition for getting things they really need."[36]

Q 4:12   What are the federal income tax rules as to timing of the deductibility of a contribution by a corporation?

Presumably, this question pertains to a charitable contribution made by a *regular* corporation (Q 1:20).

Generally, a federal income tax charitable contribution deduction for a gift made by a corporation arises at the time of, and for the year in which, the deduction is made. A corporation that reports its taxable income using the accrual method of accounting may, however, at its election, deduct charitable contributions paid within $2\frac{1}{2}$ months after the close of its tax year, as long as

1. The board of directors of the corporation authorized the making of the charitable contribution during the tax year, and
2. The charitable contribution is made after the close of the tax year of the corporation and within the $2\frac{1}{2}$-month period.[37]

This election must be made at the time the tax return for the tax year is filed. This is done by reporting the contribution on the return. A written declaration must be attached to the return stating that the resolution authorizing the contribution was adopted by the board of directors during the tax year involved. This declaration must be verified by a statement signed by an officer authorized to sign the return that it is made under penalties of perjury. There must also be attached to the return when filed a copy of the resolution of the board of directors authorizing the contribution.[38]

To satisfy this rule, contributions of property need not be segregated by year. Also, there is no requirement that the donees be identified at the time the resolution is adopted.[39]

Q 4:13   What are the federal income tax rules for deductibility of a charitable contribution by a partnership?

The taxable income of a partnership generally is computed in the same manner as is the case with individuals. The charitable contribution deduction, however, is not allowed to the partnership.[40] Rather, each partner takes into account separately the partner's distributive share of the partnership's charitable contributions.[41]

A partner's distributive share of charitable contributions made by a partnership during a tax year of the partnership is allowed as a charitable deduction on the partner's tax return for the partner's tax year with or within which the tax year of the partnership ends.[42] The aggregate of the partner's share of partnership contributions and the partner's own (directly made) contributions are subject to the various percentage limitations on annual deductibility (Q 4:3–Q 4:7).

Moreover, there is another aspect of the tax law that becomes invoked when a charitable gift is made out of a partnership: adjustment of the partner's basis in his or her (or its) interest in the partnership. This requires, by way of explanation, some background on this subject.

When a partnership makes a charitable contribution of property, the basis of each partner's interest in the partnership is decreased (but not below zero) by the amount of the partner's share of the partnership's basis in the property contributed.[43]

The adjusted basis of a partner's interest in a partnership must be increased by the sum of the partner's distributive share for the tax year and prior tax years of the taxable income of the partnership, the income of the partnership that is exempt from tax, and the excess of the deductions for depletion over the basis of the property subject to depletion.[44] The adjusted basis of a partner's interest in a partnership must be decreased (but not below zero) by distributions by the partnership, as well as by the sum of the partner's distributive share for the tax year and prior tax years of the losses of the partnership and expenditures of the partnership that are not deductible in computing taxable income and not properly chargeable to capital account.[45]

These adjustments to the basis of a partner's interest in a partner-ship are necessary to prevent inappropriate or unintended benefits or detriments to the partners. Generally, the basis of a partner's interest in a partnership is adjusted to reflect the tax allocations of the partner-ship to that partner. This adjustment ensures that the income and loss of the partnership are taken into account by its partners only once. Also, adjustments must be made to reflect certain nontaxable events in the partnership.[46] For example, a partner's share of nontaxable income (such as exempt income) is added to the basis of the partner's interest because, absent a basis adjustment, the partner could recognize gain with respect to the tax-exempt income (such as on a sale or redemption of the partner's interest) and the benefit of the tax-exempt income would be lost to the partner. Likewise, a partner's share of nonde-ductible expenditures must be deducted from the partner's basis in or-der to prevent that amount from giving rise to a loss to the partner on a sale or redemption of the partner's interest in the partnership.

In determining whether a transaction results in exempt income[47] or a nondeductible noncapital expenditure,[48] the inquiry must be whether the transaction has a permanent effect on the partnership's basis in its assets, without a corresponding current or future effect on its taxable income.

With this as background, perhaps an example will enhance these points. A and B each contribute an equal amount of money to form a general partnership. Under the partnership agreement, each item of in-come, gain, loss, and deduction of the partnership is allocated 50 per-cent to A and 50 percent to B. This partnership has unencumbered property, having a basis of $60,000 and a fair market value of $100,000. The partnership contributes the property to a charitable organization.

NOTE: This property is not of the type that requires reduction of the char-itable deduction by elements of ordinary income or capital gain (Q 4:5).

As discussed, the contribution of this property by this partnership is not taken into account in computing the partnership's taxable in-come. Consequently, the contribution results in a permanent decrease in the aggregate basis of the assets of the partnership that is not taken into account by the partnership in determining its taxable income and is not taken into account for federal income tax purposes in any other manner. Therefore, the contribution of the property, and the resulting permanent decrease in partnership basis, is an expenditure of the part-nership that is not deductible in computing its taxable income and not properly chargeable to capital account.

Reducing the partners' bases in their partnership interests by their respective shares of the permanent decrease in the partnership's basis in its assets preserves the intended benefit of providing a deduction for the fair market value of appreciated property without recognition of the appreciation. By contrast, reducing the partners' bases in their partnership interests by the fair market value of the contributed property would subsequently cause the partners to recognize gain (or a reduced loss), such as on a disposition of their partnership interests, attributable to the unrecognized appreciation in this contributed property at the time of the contribution.

In the example, under the partnership agreement, partnership items are allocated equally between A and B. Accordingly, the basis of each of A's and B's interests in the partnership is reduced by $30,000 (50% of $60,000).

Q 4:14   What are the federal income tax rules for deductibility of a charitable contribution by an S corporation?

S corporations (Q 1:18) are treated, for tax purposes, essentially the same as partnerships. Thus, the charitable contribution deduction is not allowed to the S corporation but is taken by each shareholder on an allocable basis.

Q 4:15   What are the federal income tax rules for deductibility of a charitable contribution by a limited liability company?

Limited liability companies[49] are treated, for tax purposes, essentially the same as partnerships. Thus, the charitable contribution deduction is not allowed to the limited liability company but is taken by each member on an allocable basis.

Q 4:16   Is the use of the gift property relevant in determining the amount of the charitable contribution deduction?

In some circumstances, the actual use of the property can be a factor in determining the amount of the charitable contribution deduction. The rule is that where the property contributed is tangible personal property and where the charitable donee uses the property for a non-charitable purpose, the contribution deduction must be reduced by the amount of the long-term capital gain inherent in the property.[50]

CAUTION: This rule can be troublesome in the context of the charitable auction. It is common for someone to make a gift of an item to be auctioned by the charity. The property that is the subject of the gift is often a painting, some other work of art, an item of furniture, and the

like—things that are tangible personal property. Sale soon after donation is an unrelated use. Thus, the charitable deduction for gifts of this
nature is confined to the donor's basis in the property (Q 4:5).

Q 4:17   Is there anything unique about gifts of works of art to charitable organizations?

Certainly, there usually is a federal income tax contribution deduction
for a gift of a work of art to a charitable organization. In general, this
deduction is an amount equal to the fair market value of the property
(Q 4:5).

There are, however, two exceptions that are particularly applicable
in this context:

1. The work of art that is contributed may be the creation of the
   donor, in which case the deduction is confined to the donor's
   basis in the property (Q 4:23).
2. The work of art may be put to an unrelated use by the charitable
   recipient, in which case the deduction is confined to the donor's
   basis in the property (Q 4:16).

Of these two exceptions, the second is most likely to occur. A work
of art is an item of *tangible personal property*. There is a special rule as
to gifts of this nature, which may be reiterated in this context. The rule
is this: where a gift of tangible personal property is made to a charity,
the amount of the charitable deduction that would otherwise be determined must be reduced by the amount of gain which would have been
long-term capital gain if the property contributed had been sold by the
donor at its fair market value, determined at the time of the contribution, where the use by the donee is unrelated to its tax-exempt purposes (*id.*).

The greatest controversy surrounding the charitable deduction of
a work of art is likely to be the value of the item. Not infrequently, there
is a dispute between the IRS and a donor as to the fair market value of a
work of art. Usually, these disputes are settled; sometimes they are resolved by a court—most frequently the U.S. Tax Court.

COMMENT 1: The appropriate value of an item of property is a question of fact, not law. Judges are not trained as appraisers; therefore
this field is rife with the use of expert witnesses. Not infrequently, the
value of property in these circumstances is arrived at with the court
splitting the difference between the value advanced by the donor's expert and that asserted by the government's expert.[51]

COMMENT 2: This is a field where donors can get rather creative and promoters of various art-based tax shelters proliferate. In turn, judges can become frustrated, cynical, or wry. Here is an example of the latter: "This was an interesting tax-saving arrangement devised as an art transaction, but the art will have to be treasured for art's sake and not as a tax deduction."[52]

NOTE: The IRS has devised a procedure by which a donor of a work of art to charity can reach agreement with the IRS as to the value of the item.[53]

Q 4:18   What is the tax law consequence of a loan of a work of art to a charitable organization?

As the question indicates, rather than *contribute* a work of art to a charitable organization, a person may decide to *loan* the artwork to a charity. This type of transfer does not give rise to a federal *income* tax charitable contribution deduction. The transaction is, nonetheless, a gift.

The transaction is disregarded as a transfer for *gift* tax purposes, however, where

1. The recipient organization is a charitable entity.
2. The use of the artwork by the charitable donee is related to the purpose or function constituting the basis for its tax exemption.
3. The artwork involved is an archaeological, historic, or creative item of tangible personal property.[54]

Q 4:19   What about charitable gifts of gems?

The law concerning the contribution of gems to charity essentially is that pertaining to gifts of works of art (Q 4:17). The specter of *tax shelter abuse* hangs over these gifts, however, because of the various deduction promotion schemes in this area that have unfolded in recent years.

Once again, the principal issue in this setting is the value of the items transferred. In one case, the claimed value was $80,680; the court held that the value was $16,800.[55] In another, the asserted value was $70,000; the court decided the value was $50,000.[56] Often, a court will confine the deduction value to the donor's cost basis in the gems.[57]

Q 4:20   Is there a charitable deduction for a gift of scientific research property?

Special federal tax rules govern the deductibility of charitable contributions of scientific research property.[58] To qualify under these rules, the property that is the subject of the gift must be the following:

1. Tangible personal property.
2. Stock in trade of a corporation or other property of a kind which would properly be included in the inventory of the corporation if on hand at the close of the tax year, or property held by the corporation primarily for sale to customers in the ordinary course of its trade or business.[59]

This deduction is only available for *regular* (C) corporations (Q 1:18). Thus, it is not available for a small business (S) corporation (Q 1:19), a personal holding company,[60] or a service corporation.[61]

In addition to the foregoing, for this charitable deduction to be available, all of these requirements must be satisfied:

1. The contribution must be to an *eligible institution of higher education* or an *eligible scientific research organization*. The former normally maintains a regular faculty and curriculum, normally has a regularly enrolled body of students in attendance at the place where its educational activities are regularly carried on, and meets other criteria.[62] Basically, the latter cannot be a private foundation (Q 2:2) and must be organized and operated primarily to conduct scientific research (see below).
2. The property must be constructed by the donor corporation.
3. The contribution must be made not later than two years after the date the construction of the property is substantially completed.
4. The original use of the property must be by the charitable recipient.
5. The property must be scientific equipment or apparatus, substantially all of the use of which by the charitable recipient is for research or experimentation, or for research training, in the United States in physical or biological sciences.
6. The property must not be transferred by the charitable recipient in exchange for money, other property, or services.
7. The corporation must receive from the charitable recipient a written statement representing that its use and disposition of

the property will be in accordance with the fifth and sixth of these requirements.

This deduction is computed in the same manner as is the case with respect to the special rule concerning gifts of inventory (Q 4:11).

Q 4:21   Is there a charitable deduction for a gift of computer technology and equipment?

Special federal tax rules govern the deductibility of charitable contributions of computer technology and equipment.[63] This deduction is confined to gifts for elementary or secondary school purposes.

NOTE: This deduction is not available for a contribution made during a tax year beginning after December 31, 2000.

This special deduction is termed a *qualified elementary or secondary educational contribution*. The property that is eligible for this deduction must be computer technology or equipment that is inventory or depreciable trade or business property in the hands of the donor. The gift must be made by a corporation.

NOTE: Once again (Q 4:11, Q 4:20), the corporation must be a C corporation (Q 1:18).

To be deductible, the contribution must satisfy the following criteria:

1. The contribution must be to an operating educational institution or a tax-exempt charitable entity that is organized primarily for purposes of supporting elementary and secondary education.

2. The contribution must be made no later than two years after the date the donor acquired the property (or, in the case of property constructed by the donor, the date the construction of the property was substantially completed).

3. The original use of the property must be by the donor or donee.

4. Substantially all of the use of the property by the donee must be for use within the United States for educational purposes in any of the grades K–12 that are related to the purpose or function of the organization.

5. The property may not be transferred by the donee in exchange for money, other property, or services, except for shipping, installation, and transfer costs.

6. The property must fit productively into the entity's education plan.

7. The property contributed must be computer software, computer or peripheral equipment, or fiber optic cable related to computer use.

NOTE: Not surprisingly, given the size of the Internal Revenue Code, the federal tax law provides a definition for each of these terms.[64]

A qualifying contribution may be made to a private foundation if the gift satisfies the second and fifth of these criteria, and, within 30 days of the gift, the foundation grants the property to a qualified recipient that satisfies the fourth through the sixth of these criteria and notifies the donor of the grant.

This deduction is computed in the same manner as is the case with respect to the special rule concerning gifts of inventory (Q 4:11).

Q 4:22 Is there a federal income tax deduction for a gift of real property for conservation purposes?

Yes. Special federal tax rules pertain to contributions to charity of real property for conservation purposes. These rules are an exception to the general rule that there is no charitable contribution for contributions of *partial interests* in property (Q 5:2). This exception involves the *qualified conservation contribution*.[65]

NOTE: The rules about to be discussed are in the context of the *income tax* charitable contribution deduction for qualified conservation contributions. There are, however, somewhat comparable rules in the *estate tax* and *gift tax* charitable deduction settings.

A qualified conservation contribution has three fundamental characteristics: it is a contribution

1. Of a *qualified real property interest*,
2. To a *qualified organization*,
3. Exclusively for *conservation purposes*.

A qualified real property interest is one of the following interests in real property:

1. The entire interest of the donor in the property (other than a qualified mineral interest).

NOTE: A *qualified mineral interest* is the donor's interest in subsurface oil, gas, or other minerals, and the right to access to these minerals.

CAUTION: A real property interest is not treated as an entire interest in the property (other than a qualified mineral interest) if the property in which the donor's interest exists was divided prior to the contribution in order to enable the donor to retain control of more than a qualified mineral interest or to reduce the real property interest contributed (with an exception for certain minor interests).

---

2. A remainder interest (Q 5:2).
3. A restriction (granted in perpetuity) on the use which may be made of the real property.

NOTE: A form of qualified real property interest is the *perpetual conservation restriction*. This is a restriction granted in perpetuity on the use which may be made of real property, including an easement or other interest in real property that under state law has attributes similar to an easement (such as a restrictive covenant).

A qualified organization is an entity which is one of the following:

1. A unit of government.
2. A publicly supported charitable organization which is the *donative* type (Q 2:7).
3. A publicly supported charitable organization which is the *service provider* type (Q 2:8).
4. A *supporting organization* (Q 2:15) that is controlled by one or more of the foregoing three types of organizations.

In addition, to be a qualified donee, an organization must have a commitment to protect the conservation purposes of the donation, and have the resources to enforce the restrictions. A qualified organization is not required to set aside funds to enforce the restrictions that are the subject of the contribution. In the instrument of conveyance, the donor must prohibit the donee from subsequently transferring the interest unless it requires, as a condition of the subsequent transfer, that the conservation purposes which the contribution was originally intended to advance be carried out.

The term *conservation purpose* means one of the following:

1. Preservation of land areas for outdoor recreation by, or for the education of, the general public.

> **NOTE:** This purpose includes the preservation of a water area for the use of the public for boating or fishing, or a nature or hiking trail for the use of the public.

2. Protection of a relatively natural habitat of fish, wildlife, or plants, or similar ecosystem.

> **NOTE:** This standard allows for alteration of the habitat or environment to some extent by human activity. For example, the preservation of a lake formed by a man-made dam qualifies if the lake is a natural feeding area for a wildlife community that includes rare, endangered, or threatened native species.

3. Preservation of open space (including farmland and forest land) where the preservation

- Is for the scenic enjoyment of the general public, or
- Is pursuant to a clearly delineated federal, state, or local governmental conservation policy, and
- As to either category, will yield a significant public benefit.

> **NOTE 1:** A governmental policy in this regard must be more than a general declaration of conservation goals by a single official or legislative body. The requirement is met by contributions that further a specified, identified conservation project, that preserve a wild or scenic river, or that protect the scenic, ecological, or historic character of land that is contiguous to or an integral part of the surroundings of existing recreation or conservation sites.

> **NOTE 2:** The tax regulations contain criteria for evaluating and applying phrases such as *scenic enjoyment* and *significant public benefit.*

4. Preservation of an historically important land area or a certified historic structure.

NOTE 1: An *historically important land* area includes:

- An independently significant land area, including any related historic structures that meet the National Register Criteria for Evaluation.
- Any land area within a registered historic district, including any buildings on the land area that can reasonably be considered as contributing to the significance of the district.
- Any land area adjacent to a property listed individually in the National Register of Historic Places, in a case where the physical or environmental features of the land area contribute to the historic or cultural integrity of the property.

NOTE 2: A *certified historic structure* is a building, structure, or land area which is listed in the National Register, located in a registered historic district and is certified by the Secretary of the Interior to the Secretary of the Treasury as being of historic significance to the district.

To satisfy these rules, a contribution must be *exclusively* for conservation purposes. A conservation deduction will not be denied, however, where an incidental benefit inures to the donor merely as a result of conservation restrictions limiting the uses to which the donor's property may be put. One of the requirements in this regard is that the conservation purpose must be protected in perpetuity.

COMMENT: As an example of this last requirement, a court held that a grant of an easement over the façades of the donors' interests in a condominium apartment building was not a qualified conservation contribution because it was not contributed exclusively for conservation purposes, in that the easement was not protected in perpetuity because a security interest in the building had priority over the easement.[66]

This type of gift raises (once again) the matter of valuation. The amount of the charitable contribution deduction, in the case of a contribution of a donor's entire interest in conservation property (other than a qualified mineral interest), is the fair market value of the surface rights in the property contributed.

Two subrules:

1. In the case of a contribution of a remainder interest in real property, depreciation and depletion of the property must be taken into account in determining the value of the interest.
2. The value of a charitable contribution of a perpetual conservation restriction is the fair market value of the restriction at the time of the contribution.

If a donor makes a qualified conservation contribution and claims a charitable contribution deduction for it, the donor must maintain written records of

1. The fair market value of the underlying property before and after the contribution.
2. The conservation purpose furthered by the contribution.

NOTE: This is a *substantiation* requirement. This requirement is in addition to the general·charitable contribution substantiation requirements (Q 4:37).

Q 4:23   Is there a federal income tax charitable contribution deduction for a gift of property created by the donor?

Yes, but an individual may make a contribution to a charitable organization of an item of property that was created by the donor, such as a painting or a manuscript. The charitable deduction for this type of gift is not based on the fair market value of the property. Instead, it is confined to the donor's cost basis in the property.

This result is occasioned by the rule that requires a reduction in the charitable contribution deduction, created by a gift of property, by an amount equal to the amount of gain that would not have been long-term capital gain had the property been sold by the donor at its fair market value at the time of the contribution (Q 4:5). The federal tax law excludes from the definition of the term *capital asset* a copyright, a literary, musical, or artistic composition, a letter or memorandum, or similar property, held by

1. An individual whose personal efforts created the property,
2. In the case of a letter, memorandum, or similar property, a person for whom material of this nature was prepared or produced, or

3. A person in whose hands the basis of the property of this nature is determined, for purposes of determining gain from a sale or exchange, in whole or in part by reference to the basis of the property in the hands of a person described in either of the foregoing two categories.[67]

Thus, as noted, this charitable contribution deduction is confined to the amount equal to the cost to the donor of the creation of the item of property.

Q 4:24   What about gifts to charity of commodity futures contracts?

This is an unexpected question. There cannot be too many instances where a professional fund-raiser is confronted with a charitable contribution of commodity futures contracts.

Nonetheless, the matter occasionally arises. It has been the subject of considerable litigation—six court opinions to date, all of them involving the same donors. Basically, the evolving rule is that a charitable deduction is available for the gift—but the donor must recognize as income the long-term capital gain portion of the contracts.

This question was raised as the result of a case involving an individual who donated commodities futures contracts to a charitable organization. The law was clear at the time of the gifts (1974–1978, and 1980) that the contribution would give rise to a charitable deduction for the fair market value of the contracts and that the donor would not realize any capital gain or loss (as long as certain conditions were satisfied, which they were).

The tax law contains certain *marked-to-market* provisions, concerning the transfer of commodity futures contracts.[68] These rules generally require that a transfer of this nature must result in realization as income of the amount of the capital gain inherent in the contracts. The law as to these contracts was adjusted in 1981, with the revised law providing that gains or losses from any termination of a person's obligations or rights under these contracts are treated as 60 percent long-term capital gain or loss and 40 percent short-term capital gain or loss. This change in the law posed a problem for this donor, in that there is no charitable contribution deduction for the value of donated property to the extent that it gives rise to short-term gain to the donor had the donor sold the property (Q 4:5).

The donor attempted to solve this problem by contributing to charity only the portion of the contracts that was characterized as long-term capital gain.

These rules instruct taxpayers as to the correct method of income recognition when they sell or otherwise transfer futures contracts. These contracts are annually treated as if they were sold for fair market value

on the final business day of the tax year. As every contract is construc-
tively sold each year, a taxpayer must recognize accrued gains and losses
annually by marking the contracts to market. This rule as to constructive
recognition of accrued gain is an exception to the general rule, by which
recognition of any capital gain or loss is delayed until the time of sale or
exchange. The IRS asserted—and a court of appeals agreed—that these
tax rules apply in the instance of charitable gifts of these contracts.

The statute lists a variety of ways that a futures contract can be terminated or transferred: "by offsetting, by taking or making delivery, by
exercise or being exercised, by assignment or being assigned, by lapse,
or otherwise."[69] It was the word *otherwise* that was held to embrace
transfers by charitable gift. The trial court mused that the language "describe[s] economic activity that seems fundamentally different from
charitable giving."[70] But the appellate court wrote that the mark-to-mar-
ket rules "appear to govern all terminations and transfers of futures contracts," adding that "[t]here is no reason for excluding charitable
donations from the definition of transfer."[71] The court of appeals decided
that the plain language of the statute mandates the marking of contracts
to market even when they are contributed to a charitable organization.
The appellate court was unwilling to engraft an "additional exception to
what is an already complex tax code."[72]

COMMENT: This donor attempted a final argument: Persons are able
to donate other types of property to charity without realizing capital
gains as income. Although the court of appeals agreed with this view, it
stated that Congress has created a rule that treats futures contracts differently in a variety of contexts (including charitable giving). The court
said that if Congress wants to create an exception in this setting for
charitable gifts, it can do so. Concluded this court: "Without such a provision, we think it an inappropriate arrogation of legislative power for a
court to amend the statute under the guise of judicial construction."[73]

Q 4:25   What about gifts to charity from retirement plans?

These gifts can be made but there is a considerable tax problem. Under
existing law, amounts in a retirement plan are includable in income
when withdrawn (except to the extent the withdrawal represents a return of after-tax contributions). Also, generally there is a 10 percent
penalty for an early withdrawal before attainment of age 59 1/2.[74] A charitable contribution from a retirement arrangement (including an individual retirement account) triggers these adverse tax consequences.

Congress passed a major tax bill in 1999, which was vetoed. That legislation would have created an exclusion from gross income for qualified

charitable distributions from an individual retirement arrangement to a charitable organization.[75] This distribution would be one made by an individual after age 70½ and made directly to the charity. This rule would have been effective with respect to distributions after December 31, 2002.

It is quite likely that a proposal of this nature will be a part of a forthcoming tax bill.

NOTE: Under this proposal, the distribution would have to be made *to* a charitable organization. The Senate version of the legislation, however, would have also permitted distributions of this nature to charitable remainder trusts (Q 5:6). to pooled income funds (Q 5:17), or for the issuance of charitable gift annuities (Q 5:32).

Q 4:26 Is there a federal income tax charitable contribution deduction for a gift of services?

No. The federal tax law does not allow for a charitable contribution deduction for the value of services provided to a charitable organization as a gift.[76] For example, a lawyer may contribute to a charitable organization, as an item to be bid on at the charity's fund-raising auction, his or her services in the writing of a will. There is no charitable contribution deduction for the value (based on the lawyer's hourly rate) of this type of gift.[77]

NOTE 1: There is another reason why a gift of services is not deductible: there is no charitable deduction for gifts of *property* created by the donor (Q 4:23).

NOTE 2: Some donors and their advisors seem to be unaware of this rule; charitable deductions for gifts of services are being claimed. The professional fund-raiser does not want to be in the position of having even insinuated that a charitable deduction is available in this setting.

In its annual information return, a tax-exempt organization can indicate the value of donated services received as gifts.[78] The organization cannot, however, include this value as revenue, expense the services, or (if it is a charitable organization) take the value into account in calculating public support.

NOTE: By contrast, in some instances, the out-of-pocket expenses incurred by volunteers may be deductible as charitable contributions. This can occur where the expenses are necessary to the accomplishment of the organization's charitable purposes.[79]

Q 4:27   Is there a federal income tax charitable contribution deduction for a gift of the right to use materials, equipment, or facilities?

No. The federal tax law does not allow for a charitable contribution deduction for the use of materials, equipment, or facilities provided to a charitable organization as a gift.[80] For example, the owner of an office building may contribute office space in the building to a charity. There is no charitable contribution deduction for this type of gift. Likewise, the owner of a beach house may contribute to a charity, as an item to be bid on at a fund-raising auction, a two-week stay at the house. No contribution deduction is available for this type of gift.

NOTE: Charitable deductions for gifts of the use of property, made in the context of auction fund-raising, are undoubtedly more prevalent than deductions for gifts of services (Q 4:26). Again, the professional fund-raiser should avoid situations where he or she is perceived as having suggested that a charitable deduction is available in this setting.

In its annual information return, a tax-exempt organization can indicate the value of materials, equipment, or facilities received as gifts.[81] The organization cannot, however, include this value as revenue, expense the materials or the like, or (if it is a charitable organization) take the value into account in calculating public support.

CAUTION: A common example of this situation is a gift to a charity of the right to use a vacation home for one or two weeks, to be auctioned by the charity. The value of the fair rental amount foregone by the property owner is not the basis for a federal income tax charitable contribution deduction. Moreover, use of the property by the successful bidder at the auction is considered *personal use* by the owner, for purposes of determining any business expense deduction allowable with respect to the property.[82]

Q 4:28   Is there a charitable contribution deduction for a gift of a used vehicle?

Sometimes. The IRS is greatly troubled about gifts of used vehicles, so it is important for a charity to be cautious when soliciting gifts of this nature. In materials published in the fall of 1999, the IRS wrote that it is of the view that the matter of vehicle (mostly cars) donation programs is a "growing area of noncompliance."[83] The IRS is not concerned with charities that occasionally receive cars by gift and resell them. It likewise is not concerned with charities that obtain cars by gift and use them in their program (such as sheltered workshops) or refurbish them for the benefit of the needy. What the IRS is principally troubled about is the use of "third party entrepreneurs"—who receive the cars directly, dispose of them (such as by auction or sale to scrap dealers), and pay to the charity a flat fee or set amount (often a small amount) per car. These latter situations the IRS has dubbed "suspect vehicle donation plans or programs."

There are a dozen issues of law caught up in this matter of suspect vehicle donation plans.

Clearly, for the donor, a critical issue is valuation. The value of a car can be ascertained by reference to the Blue Book. Still, the value will vary depending on factors such as condition and mileage. Some car donation plan advertisements state that donors can claim a charitable deduction based on full Blue Book value—even if the car isn't running (or may be missing an engine or transmission). At best, then, the deduction is confined to actual fair market value of the vehicle.

This matter of valuation is not confined to the donor. If the gift has a value of $250 or more, the charity must—if the deduction is to be allowed—substantiate the gift (Q 4:37). This includes providing the donor with a description of the property contributed. If the value exceeds $5,000, the donor must obtain an independent appraisal of the vehicle (Q 4:39). Both parties should be careful, in that there are penalties for aiding and abetting in the preparation of a false tax return (see below).

Where cars are given to a charity and the charity disposes of them, the activity is not taxable as an unrelated business because of the *donated good exception* (Q 6:25). If the car is transferred directly to a third party entrepreneur, that exception is not available. In some instances, the payments to the charity may be properly characterized as tax-excludable royalties (Q 6:27). The IRS, however, has staked out the position that even if the payments would otherwise constitute royalties, the payments would not be excludable from the unrelated income tax because the charity is providing services in conjunction with the transactions—by providing the necessary substantiation documents and acknowledging appraisals.

These suspect vehicle donation plans raise another issue. To be deductible, a gift must be *to* or *for the use of* a charitable organization. To be to a charity, the gift must be made under circumstances where the donee has full control of the donation and discretion as to its use (Q 1:13). In these instances, the "gift" often is to the third party, not the charity—in which case there is no charitable deduction to begin with. A gift for the use of a charity means that the donation is made in trust or similar arrangement—and that is not likely to be the case in this context.

The IRS has raised the issue of applicability of the *private benefit doctrine* (Q 1:11). The IRS posits situations where an automobile dealer or some other third party is the "true beneficiary" of the plan. The charity is cast as "lending" its tax-exempt status to facilitate the transactions.

If the private benefit is more than insubstantial, the tax exemption of the charity may be at risk.

The IRS has also raised the possibility of applicability of the *private inurement doctrine* (Q 1:10). Where the third party is an insider, that doctrine could be implicated. The position of the IRS is that there is no such thing as incidental private inurement, so transgression of that doctrine also may endanger the organization's tax-exempt status.

The intermediate sanctions penalties may be applicable, where the transaction constitutes an *excess benefit transaction* and the charity's dealings are with a *disqualified person.*

As noted, there is a penalty for an aiding and abetting in the preparation of false or fraudulent tax documents that results in an understatement of tax liability.[84] There also is a penalty for organizing and selling abusive tax shelters.[85] The latter penalty can be imposed on promoters, salespersons, and their assistants.

Thus, if a charity attempts to delegate its paperwork obligations pursuant to the substantiation requirements and/or its obligations with respect to qualified written appraisals, and the result is one or more documents that an individual can use to understate income tax liability, these penalties could be applicable to the charity. The factual issue would be: Did the charity know (or have reason to believe) [86] that its actions resulted in a tax understatement? Even if the charity did not delegate any obligations, there may still be penalties if, as the IRS put it, "no deduction is appropriate."

Finally, the IRS pointed out that even where some contribution deduction is appropriate, there may be an overstatement of a tax deduction (which also can trigger penalties). The IRS wrote of a "failure to properly supervise excessive claims concerning deductibility." This could happen if a charity permits a third party entrepreneur to make claims of that nature—such as advertising full Blue Book value deductions for gifts of cars lacking motors.

Q 4:29 What is a *restricted* gift?

A *restricted* gift is a contribution to a charitable organization where one or more restrictions (limitations, conditions) are imposed on the use or application of the gift. In a broad sense, there are two types of restricted gifts. One category of restricted gift is where the restriction is imposed on the gift by the donor. The other category is where the restriction on the gift is imposed by the board of trustees or directors of the recipient charitable organization. Usually, the term *restricted* gift is employed only to describe the first type of restricted gift.

Where the restriction was imposed by the donor, it becomes the obligation of the charitable organization—once it has accepted the encumbered gift—to use the restricted money or property in a manner that conforms to the restriction. This is because the gift restriction is considered to be imposed by contract.

COMMENT: If, of course, the restriction is imposed by the charity's governing board, the board (or a subsequent one) can remove the restriction—as long as in doing so the body does not violate the established legal rights of others.

Typical restrictions of this nature include the mandate that the gift or its proceeds be used for scholarships, a chair at a university, an award program, the construction and/or maintenance of a building, or an endowment fund (Q 4:30).

Aside from the terms of the restriction, there is an overarching need to be certain that the gift property is used for charitable ends (unless it is investment property). Difficulties in this area can be reduced to the extent the restriction is general. If even a funded program is discontinued, there may be other uses of the property that are within the range of the restriction.

NOTE: This may require some creative reading of the restriction. Again, the ease of compliance with the language of the restriction is in direct correlation with the breadth of the restriction.

If there is no one living to challenge an actual or alleged deviation from the restriction, the organization should consider use of the restricted property in a manner as close to the bounds of the restriction (but presumably not in literal compliance) as possible. This is a "judgment call," based on the facts and circumstances at the time. Above all, the organization should be prudent and act in good faith when making this type of management decision.

If there is no reasonable way to conform with the restriction, the organization has these options:

1. If the donor is still alive, obtain a written waiver of the restriction, perhaps replacing it with a restriction that the organization can currently satisfy.
2. Make a grant of the funds and/or property to another organization that can satisfy the restriction.
3. Take the matter into court in an effort to have the restriction revised or eliminated.

There are other tax issues to contend with. Generally, restrictions of the type referenced above will not jeopardize, in whole or in part, the donor's charitable contribution deduction. If the restriction would cause the charity to do something illegal or contrary to public policy, the restriction may not be enforceable. Or, to the other extreme, compliance with the restriction may endanger the charity's tax-exempt status. (A question may arise, however, as to why the charity accepted the gift.)

A restriction accompanying a gift may raise a question as to whether, in fact, the transaction amounts to a completed gift. At stake here is the donor's charitable deduction, inasmuch as there must be a true gift before there can be a charitable contribution deduction (Q 1:14). This can particularly be a problem where the donor has an ongoing involvement in the expenditure and/or investment of the gift funds or property. There can be an argument that the restriction prevents the transaction from being a completed gift—that is, a transfer by which the transferor parts with all of his or her right, title, and interest in the property—so that there is no gift and thus no charitable contribution deduction. Other areas of the law where questions of this nature are being raised concern supporting organizations (Q 2:15) and donor-advised funds (Q 4:36).

Q 4:30   What is an *endowment* gift?

An *endowment* gift is a form of restricted gift (Q 4:29). It is a gift that is restricted for placement in one or more endowment funds of the recipient charitable organization. Again, this type of restriction can be imposed on the gift by the donor or by the governing board of the charitable organization. Also, again, usually the term *endowment* gift is used only to describe the first type of restricted gift.

An endowment gift is a contribution where the charity is obligated to place the gift into one or more funds. Usually, the principal of the gift (the money and/or property transferred) must be retained in the fund and invested. That is, the gift item is not to be spent for program purposes. The income from the principal, however, is usually available for program purposes.

The endowment fund need not be a separate legal entity. It is a component of the charitable organization, best evidenced by a board resolution. Its tax-exempt status is that of the organization itself. It is often desirable to have a separate bank and/or investment account for the endowment fund. Some organizations choose nonetheless to cause the endowment fund to be in a separate entity, which itself is a charitable organization. Often, this separate entity is a supporting organization (Q 2:15).

The endowment fund can be supportive of the charitable organization's entire range of programs. It can also be supportive of just one aspect of the organization, such as maintenance of a building, funding of a scholarship program, or funding of a research effort. A charitable organization can have several endowment funds.

CAUTION: There is a trap lurking in this blend of the concept of an endowment fund and the use of a supporting organization. As is discussed elsewhere, certain tax-exempt organizations that are not charitable ones can have a supporting organization (Q 2:22). A common model is a membership association that is tax-exempt as a business league (Q 1:19) with a supporting organization. In this instance, the supporting organization cannot be or maintain an endowment fund that is generally supportive of the association—because that would be a substantial noncharitable purpose (even though it would be a form of support or benefit). Nonetheless, the supporting organization could maintain an endowment fund to be supportive of only the charitable and educational programs of the association. With that approach, the supporting organization could make restricted grants to the association.

Q 4:31 When is a gift of a note deductible for federal income tax purposes?

The making of a note, promising to pay money and/or transfer property, to a charitable organization, and delivery of the note to the charity, does not create a charitable contribution deduction. This is because a mere promise to pay does not effect transfer of title to the property.[87] Of course, when the money and/or property is actually transferred to the charitable donee, in satisfaction of the requirements of the note, an income tax charitable contribution deduction results (perhaps subject to one or more limitations).[88]

NOTE: These distinctions are based on the requirement that a charitable deduction is available only for the year in which the contribution is actually made (Q 4:9). Delivery of a note is not payment of the amount it represents.

A note in these circumstances may bear interest, or purport to bear interest. The tax consequences of the payment of the interest are dependent on the enforceability of the note. Where the note is enforceable, the payment of interest on the note is not likely to be deductible as an interest expense. If the note is not enforceable, the additional amounts paid are not interest for tax purposes but are deductible as charitable contributions.[89]

Q 4:32 When is a gift of an option deductible for federal income tax purposes?

First, it may be helpful to define what it is we are considering. A person may own an item of property and create an option by which another person may purchase the property at a certain price at or during a certain time. An option may be created for or transferred to a charitable organization.

There is no federal income tax charitable contribution deduction, however, for the transfer of an option to a charitable organization. Rather, the charitable deduction (such as it may be) arises at the time the option is exercised by the charitable donee.[90]

Thus, the transfer to a charitable organization of an option by the creator of the option is similar to the transfer of a note or pledge by the maker (Q 4:31). In the note situation, there is a promise to pay money at a future date; in the pledge situation, there is a promise to pay money or transfer some other property, or to do both, at a future date. In the option situation, there is a promise to sell property at a future date.

NOTE: These rules can be interrelated with the private foundation restrictions. One such instance involved a pledge by a corporation of an option on its common stock to a private foundation. The option document permitted the foundation to transfer the option to one or more charitable organizations. The foundation decided to not exercise the option. The corporation was a disqualified person with respect to the foundation;[91] the transaction would have been an act of self-dealing.[92] Thus, the foundation will sell the option, at its fair market value, to an unrelated charitable organization. The IRS ruled that the corporation will be entitled to a charitable contribution deduction in the year the charitable organization exercises the option and that the amount of the contribution will be the excess of the fair market value of the stock at the time the option is exercised over the exercise price.[93]

Q 4:33 When is a gift of property subject to an option deductible for federal income tax purposes?

In the case of a gift of property subject to an option, the deductible amount is calculated at the time the option is exercised (Q 4:32). Suppose, however, there is no exercise of the option.

In one instance, an S corporation (Q 1:19) executed a deed, contributing a tract of land to a charitable organization. The corporation, however, retained an option to repurchase the land for a nominal amount. The IRS concluded that there was more than a remote possibility that the option would be exercised.

In this case, the gift was made in 1993. The option was set to expire in 1995. For 1993, each of the shareholders of the corporation claimed a charitable contribution deduction for their share of the fair market value of the property. The IRS, however, determined that because of the option, there could not be charitable deductions for the shareholders for 1993 but that the deductions could be taken with respect to 1995.[94]

Q 4:34   What is a *bargain sale*?

A *bargain sale* is a transfer of property to a charitable organization which is in part a sale or exchange of the property and in part a charitable contribution of the property.[95] Basically, a bargain sale is a sale of an item of property to a charitable organization at a price that is an amount that is less than the fair market value of the property, with the amount equal to the fair market value of the property less the amount that is the sales price regarded as a contribution to the charitable organization.

CAUTION: The deduction reduction rule (Q 4:5) can apply in the bargain sale setting.

There must be allocated to the contribution portion of the property that element of the adjusted basis of the entire property that bears the same ratio to the total adjusted basis as the fair market value of the contributed portion of the property bears to the fair market value of the entire property. Furthermore, for these purposes, there must be allocated to the contributed portion of the property the amount of gain that is not recognized on the bargain sale, but that would have been recognized if the contributed portion of the property had been sold by the donor at its fair market value at the time of its contribution to the charitable organization.[96]

Q 4:35   Is a donor, to receive a charitable contribution deduction for a gift, required to give the entirety of the donor's interest in the property?

No. In certain circumstances, a donor may make a gift to a charitable organization of only a portion of the donor's interest in the property. There can be a charitable contribution deduction arising as a result of the gift, for the portion of the gift destined for charity.

This type of a gift is known as a *partial interest* gift. This means, of course, that the donor is contributing only a portion of the interest in the property to charity. For a charitable deduction to be available, however, there are some very technical rules that must be complied with.

Generally, there is no charitable deduction for a partial interest gift.[97] Here, though, is a situation where the exception to the rule is larger than the application of the general rule. The prevailing way to make a partial interest gift is to do so by means of a *split-interest trust*. This is the vehicle commonly used to conceptually divide the property into the two component interests: income interest and remainder interest (Q 5:2).

Usually, a qualified split-interest trust is required if a charitable contribution deduction is to be available.[98] Split-interest trusts are charitable remainder trusts (Q 5:6), pooled income funds (Q 5:17), and charitable lead trusts (Q 5:31).

There are some exceptions to these general requirements of a split-interest trust in this type of giving. The principal exception is the charitable gift annuity, which utilizes a contract rather than a trust (Q 5:32). Other approaches can also generate a charitable contribution deduction (Q 5:33).

Thus, in this setting, it is not enough to create a remainder interest for a charity. It is critical to create a remainder interest, the gift of which yields a charitable contribution deduction. There are only a few ways in which a remainder interest can be the subject of a charitable contribution deduction. Absent qualification of an eligible partial interest (almost always a qualifying remainder interest), there is no charitable contribution deduction for the gift.

Q 4:36   Mention was made of donor-advised funds. What is the concern of the IRS with them?

Donor-advised funds trouble the IRS for three basic reasons. Before discussing these reasons, however, let's define the term *donor-advised fund*. This type of fund is an entity, or a fund (or account) within an entity, that is the recipient of a transfer of money or property from a person (including one or more individuals, a business, or a grant-making foundation). The transferor has the ability (we shall avoid calling it a *right*) to make recommendations (that is, advise) as to subsequent uses of the money and/or property, such as investment practices and/or dispositions (grants) from the fund to charitable organizations. The parties to a transaction of this nature want the transfer to be considered, for federal tax charitable deduction purposes, a *gift* (Q 1:14).

There are several manifestations of donor-advised funds. It is not common for a single donor-advised fund to be a separate entity. Rather, the typical donor-advised fund is part of a grouping of funds of this nature. A community foundation, for example, has as one of its major functions the solicitation and maintenance of these funds. More recently, charitable gift funds, some affiliated with investment companies, have come into existence. Considerable controversy has erupted over the newer forms of donor-advised funds, in part because of complaints from community foundations.

NOTE: These entities are not the same as *donor-directed* funds. With these funds, the donor or someone else has a legally enforceable right to direct investment and/or grant-making policies.

The first of the issues is whether a donor-advised fund or, more likely, a collection or aggregate of donor-advised funds can qualify for tax exemption as a charitable organization (Q 1:8). The IRS has lost on this issue in the courts,[99] yet continues to believe that some or all of these funds do not merit exemption. The IRS believes that many of these funds, particularly outside the community foundation setting, are operated primarily for nonexempt, commercial purposes and/or are generating unwarranted private benefit. A derogatory term that some use to describe these organizations is *accommodation charities*. The thought is that these collectives of donor-advised funds do nothing themselves that is charitable; they are merely an investment and administrative manager of the funds.

CAUTION: The IRS has gone so far as to characterize some of these funds as "aggressive tax avoidance schemes."[100]

The second, and related issue, is that of donor control. This issue goes both to eligibility for tax-exempt status (Q 1:7) and the question as to whether there has been a completed gift (Q 1:13). In the principal court case on the point, the district court held that the fund involved failed to qualify as a charitable organization because the control the donors could exercise over the investment and distribution of contributions was inconsistent with tax exemption.[101] On appeal, the court ordered the district court to rule in favor of the fund on the exemption issue.[102]

The reason the appellate court vacated the district court's decision was that the provision authorizing subsequent donor control over gifts was eliminated from the fund's operating document. The IRS argued that the administrative record nonetheless showed that the fund "would not take complete control over the contributions." The government asserted that the fund would adhere to the "directions" of its donors as to investment and distribution of gift funds. The amendment of the document was seen as not preventing the fund from providing "investment services" for donors and "acting as an administrative conduit for its donors' funds."[103]

The IRS wrote that it will continue to review the "issue of donor control in donor-advised funds." It noted that a case pending in the U.S. Court of Federal Claims[104] "may affect the future development" of this issue.

The IRS asserted that the donor-advised fund that qualifies as a tax-exempt charitable entity must have "appropriate control over the donated funds."[105] The agency reiterated that in measuring levels of control, the material restriction rules relating to the termination of private foundation status[106] are applied. The IRS added that these criteria are applied to donor-advised funds in trust form that endeavor to be treated as component funds of a community foundation, so that the charitable entity can be regarded as a publicly supported charity.[107]

Also, the IRS expects, if tax exemption is to be recognized, donor-advised funds to adhere to certain of the private foundation rules. The following representations are expected[108]:

1. The organization expects that its grants for the year will equal or exceed 5 percent of its average net assets on a fiscal year rolling basis. (This is adherence to the mandatory payout requirements for private foundations.[109]) If this level of grant activity is not attained, the organization will identify the named accounts (donor-advised funds) from which grants over the same period totaled less than 5 percent of each account's average assets. The organization will contact the "donor-advisors" of these accounts to request that they recommend grants of at least this amount. If a donor-advisor does not provide the qualified grant recommendations, the organization is authorized to transfer an amount up to 5 percent of assets from the donor-advisor's named account to the charity or charities selected by the organization.

2. The organization will add language to its promotional materials which states that the organization will investigate allegations of improper use of grant funds for the private benefit of donor-advisors.

3. The organization will add language to its grantee letters to the effect that grants are to be used by grantees exclusively in furtherance of charitable purposes and cannot be used for the private benefit of donor-advisors. (This is intended to parallel the expenditure responsibility requirements for private foundations.[110])

The third issue is whether these funds are publicly supported (Q 2:7). At the present, the gifts made to donor-advised funds are treated, by the funds, as public support. Some in the IRS are of the view that the donor-advised fund (or aggregate of them) should be regarded as a pass-through entity or conduit, so that the funds paid out are only public support in the hands of the charities that receive grants from the donor-advised funds.

Currently, the amounts transferred to a donor-advised fund are forms of public support, as are grants from them. This issue is in court.[111]

Q 4:37   What are the charitable contribution *substantiation* rules?

A donor to a charitable organization of a separate charitable contribution of $250 or more in a tax year must, to have a charitable deduction for the gift, obtain written substantiation from the donee organization.[112] The requisite *contemporaneous written acknowledgment* must state (1) the amount of money and a description (but not value) of any property other than money that was contributed, (2) whether the donee organization provided any goods or services in consideration for any money or property contributed, and (3) a description and good-faith estimate of the value of any goods or services involved.

Q 4:38   What are the *quid pro quo contribution* rules?

If a charitable organization receives a quid pro quo contribution in excess of $75, the organization must, in connection with the solicitation or receipt of the contribution, provide a written statement that (1) informs the donor that the amount of the contribution for federal income tax purposes is limited to the excess of the amount of any money and the value of any property other than money contributed by the donor over the value of the goods or services provided by the organization and (2) provides the donor with a good-faith estimate of the value of the goods or services.[113]

There is a penalty for violation of these requirements.[114]

Q 4:39   What are the charitable gift appraisal requirements?

As a general rule, if the claimed value of an item of property (or group of similar items of property), which is the subject of a charitable contribution deduction, is in excess of $5,000, there must be an independent appraisal of the property. An *appraisal summary* must be attached to the tax return involved. This requirement must be complied with if the charitable deduction is to be allowed.[115]

CHAPTER 5

Planned Giving

Planned giving may be the most important type of charitable giving. (Certainly, the most funds are raised this way.) If so, the subject should be of the greatest interest to every professional fund-raiser.

Yet, there is a problem. No form of charitable giving presents more mystery or generates more confusion than planned giving. Even though this type of giving yields the greatest benefits to donors, too many charitable organizations avoid planned giving, out of fear of its complexities and because of the pressure to raise funds for immediate use. There are intricacies with this type of giving, to be sure, but none is so overwhelming as to be a legitimate basis for not having a planned giving program. The challenge for many organizations is the prompt establishment of this type of program, in addition to their other fund-raising efforts.

The rules concerning planned giving can be somewhat involved, particularly those pertaining to charitable remainder trusts. Out of complexity comes planning opportunities, and planners do not always use these opportunities in ways that are desirable for the charitable community. In other words, there can be abuse. With 30 years' experience with the rules in their statutory form, Congress and the Treasury Department have, in recent months, found it necessary to usher in new rules in the planned giving arena. These developments, of course, enhance the intricacy of these rules of law.

Here are the questions most frequently asked by professional fund-raisers (or that should be asked by them) about the basic principles of law applicable in the realm of planned giving—and the answers to them.

Q 5:1   What is *planned giving*?

The phrase *planned giving* refers to techniques of charitable giving where the contributions are large in amount (and thus so too are the charitable deductions), are usually of property (often property that has appreciated in value), and normally are carefully integrated with the financial and estate plans of the donor or donors. This approach to charitable giving is referred to as *planned* giving because of the time and planning that is devoted (or should be devoted), certainly by the donor(s) and often by the charitable donee, to designing the gift transaction.

The relationship of this type of gift to a donor's financial needs and desires is a critical factor. The donor often structures the gift so that he or she (and sometimes it) receives income as a consequence of the transaction. Usually, this benefit is technically accomplished by creating, in the donated property (sometimes being or including money) one or more *income interests* and one or more *remainder interests* (Q 5:2).

COMMENT: Two of the most difficult and frustrating aspects for the fund-raiser in obtaining planned gifts are (1) causing prospective contributors to devote a sufficient amount of their attention to an explanation of how planned giving works and (2) convincing them that they will receive income (or more of it) as the result of an act of charity. This is, to many, such a foreign and inherently inconsistent concept that they will have great trouble grasping it. Additional difficulties can ensue when an income return is to be coupled with a sizable charitable contribution deduction. These obstacles can become even more considerable when it is explained that non-income-producing property can be converted to income-producing property, that the income to be received is greater or more tax-advantaged than that being generated before the gift transaction, and/or that an immense amount of capital gains tax can be avoided. The challenge to the charitable gift planner is to get the prospective donor(s) beyond these barriers. Once that is accomplished, the rewards (financial and psychic) are great for all concerned.

Planned gifts are of two fundamental types: the gift made (1) during the donor's or donors' lifetime(s) by means of a trust or other instrument or (2) by will, so that the contributed property comes out of the decedent's estate (a bequest or devise).

Contributions of property to charity are usually made as gifts of the property in its entirety. That is, the donor transfers all of his, her, or its title to and interest in the property to the charitable donee. By contrast, the maker of a planned gift generally contributes something less than the donor's complete interest in the property. In the parlance of the law, this is known as a contribution of a *partial interest*; planned giving is usually partial interest giving. These partial interests are either income interests or remainder interests.[1]

NOTE: For a charitable contribution deduction to be available, the gift must be to (or for the use of) a charitable organization. The various planned gift vehicles are not charities—they are conduits for charities. Nonetheless, a charitable deduction arises when a gift is made to, for example, a charitable remainder trust or a pooled income fund. Technically, this deduction is for the remainder interest contributed to the charity; the giving vehicle is merely the intermediary that facilitates this type of gift.

Q 5:2   What are *income interests* and *remainder interests*?

The notions of income interests and remainder interests are legal fictions; they are concepts of rights of ownership inherent in any item of property. In theory, then, every item of property has within it at least one income interest and at least one remainder interest. This is the case whether the property is a security, work of art, or parcel of land.

An *income interest* in a property is a function of the income generated by the property. A person may be entitled, by the terms of a legally binding document (Q 5:3), to all or some portion of the income from a property for a period of time. This person thus has a right to this income flow, and is said to have an income interest in the property. Two or more persons (such as husband and wife) may have income interests in the same item of property. These income interests may be held concurrently or consecutively.

The *remainder interest* in an item of property is reflective of the projected value of the property, and/or property produced by investment or reinvestment, at some future time. The income interest(s) and remainder interest(s) in a property constitute the totality of these interests in the property. Thus, the remainder interest(s) in an item of property become the entirety of such interest(s) in the property once the income interest(s) have expired.

These interests are principally measured by the following factors:

1. The value of the property,
2. The age of the person or persons that have the income interest(s),
3. The period of time that the income interests are to exist, and/or
4. The frequency of the income payout.

In the planned giving setting, the computation of the value of an income interest and a remainder interest is made by means of actuarial tables, most often those promulgated by the Department of the Treasury, and an interest rate component (Q 5:15, Q 5:23).

For the most part, a planned gift is a gift of an income interest or a remainder interest in an item of property. Commonly, the contribution is of the remainder interest in property. In the case of a remainder interest gift, by creating an income interest (or, perhaps more accurately, retaining an income interest), the donor(s) forms the basis for receiving a flow of income as the result of the contribution. This is known as *partial interest* giving.

When a gift of a remainder interest in property is made to a charitable organization, the charity does not acquire the property represented by that interest from the planned gift vehicle until the income interest or interests have expired. When a gift of a remainder interest is made by a donor during his or her lifetime, the contributor receives the income tax charitable contribution deduction for the tax year in which the recipient charity's interest in the property is created. A gift of an income interest in property to a charity enables the donee to receive the income at the outset and to continue to do so as long as the income interest remains in existence.

Q 5:3   How are these interests created?

Income and remainder interests in property are most frequently created by means of a trust. This is the vehicle that is used to conceptually divide the property into the two component interests. The law terms these trusts *split-interest trusts*. Usually, a qualified split-interest trust is required if a charitable contribution deduction is to be available.[2] Split-interest trusts are charitable remainder trusts (Q 5:6), pooled income funds (Q 5:17), and charitable lead trusts (Q 5:31).

There are exceptions to these general requirements of a split-interest trust in planned giving. The principal exception is the charitable gift annuity, which is created by means of a contract rather than a trust (Q 5:32). Other approaches can also generate a charitable contribution deduction (Q 5:33).

In the planned giving setting, however, it is not enough to create a remainder interest. It is also critical to create a remainder interest, the gift of which yields a charitable contribution deduction. Absent qualification of an eligible partial interest (usually a qualifying remainder interest), there is no charitable contribution deduction.[3] The qualifying remainder interest vehicles are those mentioned earlier: the charitable remainder trust and the pooled income fund.

Q 5:4   What are the tax consequences of a charitable gift of a remainder interest?

For a gift of a remainder interest in property to a charitable organization, made by the donor(s) during lifetime, the federal income tax advantages are manifold. Let's assume a single donor. The donor creates an income flow, for him or her or someone else, as the result of the gift; this income may be preferentially taxed. The donor receives a charitable contribution deduction for the gift of the remainder interest, which will reduce or maybe even eliminate the tax on the income from the property. The property that is the subject of the gift may have appreciated in value in the hands of the donor (*appreciated property*); if that is the case, the capital gains tax that would have been paid had the property been sold by the donor is avoided. The trustee of the charitable remainder trust may dispose of the gift property and reinvest the proceeds in property that generates more capital gain or more income. Because the trust is generally tax-exempt, any capital gain from such a transaction is not taxed, nor is the income earned by the trust.

Moreover, the donor can become the beneficiary of professional fund management services provided to the trust. All of these benefits can be available while, simultaneously, the donor is satisfying his or her charitable desires—and doing so at a level that, absent these tax incentives, would not be possible.

A contribution of a remainder interest by means of an estate gives rise to an estate tax charitable contribution deduction.[4]

Q 5:5   It was said that a charitable remainder trust generally is tax-exempt. Why the qualification?

Nearly all charitable remainder trusts are tax-exempt. Nonetheless, this type of trust is not exempt if it has unrelated business taxable income.[5] (This type of income is the subject of Chapter 6.) In making this determination, the exempt purposes of the remainder interest charitable beneficiary are used to ascertain relatedness.[6]

NOTE 1: A charitable remainder trust with unrelated business taxable income is taxable on all of its net income, not just the unrelated income (as is the case with most tax-exempt organizations).[7] A charitable remainder trust with unrelated business income that is not taxable (such as because of offsetting deductions or the specific deduction) does not have income that is taxable under this rule.

NOTE 2: A pooled income fund is not a tax-exempt organization in the conventional sense of that word. It receives, however, a deduction for its income distributions and for the amounts destined for charitable purposes—and thus ends up, as a practical matter, exempt from income taxation.

Q 5:6   What is a *charitable remainder trust*?

A *charitable remainder trust* is a type of split-interest trust (Q 5:3).[8] As the name indicates, it is a trust that has been used to create a remainder interest (Q 5:2), with that interest in the gift property designated for one or more charitable organizations. Each charitable remainder trust is designed and written specifically for the particular circumstances of the donor(s). The donor(s) receives a charitable contribution deduction for the transfer of the remainder interest.

A qualified charitable remainder trust must provide for a specified distribution of income, at least annually, to one or more beneficiaries, at least one of which is *not* a charity. The flow of income must be for a life or lives, or for a term not to exceed 20 years. An irrevocable remainder interest must be held for the benefit of the charity or paid over to it. The noncharitable beneficiaries are the holders of the income interests and the charitable organization has the remainder interest. Most types of property can be contributed to a charitable remainder trust (Q 5:9).

Conventionally, once the income interests expire, the assets in a charitable remainder trust are distributed to, or for the use of, the charitable organization that is the remainder interest beneficiary. It does not happen very often, but the property in the trust may, instead of being distributed to the charity, be retained in the trust for use for charitable purposes.

CAUTION: If the second option is selected, the trust will have to be qualified for tax-exempt status as a charity. It is almost certain to constitute a private foundation (Q 2:2).

Usually, a bank or similar financial institution serves as the trustee of a charitable remainder trust. This institution should have the capacity to administer the trust, make appropriate investments, and timely adhere to all income and gain distributions and reporting requirements. In some instances, the charitable organization that is the remainder interest beneficiary acts as the trustee.[9]

CAUTION: This is a subject of state law. In some states, a charitable organization cannot serve as a trustee. State law, then, obviously must be looked into before a trust arrangement is finalized.

A donor or related party may be the trustee of a charitable remainder trust. Caution must be exercised here, however, to avoid triggering the *grantor trust* rules, which, among other outcomes, cause the gain from the sale of appreciated property (Q 5:4) by the trust to be taxed to the grantor/donor.

Generally, a charitable remainder trust is a tax-exempt organization (Q 5:5).

Q 5:7   Are there different types of charitable remainder trusts?

Yes. At the present time, there are five types of charitable remainder trusts. One of these is the *charitable remainder annuity trust* (CRAT) and the other four are variations of the *charitable remainder unitrust* (CRUT). The prime distinction among these trusts is the manner in which the income to be paid from the trust to those holding income interests is determined.

NOTE: Another important distinction between a CRAT and a CRUT is that additional contributions can be made to a CRUT but not to a CRAT.

A qualified CRAT must have the following features:

1. The income payments from the trust are in the form of a fixed amount—an annuity—or what the law terms a *sum certain*.
2. This sum certain must be at least 5 percent of the initial net fair market value of all property placed in the trust and may not exceed 50 percent of that value.
3. This sum certain (or *annuity amount*) must be paid, at least annually, to one or more persons (at least one of which is not a charity).
4. If the annuity amount beneficiary is an individual, that person must be living at the time of creation of the trust.
5. The annuity amount payment period may be for a term of years, not in excess of 20, or for the life or lives of the annuity amount beneficiary or beneficiaries.

6. No amounts, other than the annuity amounts, may be paid to or for the use of any person other than a charitable organization.

7. Following the close of the annuity payment period, the remainder interest in the trust must be transferred to, or for the use of, a charitable organization or retained by the trust for a charitable use.

8. The value of the remainder interest (Q 5:15) must be at least 10 percent of the initial net fair market value of all property placed in the trust.[10]

NOTE: The criteria in items number 2 and 8 above went into effect in 1997.

As an example of the annuity amount, a CRAT is funded with $100,000 worth of property; the income payout amount is set at $5,000. Thus, $5,000 must be paid annually to one or more income interest beneficiaries.

NOTE 1: It is said throughout that the income interest amounts must be paid *annually*. This refers to the total amount of income that is required to be paid out each year. The actual payout may be more frequent, such as semiannually or quarterly. (See the fourth factor in Q 5:2.)

NOTE 2: In addition to the above rules concerning qualified CRATs, to the extent the remainder interest is in *qualified employer securities*,[11] the securities may be transferred to an employee stock ownership plan[12] as long as the transfer constitutes a *qualified gratuitous transfer*.[13]

One of the CRUTs is the standard CRUT, or SCRUT. A qualified SCRUT must have the following features:

1. The income payments from the trust are an amount equal to a fixed percentage of the net fair market value of its assets, valued annually.

2. This fixed percentage must be at least 5 percent of the net fair market value of the assets, valued annually, and may not exceed 50 percent of that value.

3. This income amount (or *unitrust amount*) must be paid, at least annually, to one or more persons (at least one of which is not a charity).

4. If the unitrust amount beneficiary is an individual, that person must be living at the time of creation of the trust.

5. The unitrust amount payment period may be for a term of years, not in excess of 20, or for the life or lives of the unitrust amount beneficiary or beneficiaries.

6. No amounts, other than the unitrust amounts, may be paid to or for the use of any person other than a charitable organization.

7. Following the close of the unitrust payment period, the remainder interest in the trust must be transferred to, or for the use of, a charitable organization or retained by the trust for a charitable use.

8. With respect to each contribution of property to the trust, the value of the remainder interest (Q 5:15) in the property must be at least 10 percent of the net fair market value of the property as of the date the property is contributed to the trust.[14]

NOTE: The criteria in items number 2 and 8 above went into effect in 1997.

The SCRUT is also thus known as the *fixed percentage CRUT*.[15] Thus, the amount paid out each year to the income interest beneficiaries can fluctuate from year to year. As an example of a standard unitrust amount, a SCRUT is funded with $100,000 worth of property; the percentage selected is 5 percent. In year 1, the income payout amount is $5,000. Thus, $5,000 must be paid that year to one or more income interest beneficiaries. The value of the trust's assets for year 2 is $105,000; the payout amount is $5,250. The value of the trust's assets for year 3 is $110,000; the payout amount is $5,500. The value of the trust's assets for year 4 is $95,000; the payout amount is $4,750.

There are two types of CRUTs that are known as *income exception CRUTs*. This means that the payout rules for SCRUTs need not be followed. This approach is usually used where the contributed property does not generate enough income (perhaps none) to enable the trust to comport with the 5 percent rule.

One of these types of CRUTs enables the income to flow to the income interest beneficiary or beneficiaries once there is any income generated in the trust.[16] This amount may be less than the 5 percent amount. Here, the unitrust amount is the lesser of the fixed percentage amount or the trust's annual net income. Here, the income payments begin once a suitable amount of income begins to flow into the trust. That is, the income payments may begin at a future point in time and are only prospective. This form of CRUT is the net income CRUT—or NICRUT.[17]

For example, the property transferred to a NICRUT has a fair market value of $100,000, but it is non-income producing (e.g., it is unimproved real estate). Two years elapse before the property can be sold. The property is sold early into year 3 and the proceeds invested; the investment return for that year is 3 percent. This NICRUT would make no distributions in years 1 and 2, and distribute the 3 percent amount in year 3.

The other of these types of CRUTs is similar to the NICRUT but the trust instrument provides that for the years in which there was no or an insufficient distribution, the trust can, once the investment policy generates adequate income, not only begin to pay the income interest beneficiaries the full amount of the determined unitrust payments but also make payments that make up for the distribution deficiencies in prior years.[18] This type of trust can thus make catch-up—or makeup—payments once the non-income-producing asset is sold. Thus, in this case, the unitrust amount is determined under the net income method, with that amount also including any amount of income that exceeds the current year's fixed percentage amount to make up for any shortfall in payments from prior years when the trust's income was less than the fixed percentage amount. This net income makeup CRUT is the NIMCRUT.[19]

For example, the property transferred to a NIMCRUT has a fair market value of $100,000, but it is non-income producing (e.g., it is unimproved real estate). The fixed percentage is 5 percent. Two years elapse before the property can be sold. The property is sold early into year 3 and the proceeds invested; the investment return for that year is 3 percent. In years 4 and 5, the return is 5 percent. In years 6 and 7, the return is 8 percent. This NIMCRUT would make no distributions in years 1 and 2, distribute the 3 percent amount in year 3, distribute the 5 percent amount in years 4 through 7, and start using the excess (over 5 percent) income amounts received in years 6 and 7 to make up for the deficiencies in payouts in years 1 through 3.

NOTE: Again, these trusts do not normally pay income taxes (Q 5:5). Thus, if the non-income-producing property was highly appreciated in value, the sales proceeds are not reduced by capital gains taxes, which means that the full amount of the sales proceeds can be invested in income-producing property. This produces the maximum asset base to generate income in furtherance of the NIMCRUT approach.

TIP: The makeup feature selected will have an impact on the charitable deduction for the gift of the remainder interest. Because the makeup feature that allows for retroactive payments can provide more income to the income beneficiary (or beneficiaries) than the prospective makeup feature, the income interest is likely to be greater and, correspondingly, the remainder interest is that much less. The result: a smaller charitable deduction when the retroactive income makeup provision is used.

The fourth type of CRUT is the flip unitrust—the FLIPCRUT. In the case of a FLIPCRUT, its governing instrument provides that the CRUT will convert (flip) once from one of the income exception methods—the NICRUT or NIMCRUT—to the fixed percentage method—the SCRUT—for purposes of calculating the unitrust amount.[20] The conversion is allowed, however, only if the specific date or single event triggering the flip (*triggering event*) is outside the control of, or not discretionary with, the trustee or any other person or persons.[21]

Permissible triggering events with respect to an individual include marriage, divorce, death, or birth.[22] The sale of an unmarketable asset, such as real estate, is a permissible triggering event.[23] Examples of impermissible triggering events include the sale of marketable assets and a request from the unitrust amount beneficiary or that recipient's financial advisor that the CRUT's payout mechanism be converted to the fixed percentage method.

The conversion to the fixed percentage method must occur at the beginning of the tax year that immediately follows the tax year in which the triggering date or event occurs.[24] Any makeup amount is forfeited when the trust converts to the fixed percentage method.

The term *unmarketable assets* means assets other than cash, cash equivalents, or assets that can be readily sold or exchanged for cash or cash equivalents. Unmarketable assets include real property, closely held stock, and unregistered securities for which there is no available exemption under the securities laws permitting public sale.[25]

Thus, where these rules are satisfied, a donor can fund a CRUT with unmarketable assets that produce little or no income. The donor likely wants the income beneficiary or beneficiaries of the CRUT to receive a steady stream of payments based on the total return available from the value of the assets. Of course, these payments cannot be made until the unmarketable assets can be converted into liquid (marketable) assets that can be used to generate income to pay the fixed percentage amount.

Using these FLIPCRUT rules, a donor can establish a CRUT that uses one of the two income exception methods in calculating the unitrust amount until the unmarketable assets are sold. Following the sale, the CRUT's payout method would be altered so that the fixed percentage method is used to calculate the unitrust amount. Thus, the permissible FLIPCRUT patterns are a NICRUT flipped to a SCRUT or a NIMCRUT flipped to a SCRUT.

NOTE 1: The FLIPCRUT rules are effective for CRUTs created on or after December 10, 1998.[26] Income exception CRUTs created before, on, or after that date, containing nonqualifying flip provisions, can, however, be reformed to add permitted provisions allowing a flip to the fixed percentage method.[27] Adding the conversion language to a CRUT will not cause it to fail to function as a charitable remainder trust and will not be an act of self-dealing[28] if the trustee of the CRUT initiated legal proceedings to reform the CRUT by June 8, 1999, as long as the triggering event does not occur in a year prior to the year in which the court involved issued the order reforming the trust.[29]

NOTE 2: The conversion permitted by this law is the only allowable type of CRUT flip. (Any other type of conversion will cause the trust to fail to constitute a charitable remainder trust.) Thus, for example, a SCRUT cannot convert to a NICRUT or a NIMCRUT. For that matter, a CRAT cannot convert to a CRUT, nor can a CRUT convert to a CRAT.

NOTE 3: The rules as to qualified gratuitous transfers of qualified employer securities also apply in the case of CRUTs.

COMMENT: One wag, who will not be embarrassed by identification in this space, observed that a charitable remainder trust that fails to qualify as one of the five eligible types is a . . . FLOPTRUST.

Q 5:8   What types of charitable organizations can be remainder interest beneficiaries of charitable remainder trusts?

There are no limitations on the types of charitable organizations that can be beneficiaries of charitable remainder trusts. That is, these organizations can be either public charities (Q 2:1) or private foundations (Q 2:2).

NOTE: Thus, the rule in this regard is different from the case with respect to pooled income funds (Q 5:18).

TIP: The percentage limitations on deductible charitable giving (Q 4:3–Q 4:7) need to be taken into account. For example, a contribution of appreciated property (Q 4:5) to a public charity is subject to the 30 percent limitation, while the same gift made to a private foundation is subject to a 20 percent limitation. These percentages do not just apply when a gift is made outright; these percentages apply when the gift is made by means of a charitable remainder trust. Here can be a problem: if the trust instrument does not expressly confine the charitable beneficiary or beneficiaries to a public charity or public charities, the 20 percent limitation will be imposed on the deduction, because of the possibility that the property will be transferred to a private foundation (Q 4:8). (Also, the gift deduction may be confined to the donor's basis in the property (Q 4:5).)

Q 5:9 What types of gift property are suitable for charitable remainder trusts?

For the most part, nearly any type of personal or real property may be contributed to a charitable remainder trust. (Money may also be given.) Commonly, the properties contributed (aside from money) are securities (stocks and/or bonds) and real estate. Because of the payout requirement (Q 5:6), however, it is necessary to be concerned about whether the property is income-producing or can be readily converted to income production.

There can be some tax difficulties when property is transferred to a charitable remainder trust. Many of these problems arise when an item of tangible personal property is contributed to a charity by means of a charitable remainder trust. Principally there are three of these conundrums (Q 5:12). Also, properties encumbered with debt can pose some tax problems (Q 5:10).

CAUTION: This matter of property in remainder trusts is not confined to property originally contributed by gift. There can be problems arising from property that has become investment property. The issue is whether there is any unrelated business taxable income (Q 5:5).

Q 5:10 What happens if property contributed to a charitable remainder trust is encumbered with debt?

If property encumbered with debt is transferred to a charitable remainder trust, the result is likely to be unrelated debt-financed income. This is because the debt is an *acquisition indebtedness*.[30] The receipt of unrelated debt-financed income, if it is unrelated business taxable income, will cause the trust to lose its tax-exempt status for each year in which that type of income is received (Q 5:5).

Q 5:11 What happens when an option is transferred to a charitable remainder trust?

The answer depends on the type of property that underlies the option. If the underlying property could be transferred directly to the trust, the transfer of the option raises only the matter of the timing of the gift. This is because there is no charitable deduction for the gift until the option is exercised (Q 4:32). If the property would be inappropriate for transfer directly to the trust, however, the transfer of the option would cause the trust to lose its tax-exempt status (Q 5:5).

A basic principle underpinning the law of charitable remainder trusts is that this body of law is intended to ensure that the amount a charitable organization receives following the close of the income payment period is fairly commensurate with the amount on which the donor's charitable contribution deduction was based. This type of trust must function as a charitable remainder trust in every respect from the date of its creation; that cannot happen unless each transfer to the trust qualifies for a charitable deduction. The IRS attempts to be attuned to situations where the donor may be merely using a charitable remainder trust as a means to take advantage of the tax exemption for capital gains incurred by the trust (Q 5:4).

Encumbered property in a charitable remainder trust can jeopardize the trust's tax-exempt status (Q 5:10). Where an option to purchase this type of property, rather than the property itself, is transferred to a charitable remainder trust, the IRS will assume that the donor is attempting to avoid the adverse consequences attendant to a transfer of the property directly to the trust. If the option is used in an attempt to sidestep these tax consequences, the IRS will disqualify the trust as a charitable remainder trust.[31]

Q 5:12   What happens when an item of tangible personal property is transferred to a charitable remainder trust?

The transfer of an item of tangible personal property to a charitable remainder trust does not inherently cause any problems with respect to qualification of the trust under the federal tax law. Nonetheless, three aspects of the general charitable giving laws are implicated.

A charitable contribution of a future interest in tangible personal property is treated, for federal income tax purposes, as having been made only when all intervening interests in, and rights to, the actual possession or enjoyment of the property have expired or are held by persons other than the donor or those closely related to the donor.[32] By contributing this type of property to the trust, the donor is creating and retaining an income interest in it, thus triggering this rule as to future interests. There would be an income tax charitable contribution, however, when the trustee of the trust sold the property because there would be an income interest in the proceeds of the sale.

Where there is a charitable contribution of tangible personal property and the charitable donee uses the property in a manner that is unrelated to its tax-exempt purpose (Q 5:5), the amount of the deduction must be reduced by the amount of the gain that would have been long-term capital gain if the property had been sold for its fair market value.[33] Usually, gifts of this nature involve long-term capital assets and it is contemplated that the trust will sell the property. The sale would be an unrelated use. Therefore, the donor's charitable contribution deduction (already confined to that for a remainder interest and in existence only after the sale) would have to be reduced to the amount of the donor's basis in the property allocable to the remainder interest.

Where there is a charitable contribution of tangible personal property by an individual and the donee is not a public charity (Q 2:1), the charitable contribution deduction for the gift generally must be confined to an amount equal to 20 percent of the donor's adjusted gross income (Q 4:7). Where the recipient is a public charity, the limitation generally is 30 percent (Q 4:5). The trust instrument must specifically provide that the donee or donees must be public charities for the higher of these two limitations to apply.

TIP: If the trust is silent on this point, the IRS will be of the view that one or more charitable beneficiaries can be a private foundation and hold that the lower of the two limitations is the applicable one.[34] This can happen, for example, where the donor reserves a lifetime power of appointment and a testamentary power to designate the charitable organization(s) that is to receive the remainder interest—and the powers fail to confine the potential remainder interest beneficiary(ies) to a public charity(ies).

As noted, however, with tangible personal property the charitable contribution deduction does not come into being until the property is sold. The gift then is of the sales proceeds—money. In the case of charitable gifts of money, the percentage limitations generally are 50 percent for public charities (Q 4:3) and 30 percent for private foundations (Q 4:4).[35] The same considerations as noted above apply, however, in that the IRS will take the position that the lower limitation is the applicable one, unless the document expressly confines the remainder interest beneficiaries to public charities.

Q 5:13   Who can be a donor to a charitable remainder trust?

Any person—an individual, partnership, corporation, or otherwise—can be a donor to a charitable remainder trust. Usually, the donor is an individual or there may be two donors who are (related) individuals. The income payment period, in the case of an individual, can be for one or more lifetimes or for a term of years (Q 5:6). Where a corporation is the donor, the income payment period must have a limitation expressed in terms of years (*id.*).

Q 5:14   How are amounts distributed to an income interest beneficiary from a charitable remainder trust taxed?

The tax treatment accorded amounts distributed to an income interest beneficiary from a charitable remainder trust is dependent essentially on two factors: (1) the character of the amounts, for tax purposes, in the trust and (2) the application of a four-tier system for determining the sequence in which the various types of the amounts are taxed. The character of a charitable remainder trust's income is determined at the time the income is realized by the trust.

The tiering is as follows:

1. The amount is first taxed as ordinary income (that is, not amounts that are gains, or amounts treated as gains, from the sale or other disposition of capital assets), includable in the recipient's gross income, to the extent of this type of income of the trust for the year and this type of undistributed income of the trust for prior years.

2. The remaining amount (if any) is next taxed as a capital gain to the extent of the capital gain of the trust for the year and the undistributed capital gain of the trust for prior years.

> **COMMENT:** When the law as to the tax treatment of capital gains was changed in 1997, some additional complexity was introduced into this area. Shortly thereafter, the IRS issued guidance categorizing long-term capital gains and losses of charitable remainder trusts into three groups: a 28 percent group, a 25 percent group, and a 20 percent group.[36] This guidance provided that long-term capital gains in a CRT from January 1, 1997, through May 6, 1997, are in the 28 percent group.
>
> Congress then again changed this aspect of the law somewhat in 1998, causing certain long-term capital gains that would be in the 28 percent group to be in the 25 percent group or the 20 percent group. The IRS then issued guidance reflecting the alterations in this area wrought by the 1998 legislation.[37]

3. The remaining amount (if any) is next taxed as *other income* (such as tax-free interest income) to the extent of this type of in-

come of the trust for the year and this type of undistributed income of the trust for prior years.

4. The remaining amount (if any) is next treated as a distribution of trust corpus, which is not taxed.[38]

Q 5:15 How is the value of a remainder interest in a charitable remainder trust determined?

The amount of the charitable contribution deduction for a gift to charity by means of a charitable remainder trust essentially is the value of the remainder interest in the trust property.[39] The rules as to valuation of a remainder interest in a charitable remainder trust vary, depending on the type of trust involved: a charitable remainder annuity trust (CRAT) or a charitable remainder unitrust (CRUT).

CRAT

The fair market value of a remainder interest in a CRAT is its *present value*.[40]

For purposes of the charitable contribution deductions (Q 4:1), the fair market value of the remainder interest in a CRAT is the net fair market value—as of the appropriate valuation date—of the property placed in the trust, less the present value of the annuity income interest.[41] Simply stated, the value of the remainder interest is equal to the value of the property transferred to the trust less the value of the annuity interest.

Thus, valuation of a remainder interest in a CRAT requires identification of a *valuation date*. The rules for determining this date are dependent upon the type of charitable contribution deduction involved.

In the case of a gift involving an *income tax* charitable contribution deduction or a *gift tax* charitable contribution deduction, the term *valuation date* means, in general, the date on which the property is transferred to the trust by the donor.[42]

NOTE: The valuation date is not determined by the date on which the trust was created.

The present value of an annuity interest is determined basically by two factors: mortality tables promulgated by the IRS and an interest rate that is set by the Department of the Treasury[43] each month.[44]

This interest rate is equal to 120 percent of the federal mid-term rate that is in effect for the month in which the interest rate falls (rounded to the nearest $^2/_{10}$ of 1 percent). The donor may elect[45] to compute the present value of the annuity interest by use of the interest rate component for either of the two months preceding the month in which the valuation date falls.[46]

In an instance of a gift involving an *estate tax* charitable contribution deduction, the valuation date generally is the date of death. There is, however, in the estate tax context, an *alternative valuation date* which may be elected by the decedent's estate,[47] in which case the valuation date is the alternative valuation date. If the alternative valuation date is elected, and the decedent's estate also elects to use the interest rate component for one of the two months preceding the alternative valuation date, the month selected containing that date is the one used to determine the interest rate and mortality tables.[48]

The present value of an annuity is computed using rules in the estate tax regulations.[49] If the interest to be valued is the right of a person to receive an annuity that is payable, at the end of each year, for a term of years or one life, the present value of that interest is ascertained by multiplying the amount that is annually payable by the appropriate annuity actuarial factor. That factor is the one that corresponds to the applicable interest rate and the annuity period.[50]

As noted, this annuity actuarial factor assumes that the annuity is paid annually. If, however, the annuity is payable at the *end* of semiannual, quarterly, monthly, or weekly periods, the product obtained by multiplying the annuity factor by the annual annuity amount must be multiplied by an adjustment factor.[51] Likewise, an adjustment must be made if the annuity is payable at the *beginning* of one of these periods.[52] This adjustment is required to adjust (lower) the charitable deduction in reflection of the more frequent annuity payments.

Other tables are used to compute the value of a remainder interest in cases of an annuity amount determined on the basis of multiple lives.[53]

CRUT

The fair market value of a remainder interest in a CRUT is its *present value*.[54] This is the case for purposes of the charitable contribution deductions (Q 4:1).[55] The rules as to determining the valuation date are the same as those for CRATs.

These rules require determination of an *adjusted payout rate*.[56] There are rules where the unitrust payment period is for a term of years[57] and where it is for the life of an individual.[58]

NOTE 1: In certain circumstances (such as a terminal illness), there are exceptions to the use of the prescribed mortality tables.[59]

NOTE 2: A claim for a charitable deduction on a tax return for the value of a remainder interest in a CRT must be supported by a "full statement" attached to the return showing the computation of the present value of the interest.[60]

COMMENT: The charitable contribution deduction is, as discussed, based on the value of the remainder interest in a CRT. If, however, the probability that the charity will receive the remainder interest is negligible, the charitable deduction will not be allowed.[61] In one instance, where the likelihood that the remainder interest beneficiary would receive the interest was not in excess of 5 percent, the IRS disallowed the charitable contribution deduction.[62]

Other tables are used to compute the value of a remainder interest in cases of a unitrust interest determined on the basis of multiple lives.[63]

Q 5:16   Who can be a trustee of a charitable remainder trust?

Under the federal tax law, any person can be a trustee of a charitable remainder trust. This means that the trustee, or one of the trustees, can be the donor, an income interest beneficiary, the charity that is to receive the remainder interest, another individual, or a financial institution or other corporate trustee.

TIP: Caution must be exercised when causing the donor to be the trustee: the grantor trust rules ought not to be triggered. The principal consequence of application of these rules is that the capital gain resulting from the sale of trust assets would be taxed to the donor.

State law on this point should be reviewed, because of various limitations as to what entities can be trustees of trusts—charitable or otherwise.

Q 5:17   What is a *pooled income fund*?

A *pooled income fund* is a type of split-interest trust (Q 5:3).[64] It is a trust (fund) that is used to create remainder interests (Q 5:2) destined for charity.

A donor to a qualified pooled income fund receives a charitable contribution deduction for contributing the remainder interest in the donated property to charity. This use of the fund creates income interests (*id.*) in noncharitable beneficiaries. The remainder interests in the gift properties are destined for the charitable organization that maintains the fund.

The pooled income fund's basic instrument (a trust agreement or declaration of trust) is written to facilitate gifts from an unlimited amount of donors, so the essential terms of the transaction must be established in advance for all participants.

NOTE: This is an important distinction in relation to the charitable remainder trust (Q 5:6). Each charitable remainder trust is designed for the circumstances of the particular donor(s) (Q 5:27). This ability or inability to tailor the gift can be a factor in deciding which planned gift vehicle to use (Q 5:30).

The pooled income fund is—literally—a pooling of gift properties. It is sometimes characterized as functioning in the nature of a mutual fund, albeit for the benefit of charities. Although there is some truth to this— the pooled income fund *is* an investment vehicle—the funding of a pooled income fund is basically motivated by charitable intents.

Each donor to a pooled income fund contributes an irrevocable remainder interest in the gift property to or for the use of an eligible charity. The donor creates an income interest for the life of one or more beneficiaries, who must be living at the time of the transfer.

NOTE: With the charitable remainder trust, an income interest can be measured by a term of years (Q 5:6). This is not permissible in the case of pooled income funds.

The properties transferred by the donors must be commingled in the fund (so as to create the necessary pool).

Contributions to pooled income funds are generally confined to cash and readily marketable securities.

NOTE: This requirement, as well, highlights an important distinction between pooled income funds and charitable remainder trusts (Q 5:9).

The pooled income fund, by its nature, must be kept liquid, to facilitate the flow of new gift property, reinvestments, and transfers of remainder interests to the charitable organization. A pooled income fund cannot invest in tax-exempt bonds and similar instruments.

The present value of an income interest in property transferred to a pooled income fund is computed on the basis of life contingencies prescribed in the estate tax regulations and an interest rate equal to the highest yearly rate of return of the fund for the three tax years immediately preceding the tax year in which the transfer to the fund is made.[65] Special rules apply in the case of new pooled income funds (Q 5:24).

Each income interest beneficiary must receive income at least once each year.[66] The pool amount is generally determined by the rate of return earned by the fund for the year. Income beneficiaries receive their proportionate share of the fund's income. The dollar amount of the income share is based on the number of units owned by the beneficiary. Each unit must be based on the fair market value of the assets when transferred.

A pooled income fund must be maintained by one or more charitable organizations.[67] The charity must exercise control over the fund. It does not have to be the trustee of the fund, but it must have the power to remove and replace the trustee.

NOTE: Whether a charitable organization can be the trustee of a pooled income fund is a matter of state law (Q 5:25).

A donor or an income beneficiary of a pooled income fund may not be a trustee of the fund.[68] A donor may, however, be a trustee, director, or officer of the charitable organization that maintains the fund, as long as he or she does not have the general responsibilities toward the fund that are ordinarily exercised by a trustee.

NOTE: A pooled income fund can accommodate a smaller amount (value) of securities or similar property than a charitable remainder trust. From a fund-raising standpoint, this may appear counterproductive. These funds, however, offer opportunities for attracting first-time planned givers, setting the stage for larger gifts (including those to charitable remainder trusts) later.

TIP: No limits are imposed by law as to the number of pooled income funds a charitable organization may maintain. One or more funds may be used for general fund-raising purposes; others may be organized around specific investment approaches or purposes.

Q 5:18   What types of charities can be remainder interest beneficiaries of pooled income funds?

There are stringent limitations on the types of charitable organizations that can be remainder interest beneficiaries of pooled income funds. These organizations can only be certain types of public charities.

The charitable organizations that can be remainder interest beneficiaries of pooled income funds are churches, conventions and associations of churches, and integrated auxiliaries of churches; universities, colleges, and schools; hospitals, other health care providers, and medical research organizations affiliated with hospitals; foundations affiliated with government-owned and -operated colleges and universities; governmental units; and donative publicly supported charities (Q 2:3; Q 2:7).[69]

Other types of public charities—generally, service provider publicly supported charities (Q 2:8) and supporting organizations (Q 2:15)—cannot be remainder interest beneficiaries of pooled income funds.

TIP: This matter is not quite that easily delineated. In defining the categories of eligible pooled income fund remainder interest beneficiaries, the law provides that they must be *described in* a qualifying category. For example, a charitable organization may have a determination letter from the IRS classifying it as a service provider publicly supported charity, although it simultaneously meets the criteria for a donative publicly supported charity. That type of charitable organization could maintain a pooled income fund.

Q 5:19   What does it mean to *maintain* a pooled income fund?

As noted, a qualifying pooled income fund must be maintained by the public charity to or for the use of which the irrevocable remainder interest is contributed (Q 5:17). This requirement of *maintenance* is satisfied where the public charity exercises control, directly or indirectly, over the fund. For example, this requirement of control is ordinarily met when the public charity has the power to remove the trustee or trustees of the fund and designate a new trustee or trustees.[70]

A national organization that carries out its purposes through local organizations, chapters, or auxiliary bodies with which it has an identity of aims and purposes may maintain a pooled income fund in which one or more local organizations and the like that are eligible public charities have been named as recipients of the remainder interests.[71]

Q 5:20   What types of property are suitable for pooled income funds?

Generally, only property that is liquid in nature can be transferred to a pooled income fund as a charitable gift, because of the necessity of maintaining the requisite *pool* of assets (Q 5:17). Transferable property is generally money and publicly traded securities. It appears possible, however, that other types of property—such as real estate—may be transferred to a pooled income fund, if the trustee of the fund can readily sell the property.

NOTE: Oddly, there has not been a court opinion or public or private IRS ruling addressing this subject.

Q 5:21   Who can be a donor to a pooled income fund?

Only individuals can be donors to pooled income funds. The income payment periods are confined to lifetimes; pooled income fund interests cannot be determined by means of terms.[72] Consequently, a corporation cannot be a donor to a pooled income fund.

Q 5:22   How is income paid to an income interest beneficiary of a pooled income fund taxed?

An income interest beneficiary of a pooled income fund must include in his or her gross income all amounts properly paid, credited, or required to be distributed to the beneficiary during the tax year or years of the fund ending within or with his or her tax year.[73]

NOTE: The tiered system applicable in the case of charitable remainder trusts (Q 5:14) is inapplicable to payments out of a pooled income fund.

Q 5:23   How is the value of a remainder interest in a pooled income fund determined?

The fair market value of a remainder interest in a pooled income fund is its present value.[74] For purposes of the charitable contribution deductions, the present value of a remainder interest in property transferred to a pooled income fund is computed on the basis of certain life contingencies[75] and discount at a rate of interest, compounded annually, equal to the highest yearly rate of return of the fund for the three years immediately preceding the year in which the transfer of property to the fund is made.[76]

The yearly rate of return of a pooled income fund for a year generally is the percentage obtained by dividing the amount of income earned by the fund for the year involved by an amount equal to the

1. Average fair market value of the property in the fund for that year, less

2. A sum termed the *corrective term adjustment.*[77]

CAUTION: Where it appears from the facts and circumstances that the highest yearly rate of return of the fund, for the three years immediately preceding the year in which the transfer of property is made, has been purposely manipulated to be substantially less than the rate of return that would otherwise be reasonably anticipated, with the purpose of obtaining an excessive charitable deduction, that rate of return may not be used. Instead, the highest yearly rate of return of the fund must be determined by treating the fund as a new one (Q 5:24).[78]

Q 5:24   How is the rate of return calculated for a new pooled income fund?

For this purpose, a *new* pooled income fund is one that has been in existence for less than three years immediately prior to the tax year in which a transfer is made to the fund. A *deemed* rate of return must be used for any transfer to a new pooled income fund until it can compute its highest rate of return for its previous three tax years under the general rules (Q 5:23).[79]

The deemed rate of return is the interest rate (rounded to the nearest $2/10$ of 1 percent) that is 1 percent less than the highest annual average of the monthly rates used generally to calculate remainder interests (Q 5:15) for the three calendar years immediately preceding the year in which the transfer to the fund was made.

This was most recently illustrated by the method for determining the deemed rate for pooled income funds started in 1998.[80]

Q 5:25   Who can be a trustee of a pooled income fund?

The charitable organization that maintains (Q 5:19) the pooled income fund is required to exercise control over the fund. The charity does not have to be the trustee of the fund—although, as a matter of federal tax law, it can be—but it must have the power to remove and replace the trustee. A donor or an income interest beneficiary of the fund may not be a trustee.

NOTE: A donor may be a trustee, director, or officer of the charitable organization that maintains the fund, as long as he or she does not have the general responsibilities with respect to the fund that are ordinarily exercised by a trustee.

State law should be examined on this point, because of various limitations on what entities can be trustees of trusts, charitable or otherwise. For example, in some states, a charitable organization is not permitted to serve as a trustee.

Q 5:26   What happens when a charitable organization that has a pooled income fund ceases to qualify as a type of public charity that can maintain a pooled income fund?

As of the year the charitable organization ceases to constitute a type of public charity that is eligible to maintain a pooled income fund, the fund would lose its favorable tax statuses. Among other outcomes, contributions to charity by means of the fund would no longer be tax deductible as charitable gifts. Contributions made while the organization was qualified would not be adversely affected by the change in the fund's status.

NOTE: The tax regulations are silent on this subject. There is no court opinion, nor IRS public or private ruling, that addresses the point.

Q 5:27   When should a charitable remainder trust be used rather than another planned giving technique?

Because the charitable remainder trust has the broadest range of planning possibilities of any of the planned giving techniques, one way to answer this question is to say that a charitable remainder trust should be favored in any potential planned giving scenario, and used unless there is a compelling reason to utilize one of the other planned giving vehicles. Another approach is to say that a charitable remainder trust should be used only when none of the other techniques can be.

The charitable remainder trust offers the greatest flexibility in terms of the types of property that can be transferred to it (Q 5:9). A donor who wants to take advantage of a makeup feature (Q 5:7) or a conversion feature (*id.*) must use a charitable remainder unitrust. Tax-exempt securities can be transferred to a charitable remainder trust but not to a pooled income fund (Q 5:17). The charitable remainder trust offers more flexibility when it comes to selecting a trustee or trustees (Q 5:16). A donor desirous of an annuity and wishing to avoid the bargain sale rules (Q 4:34) can only use a charitable remainder annuity trust (inasmuch as these rules would be invoked where a charitable gift annuity is created (Q 5:32)). The charitable remainder trust can be tailored to the donor's circumstances more so than with any other planned gift vehicle.

Q 5:28 When should a pooled income fund be used rather than another planned giving technique?

The pooled income fund can be used where the donor of liquid property is not interested in receiving the income interest in the form of fixed income (that is, as an annuity) and feels more comfortable with an investment base that may be larger than that created by the donor's sole gift. The pooled income fund also is useful when the gift property is relatively modest in size (that is, it may be too small to be transferred to a charitable remainder trust).

COMMENT: Although the law does not address the point, most charities have a policy as to the minimum amount they will accept as a gift by means of a charitable remainder trust. A common amount is $100,000. A pooled income gift may be as low as $5,000—and some charities will accept even less if the donor has previously made a contribution to the pooled income fund.

Furthermore, the pooled income fund gift is simple to document and does not entail much cost (in part because there is no trust document to draft).

Q 5:29 What are the disadvantages of using a charitable remainder trust in relation to other planned giving techniques?

The charitable remainder trust is such a flexible vehicle, one that can be used in so many creative ways, that perhaps the greatest disadvantage in using it is the cost of designing and preparing the trust document. These are tailored to particular gift situations, so the legal fees involved could be in the thousands of dollars. Also, as noted (Q 5:28), many charitable organizations have a minimum for the value of the property they will accept by means of a charitable remainder trust. Commonly, again as noted, the starting level is $100,000, although some charitable organizations will accept these gifts as low as $25,000. Financial institutions have minimums for the amounts in trust they will manage. From a legal standpoint, there is greater likelihood of becoming entangled in the *grantor trust* rules than with any other giving technique.

COMMENT: There are some perils here, too, for the lawyers that pre-pare these documents. (Even greater perils lurk when those who write these documents are not lawyers.) Two elements in this regard do not mix well: the various types of charitable remainder trusts (Q 5:7) and the word processor. Lawyers have been known to leave in provisions, suitable for one type of remainder trust, that cause a trust to fail to qual-ify as the type of trust the donor intended. The same result can obtain when a provision is omitted. A mistake like this can have a big impact on the charitable deduction and on the amount the charity is to receive. While the IRS has been generous in allowing trust amendments to cor-rect scriveners' errors,[81] this is the stuff of malpractice suits.

Q 5:30   What are the disadvantages of using a pooled income fund in relation to other planned giving techniques?

The principal disadvantage to the use of a pooled income fund is its in-flexibility: there is not much planning that can be done with it. Also, the income interest beneficiaries of a pooled income fund have no guaran-tees as to the amount of income they will receive. They receive their al-locable shares of the fund's annual net earnings—whatever that amount may turn out to be. Furthermore, tax-exempt securities may not be con-tributed to a pooled income fund.

Q 5:31   What is a *charitable lead trust*?

In essence, a *charitable lead trust* is the reverse of a charitable remain-der trust (Q 5:6): with the lead trust, the income interest is contributed to charity and the remainder interest is destined for noncharitable ben-eficiaries.[82] Thus, the charitable lead trust is a form of split-interest trust (Q 5:3).

Under these arrangements, an income interest in property is con-tributed to a charitable organization for a term of years or for the life of one or more individuals. The remainder interest in the property is re-served to return, at the expiration of the income interests (the *lead pe-riod*), to the donor or to be transferred to one or more other remainder interest beneficiaries.

The charitable lead trust can be used to accelerate into one year a series of charitable contributions that would otherwise be made an-nually. In some circumstances, a charitable deduction is available for the transfer of an income interest in property to a charitable organiza-tion by means of a charitable lead trust. There are stringent limita-tions, however, on the deductible amount of charitable contributions of these income interests. Frequently, there is no charitable contribution deduction; the donor's motive for establishing the trust is estate planning.

Q 5:32   What is a *charitable gift annuity*?

Unlike most other forms of planned giving—which are based on a type of split-interest trust (Q 5:6, Q 5:17, Q 5:31)—the *charitable gift annuity* is arranged in an agreement between the donor and the charitable donee.[83] The donor agrees to make a payment and the donee agrees, in return, to provide the donor (and/or someone else) with an annuity. (Again, an *annuity* is a payment of a fixed amount, usually annually (Q 5:17).)

With one payment, the donor is actually engaging in two transactions: the *purchase* of an annuity and the making of a charitable *gift*. The gift component gives rise to the charitable contribution deduction. One sum (which may include one or more items of property) is transferred; the amount in excess of the portion necessary to purchase the annuity is the charitable gift portion. Because of the dual nature of the transaction, the charitable gift annuity transfer constitutes a *bargain sale* (Q 4:34).

The annuity resulting from the creation of a charitable gift annuity arrangement is a fixed amount paid at regular intervals (as noted, at least once annually). The exact amount is calculated to reflect the age of the beneficiary, which is determined at the time the calculation is made, and the annuity rate selected.

NOTE: As a matter of law, a charitable organization is free to offer whatever rate of return it wishes (staying within the ambit of reasonableness). Most charities utilize the rates periodically set by the American Council on Gift Annuities. These voluntary rates are in place to avoid unseemly "price wars" among charities pursuing these gifts. The establishment and "enforcement" of these uniform rates triggered litigation in which the Council was charged with antitrust and securities law violations.[84] In an effort to eliminate the bases for these types of lawsuits, Congress responded in 1995 with the Philanthropy Protection Act (amending the securities laws) and the Charitable Gift Annuity Antitrust Relief Act (amending the antitrust laws), the latter augmented by the Charitable Donation Antitrust Immunity Act of 1997.[85]

A portion of the annuity paid is tax-free because it is a return of capital. Where appreciated property is contributed, there will be recognition of capital gain reflecting the appreciation that is attributable to the value of the annuity. If the donor is the annuitant, the capital gain can be reported ratably over the donor's life expectancy. The tax savings occasioned by the charitable contribution deduction may, however, shelter any capital gain (resulting from creation of the annuity) from taxation.

Because the arrangement is by contract between the donor and donee, all of the assets of the charitable organization are subject to liability for the ongoing payment of the annuities.

NOTE: This is an important distinction between charitable gift annuities and other giving approaches. With most planned giving techniques, the resources for payment of income are confined to those in a split-interest trust. Here, the resources of the charity are on the line for the annuities.

For this reason, some states impose a requirement that charitable organizations establish a reserve for the payment of gift annuities. This is one reason many charitable organizations are reluctant to embark on a gift annuity program. Organizations can, however, eliminate much of the risk surrounding ongoing payment of annuities by reinsuring them.

NOTE: In general, an obligation to pay an annuity is a debt. Thus, the charitable organization involved would have acquisition indebtedness for purposes of the unrelated debt-financed income rules, were it not for a special rule.[86] To come within this rule (which gift annuity programs should and usually do), the value of the annuity must be less than 90 percent of the value of the property in the transaction, there can be no more than two income beneficiaries, there can be no guarantee as to a minimum amount of payments and no specification of a maximum amount of payments, and the annuity contract cannot provide for an adjustment of the amount of the annuity payments by reference to the income received from the transferred property or any other property.

TIP: A charitable organization that provides commercial-type insurance as a substantial part of its activities cannot be tax-exempt; this activity, even when of a lesser magnitude, is an unrelated business. Arguably, a charitable gift annuity is not a form of commercial-type insurance. To eliminate uncertainty on the point, however, there is an exception from these rules for these annuities.[87] To be eligible for this exception, a charitable deduction must be involved and the above exception from the unrelated debt-financed income rules must be available.

Q 5:33 Are there other ways to make deductible gifts of remainder interests?

Yes; there are three of them:

1. An individual may give a remainder interest in his or her personal residence or farm to charity. The individual receives a

charitable deduction for this gift without using a trust (indeed, a trust cannot be used in this context).

2. A trust is not required for a deductible gift of a remainder interest in real property when the gift is made in the form of a *qualified conservation contribution*.

3. A contribution of an undivided portion of one's entire interest in property is not regarded as a contribution of a partial interest in property.[88]

Q 5:34   What about gifts of life insurance?

Charitable contributions of life insurance policies are popular forms of giving. A gift of a policy of whole life insurance is an excellent way for an individual who has a relatively small amount of resources to make a major contribution to a charitable organization. Gifts of life insurance can be particularly attractive for younger donors.

If the life insurance policy is fully paid, the donor will receive a charitable contribution deduction for the cash surrender value or the replacement value of the policy. If the premiums are still being paid, the donor receives a charitable contribution deduction for the premium payments made during the particular tax year. For the deduction to be available, however, the donee charity must be both the beneficiary and the owner of the life insurance policy.

TIP: A policy of life insurance is valid (enforceable) only where the owner of the policy has an *insurable interest* in the life of the insured. In essence, this means that the owner and beneficiary of the policy (the same person) must be more economically advantaged with the insured alive. Examples of relationships where insurable interests exist are healthy marriages and the employment of key individuals. There is disagreement as to whether a charitable organization is better off with this type of donor dead or alive. In many instances, a charity is advantaged by having a donor of a life insurance policy alive: he or she may be an important volunteer (perhaps a trustee or officer) and/or a potential contributor of other, perhaps larger gifts.

Q 5:35   What about charitable split-dollar insurance plans?

The *charitable split-dollar insurance plan* (of which there are several varieties) essentially is a plan where a charitable organization receives one or more gifts and elects to use them to invest in a life insurance–based program, which provides death benefits to the charity and to the donor and his or her family members. This type of plan can be advantageous to a charitable organization in building a sizable endowment fund.

These plans are controversial for a variety of reasons. Some critics assail the idea that there is an "understanding" between the donor and the charity that the gift will be invested in the insurance program; the thought is that the *step transaction doctrine* (Q 1:27) would defeat the deduction because the transaction is not a completed gift in that the donor directed use of the gift proceeds. The charity, however, is legally free to use the gift proceeds as it wishes; the case law is clear that this is not a step transaction.

COMMENT: On this point, the critics are being particularly (and perhaps dangerously) hypocritical. In and out of the realm of planned giving, there are understandings and expectations between donors and donees. With donor-advised funds and community foundations, there are innumerable understandings of this nature. What about charitable remainder trusts, where decisions are made as to whether to sell the gift property or the charity's investment strategy nicely changes once the income beneficiaries reach retirement age?

Another criticism is that these split-interest insurance plans generate an unwarranted private benefit. While it is true that some versions of these plans provide greater private benefits than are properly warranted, not all of them do. At any rate, where is the major gift—planned or otherwise—that does not accord, directly or indirectly—a personal benefit to a donor or to a donor's family member?

COMMENT: A bill was introduced in the House of Representatives in 1999, in an effort to shut down charitable split-dollar insurance plans. It would cause forfeiture of any charitable contribution deduction for any transaction "which provides a personal benefit directly or indirectly to the donor or any designee of the donor."[89] If enacted, this language basically would eliminate the charitable contribution deduction.

Nonetheless, charitable organizations should avoid participation in charitable split-dollar insurance programs until these tax law issues are resolved. There is considerable opposition to these plans in Treasury and the IRS, and on Capitol Hill. Legislation is being enacted which would deny the federal income, estate, and gift tax charitable contribution deductions for any transfer to or for the use of a charitable organization if in connection with the transfer

1. The organization, directly or indirectly, pays or has previously paid any premium on any personal benefit contract with respect to the transferor, or

2. There is an understanding or expectation that any person will, directly or indirectly, pay any premium on any personal benefit contract with respect to the transferor.[90]

The phrase *personal benefit contract* will mean, with respect to the transferor, any life insurance, annuity, or endowment contract if any direct or indirect beneficiary under the contract is the transferor, any member of the transferor's family, or any other person (other than a charity) designated by the transferor.

The law will impose on a charitable organization an excise tax, in an amount equal to the premiums paid by the entity on any life insurance, annuity, or endowment contract, if the payment of the premiums is in connection with an above-described transfer for which a charitable deduction is not allowable. Payments would be treated as made by the charitable organization if they are made by any other person pursuant to an understanding or expectation of payment. (The excise tax will not apply if all of the direct and indirect beneficiaries under the contract (including any side agreement) are charities.)

A charitable organization will have to annually report to the IRS the amount of premiums that are paid during the year that are subject to the excise tax, as well as the name and identification number of each beneficiary to which the premiums relate. This reporting requirement will encompass any side agreement.

The deduction denial provision will apply to transfers after February 8, 1999. The excise tax provision will apply to premiums paid after the date of enactment. The reporting provision will apply to premiums that would be subject to the excise tax were it then effective, paid after February 8, 1999.

NOTE: This bill is of considerable potency, having been sponsored by the Chairman of the House Ways and Means Committee and the Committee's ranking minority member.

COMMENT: It would seem that a better approach in this area, rather than simply legislate away charities' ability to utilize these plans, is to develop a statute that permits charitable deductions with respect to appropriate (qualified) split-dollar insurance plans. In this way, there would be a "carve-out" for the qualified plans, rather than an outright prohibition. For example, in the face of claims of abuses in the planned giving arena, Congress did not (in 1969) eliminate planned gift arrangements but instead legislated criteria by which the charitable deductions would be available with respect to appropriate programs (Q 5:6, Q 5:17, Q 5:31, Q 5:32). This practice is ongoing to this day, with Congress not only continuing to refine the criteria for charitable remainder trusts (Q 5:6) but also, in other fund-raising contexts, carving out rules by which the gift solicitation practices are suitably permitted. A recent case in point is the qualified sponsorship payment.[91] These plans and programs, then, have not been legislated out of existence; rather, those with appropriate features are allowed.

Q 5:36   How does a charitable organization start a planned giving program?

First and foremost, in commencing a planned giving program, the members of the charitable organization's board of directors (or trustees) must be involved. (This does not mean involved as donors at this point—that stage comes later.) They must be involved—if the effort is to have any credibility and thus success—in the launching of the program. One of the important elements of this step—admittedly more from a legal than a fund-raising point of view—is the passing of a board resolution by which the program is formally created, and stating who is principally responsible for implementing it, which planned giving vehicles are to be used (at least at the outset), and the gift parameter policies. As to the latter, the resolution may include requirements that charitable remainder trust gifts be at least $100,000 and involve no more than two income beneficiary lives (Q 5:28) and that a pooled income fund gift be at least $5,000 (*id.*). This resolution would become part of the board minutes and be part of the official record at the beginning of the planned giving program; this can be helpful, should there be any questions about these decisions in later years.

A presentation—probably necessarily a relatively brief one—should be made at a board meeting on the basics of planned giving. This works best—that is, the board members are likely to pay more attention—if this miniseminar is offered by an outsider, such as a lawyer, professional development consultant, or bank trust officer. (The board might pay even more attention if the presenter is paid.) The board members should be given some written materials as part of this presentation, for reference during the meeting and for perusal afterwards.

Prototype documents should be prepared, such as forms for charitable remainder trusts and pooled income fund transfer agreements. While not likely to be of much concern to a prospective donor, these documents are certain to be of great interest to the potential donor's advisor, be it lawyer, accountant, financial planner, or similar individual, particularly if the advisor is unfamiliar with planned giving.

Registration of this fund-raising program should be undertaken in the appropriate state(s) (see Chapter 9). Marketing literature should be prepared. The organization can either write and print these materials itself or purchase them commercially.

TIP: Some organizations make the mistake of starting with every available planned giving technique and discussing them all in one (sizable) document, replete with lengthy illustrations. While impressive, few will read this material—it will probably go the way of books designed for coffee tables. It is best to have separate brochures on each of the techniques that are to be used, perhaps with an overall booklet about the charity into which the appropriate brochure(s) can be slipped. These brochures should be reasonably easy to read, with examples kept as simple as possible. Not every answer to planned giving questions needs to be provided in these materials.

The organization should then start the process of building a network or cadre of volunteers who will be planned giving advocates to the charity's constituency. This group—ideally—will include members of the board. These individuals will need some special training in planned giving. The purpose here is not to make them planned giving experts overnight—or perhaps ever—but rather to get them to the stage where they are sufficiently familiar with the subject so they can meaningfully talk to prospective donors, who are likely to be their peers.

TIP: These individuals should all be contributors of a planned gift—and hopefully comfortable in talking about that. It is also important that all board members participate. The task of launching—and maintaining—a planned giving program is made much more difficult—impossible?—when the organization's own leadership has not made a planned gift (or not even committed to one)—or, worse, will not give.

The next steps are obvious but the toughest: identifying prospective planned givers, communicating with them, and obtaining the gifts ("closing the deal"). For organizations with an emerging planned giving program, the best way to proceed is to have a staff person or a volunteer meet with the prospective contributor and work out a general plan.

TIP: One of the most important aspects of this stage—and this should be taught to the cadre of planned giving advocates—is matching the needs and interests of the donor(s) to the suitable planned giving vehicle(s). This is the "tailoring" process (Q 5:28).

Thereafter, one or more sessions with a planned giving professional can be held, where advice will be forthcoming as to the specific planned giving method(s) that is (or are) best for all parties. In complex situations, the prospective donor may interrelate with the planned giving professional. After that, a lawyer can prepare the required instrument(s).

CAUTION: The donor and the donee should each be represented by legal counsel. There can be competing interests in these settings and conflicts of interest are obvious. A common problem, however, is that the lawyer for the donor (and sometimes there isn't one, at the beginning) will not be familiar with planned giving, and will have to be helped along, preferably informally, by the lawyer for the prospective charitable donee.

As the gifts roll in and the various factors that lead to them are experienced, the staff of the charity will gain greater confidence and thus will need to rely less on outside counsel. A planned giving professional may be added to the staff. The outside planned giving professional may be kept on call and used when circumstances warrant.

One of the excuses frequently given for postponing the inauguration of a planned giving program (or ignoring the idea of such a program altogether) is that it is not suitable for a new, particularly small organization.

NOTE: Planned giving used to be called *deferred giving*, that term being reflective of the fact that the charity's receipt of its interest in the gift property (usually, the remainder interest (Q 5:2)) is deferred until some future time. The term fell out of favor because some donors became of the view that their tax benefits were what was deferred—a most disconcerting frame of mind. Still, taking into account the many organizations that find excuses for not having a planned giving program, it seems that the term *deferred giving* has a contemporary meaning.

There is no question that a university with decades of graduations or a hospital with decades of successful operations has a more solid contributor base than a community service group incorporated yesterday. But that university's or hospital's relative advantage is not an authentic reason for doing nothing. Every organization has developed or will develop a support base or it would not or will not exist. It may be that on day one, there is only one planned gift prospect, perhaps a rather tenuous one; yet that is no reason for not soliciting that prospect for a gift. The largest planned giving program in the nation started with one gift.

CHAPTER 6

Unrelated Business Activities

Of all of the major federal tax law rules applicable in the charitable fund-raising context, the rules concerning unrelated business activities may be the least familiar to the fund-raising professional. This is not surprising, since it is the rare individual (perhaps only the occasional tax lawyer) who envisions a fund-raising function as a *business*.

Nevertheless, the taxability of income derived by a charitable organization from the conduct of *unrelated business* is a key feature of the overall law applicable to charities (and other categories of tax-exempt organizations). No field of the federal tax law applicable to charities is spawning more issues and controversies than that pertaining to unrelated business activities. Many of these controversies have a direct or indirect impact on the process and the results of fund-raising for charitable purposes.

Here are the questions most frequently asked by professional fund-raisers (or that should be asked by them) about the unrelated business activities rules—and the answers to them.

Q 6:1 What does the term *business* mean?

In the eyes of the federal tax law, nearly every activity of a charitable or other tax-exempt organization is considered a business. From this perspective, an exempt organization is a bundle or cluster of businesses. These businesses include program activities—and fund-raising activities.

The technical term for *business* is *trade or business*. The phrase *trade or business* is defined by statute to mean any activity that is carried on for the production of income from the sale of goods or the performance of services.[1] That definition is, obviously, quite broad and, as noted, encompasses just about everything that a tax-exempt organization does.

It is difficult for a tax-exempt organization to convince the IRS or a court that a particular activity is not a business. The most likely instances where an exempt organization can prevail on this point is with respect to its investment activities and infrequent sales of assets. Occasionally, an organization will succeed, as illustrated by a court opinion finding that an association's monitoring activities with respect to insurance programs for its membership, where the insurance and claims processing functions were elsewhere, did not rise to the level of a trade or business.[2]

The courts and the IRS sometimes add other requirements and possibilities that may cause an activity to be regarded as a business. Thus, a business activity may be found when an exempt organization is in *competition* with for-profit enterprises.[3] The existence of *profits* (excess of revenue over expenses) may lead to a conclusion that an undertaking is a business. There may be an assertion that unrelated business is occurring solely because a fee is charged for the product or service. Moreover—and this is becoming a growing practice—the IRS or a court will jump to the conclusion that an unrelated business exists where the activity is conducted in a *commercial* manner (Q 6:11).[4]

Moreover, what may appear to be one business may in fact be several businesses. The law entertains the idea that an activity can be broken into several businesses, thereby increasing the number of businesses that comprise the operations of the exempt organization. This is known as *fragmenting* an organization's operations; the rule of law is the *fragmentation rule* (Q 6:3).

Q 6:2   What does the term *unrelated business* mean?

One of the great areas of controversy in the law of tax-exempt organizations is whether a business is a *related* one or an *unrelated* one (Q 6:5). As noted, a charitable organization is likely to have several program activities; each of them are related businesses. One or more fund-raising activities are businesses as well—but it is a rare one that is a related business.

Basically, an *unrelated business* is a business that is conducted by a tax-exempt organization, where the business is not substantially related to the achievement of the organization's exempt purposes.[5]

Q 6:3   What is the *fragmentation rule*?

The *fragmentation rule* is an important rule of law in the unrelated business income setting, because it allows for the identification, and isolation for examination purposes, of the discrete operations of a tax-exempt organization. It is used primarily by the IRS to see if there is an unrelated business tucked in among a cluster of related businesses.

Here is the rule in its specificity: an activity does not lose its identity as a trade or business if it is carried on within a larger aggregate of similar activities or within a larger complex of other endeavors that may or may not be related to the exempt purposes of the organization.[6] This means that an activity cannot be hidden from scrutiny, as to whether it is a separate business, by enveloping it with other activities.

The IRS has the authority to review each business of a charitable or other exempt organization, as if it was operating alone, in search of unrelated activity. The agency can fragment an organization into as many businesses as it can define; no court has attempted to limit the extent to which the IRS can go in this regard. For example, the administration of a university may regard the bookstore as a single operation (a business). But the IRS will see it as an aggregation of businesses, one being the sale of books, another of computers, another of appliances, and so on. The same is true with activities such as hospital and museum gift shops, associations' sales of items to their members, and the like.

Historically, the fragmentation rule has been used to break down activities into singular businesses by means of sales of items, as in the case of bookstores and gift shops. In the modern era, where it has become a common practice to segment individuals into classes for law purposes (allocation of benefits and preferences), the fragmentation rule is used to evaluate separate business operations by classes of users. Thus, in the case of membership-based fitness centers, which can be related businesses when they serve the general public (Q 6:11), the IRS will fragment the membership base into "identified groups of users" to determine if in fact the facility is available to the public.[7] Likewise, the IRS determined when the use of a university's golf course is and is not a related business by fragmenting the operation on the basis of the status of the users.[8]

Thus, the fund-raising professional may have difficulty accepting the idea that a charity's fund-raising program is a *business*.

NOTE: As will be discussed (Q 6:22), the fund-raising professional is likely to have even a harder time grappling with the concept that the fund-raising program is not a related business.

Yet, in fact, the matter is more intricate: the fund-raising program is almost certain to be a composite of businesses. The annual fund campaign is a business, just as is a capital campaign, a planned giving program, and a direct mail effort. Indeed, each special event is a business.

Q 6:4   How much unrelated business activity can a charitable organization engage in without endangering its tax exemption?

A lawyer practicing exclusively or primarily in the tax-exempt organizations field probably could do very well by having a dollar for every time that question is asked. It is, indeed, one of the most frequently asked questions in this area of the law. There is, by the way, nothing unique about charitable organizations here; this inquiry is consistently posed by representatives of nearly all categories of exempt organizations.

Basically, the management of a charitable organization should not lose sight of the fundamental fact that the entity is a nonprofit, tax-exempt, charitable (Q 1:8) organization. As such, it must be operated *primarily* for its exempt purposes (Q 1:9). If there is to be any taxable income, it will be income derived from business activities that are unrelated to the organization's charitable purpose. As long as operations are primarily for charitable purposes, the organization need not fear loss of its tax-exempt status.

Having said this, there is no mechanical formula for measuring what is *primary*. This determination is done on the basis of what the law likes to term the *facts and circumstances*.

COMMENT: In the law of tax-exempt organizations, there are many applications of a facts-and-circumstances test. One of them is in connection with the decision as to whether a person is an insider with respect to a charitable organization for purposes of the private inurement doctrine (Q 1:10). In that setting, a federal court of appeals was recently heard to whine that a facts-and-circumstances test "is no standard at all, and makes the tax status of charitable organizations and their donors a matter of the whim of the IRS."[9] This may be frustrating to a non-lawyer but often this test is the best that can be done in the real world; it frequently is preferable to some rigid rule of law, such as an absolute number or a particular percentage.

The IRS—uniformly supported by the courts[10]—heartily rejects the thought of applying any particular percentage in measuring the existence of primary activities, and thus applies this principle of law on a case-by-case basis.

TIP: Percentages are used in this and comparable contexts all the time, if only as a guide. The term *primary* has been assigned percentages in other settings; for unrelated business income purposes, it can

---

mean at least 65 percent. By comparison, the word *substantial* has been defined to mean 33$\frac{1}{3}$ percent and at least 85 percent; *substantially all* is sometimes set at 90 percent. *Incidental* is sometimes viewed as being up to 15 percent.

If these percentages have any validity—and, to a limited extent, they do for evaluation purposes—then an organization could have as much as one-third of its activities or income be unrelated. There are IRS private letter rulings upholding unrelated income in excess of 40 percent; however, in these cases, the amount of *time* devoted to the unrelated business was considerably less.

It would seem that an organization receiving over one-half of its income from unrelated business would not qualify for tax-exempt status. Yet, an IRS ruling made public in 1997 permitted ongoing exemption for a charitable entity that had unrelated business income at a rate of 98 percent, albeit with the time devoted to charitable endeavors at about 40 percent.[11]

COMMENT: It has been noted that fund-raising is a business (Q 6:2). For decades, there has been controversy over levels of charitable organizations' fund-raising costs, usually expressed as percentages. The clamor here, however, is framed as the use of charitable dollars for noncharitable ends. One court put the issue this way: "whether charities should be denied a tax exemption if their operating expenses are a very high percentage of the total charitable donations that they receive"?[12] Critics of higher-end fund-raising costs do not express their unhappiness in terms of the monies being spent for unrelated business activities.

A prudent assessment or review would cause a charitable organization to seriously evaluate its tax exemption situation if its unrelated business income annually exceeds 20 or 25 percent of total revenue. There may not be much of a problem if the unrelated income is passive (as in the nature of investment income). Otherwise, one remedy may be the establishment of a for-profit subsidiary.[13]

COMMENT: The statement that there is no mechanical formula for measuring what is *primary* is not precisely accurate. In the case of tax-exempt title-holding companies, the maximum amount of unrelated business income that they can have in a year without endangering tax exemption is 10 percent.[14] This rule does not apply with respect to any other type of exempt organization. For charitable and most other exempt organizations, 10 percent is too narrow a limitation on permissible unrelated activity.

Q 6:5   How does a charitable organization know whether an activity is a related one or an unrelated one?

This is both one of the easiest and one of the hardest questions to answer in the law of tax-exempt organizations. And, again, the difficulties here are not confined to charitable organizations.

The easy answer is that an unrelated activity is one that does not substantially advance the charitable purposes of the organization. That is, it is an activity that the organization engages in for the purpose of earning money, rather than furthering charitable objectives.

NOTE: This is why nearly every type of fund-raising activity is not a related business.

The fact that the money earned (raised) is used for charitable purposes does not alone cause the underlying activity itself to be related.

At the same time, just because an activity generates net income does not make the activity an unrelated one. It goes without saying that many related (program) activities of charitable (and other) exempt organizations generate impressive net economic returns. This test—another facts-and-circumstances one—thus looks not so much to the inherent nature of an activity but rather to the reason for engaging in it and the overall exempt purposes of the organization.

COMMENT: There are hundreds of examples of this point; here is one. The operation of a motel, considered as such, is clearly not a charitable activity. But, the operation of a motel by a supporting organization (Q 2:15) related to an exempt hospital can be a charitable activity (promotion of health) (Q 1:8). The facility enables the hospital to locate patients and family in the event of an emergency, and encourages the comfort and well-being of the patients during the time they are undergoing treatment at the hospital.[15]

The more complex answer is that the activity must be evaluated against as many as five levels of analysis. These are:

1. Is the activity a *trade or business* (Q 6:1)?
2. Is the activity *regularly carried on* (Q 6:13)?
3. Is the conduct of the activity *substantially related* to the conduct of charitable functions (Q 6:18)?
4. Is the *activity* exempted from taxation by one or more statutory exceptions (Q 6:25)?

5. Is the *income* from the activity exempted from taxation by one or more statutory exceptions (Q 6:27)?

Q 6:6   What is the rationale underlying the unrelated business income rules?

The basic structure of the unrelated business income rules was enacted in 1950. The essence of this body of law is to separate the income of a charitable or other tax-exempt organization into two categories: (1) income from one or more related businesses and (2) income from one or more unrelated businesses. The income from unrelated business is taxed basically in the same manner as if it was earned by a for-profit, taxable corporation.

The primary objective of these rules was to eliminate a source of *unfair competition* with the for-profit sector by placing the unrelated business activities of exempt organizations on the same tax basis as those conducted by nonexempt organizations, where the two are in competition.[16] Some courts place considerable emphasis on the factor of competition when assessing whether an undertaking is an unrelated business (Q 6:2). The existence or nonexistence of competition, however, is not a statutory requirement for there to be a trade or business.

Despite 50 years of application of these rules, the cries of "unfair competition" from the business sector, particularly small business owners, have not been quelled. Five decades later, the issue is not so much that unrelated business by nonprofit organizations is competitive; rather, the competition is usually derived from *related* businesses.

NOTE: Thus, the two hottest issues of the day in this area are the operation, by charitable organizations, of fitness centers and travel tours. The health industry wants the operation of fitness facilities by charitable organizations to end; so far, the IRS is ruling these enterprises are, under certain circumstances, related businesses (Q 6:11). The travel tour industry is trying to force a reduction in tours conducted by charitable and educational institutions, and is fighting proposed regulations[17] that would treat some tours as related activities (Q 6:23).

In part, this is the result of (1) shifts in the definitions of what amounts to related and unrelated enterprises (including management and investment assistance) and (2) the entry of for-profit businesses into fields of endeavor previously confined to nonprofit entities (such as health care, research, and education).

Some small business advocates want competitive practices prohibited, as a way of "leveling the playing field." Proponents of this view say that unrelated income taxation is insufficient; they fret about the fact that some consumers are attracted to, and thus take their business to, nonprofits just because they are nonprofit—a phenomenon known as the "halo effect."

Thus, the purpose of the unrelated business income tax is to equalize the economics of a transaction, irrespective of whether the vendor of a good or service is tax-exempt or taxable. If an organization can sell a product or a service and not pay income tax on the sales proceeds, that organization can charge a lower price for that product or service and have more profit remaining than an organization selling the same product or service and having to pay taxes as a cost of doing business. This ability, and occasional practices of price undercutting, is the foundation for the claim of unfair competition.

Q 6:7   Does this mean that the federal tax law considers the programs of charitable organizations as businesses?

Yes. As noted, each of a charitable organization's programs is considered a separate business. In fact, by operation of the fragmentation rule (Q 6:3), a program can entail several businesses. This phenomenon could cause a problem for charitable fund-raising—donors certainly don't think of charities as bundles of businesses—except that no one outside the unrelated business setting gives any thought to the matter.

Q 6:8   When the federal tax law regards a charitable organization as a composite of businesses, isn't that different from how these organizations view themselves?

There is no question about that, although as noted (Q 6:7) this matter is rarely contemplated by the lay public. Yet, within the unrelated business context, the disparity in perception gets more convoluted. To be more specific, the statutory definition of *business* provides that the phrase *trade or business* "includes" that definition of it. The word *includes* has opened the door for the courts and the IRS to add other requirements and possibilities that may cause an activity to be a business. Sometimes, other criteria are used—such as competition, commerciality, or profit-making—with the conclusion then jumped to that the activity is an unrelated business.

To illustrate how legal principles can evolve in strange ways, in a completely different area of the tax law, dealing with whether a gambler gambling for only personal ends is engaged in a business for expense deduction purposes, the Supreme Court held that for an activity to be considered a business, it must be carried on with a *profit motive.*[18] The Court specifically wrote that this definition of business was not to be used in other tax settings. But lower courts promptly ignored that admonition and engrafted that rule onto the definition of business for exempt organizations' law purposes.[19]

Q 6:9   Why would a charitable organization object to that additional element of the definition, concerning a profit motive? Wouldn't that rule always favor charitable organizations, causing some activities to not be businesses in the first instance?

Theoretically, perhaps; but in the real world it doesn't always work that way. In some instances, a charitable or other tax-exempt organization *wants* an activity to be considered an unrelated business. This is because net income from one unrelated activity and a net loss from another unrelated activity can be aggregated to produce a single, bottom-line item of net-net income or net-net loss.

For example, suppose a charitable organization has two unrelated activities. In a year, one produces $100,000 of net income, the other generates a $70,000 net loss. On the unrelated business income tax return (Q 6:34), the income and loss from the two activities can be blended, so that the charity pays the unrelated business income tax on only $30,000. This works, however, only when both activities are in fact *businesses*.

Suppose further that the second of these activities consistently, year-in and year-out, yields losses. The IRS is likely to take the position that because the activity always annually results in a loss, it is not being conducted with the requisite *profit motive* (Q 6:8). A loss activity may be viewed by the IRS as an *accommodation* to another party, rather than a business entered into with the intention of making a profit.[20]

COMMENT: A fearless prediction: The IRS will never assert that an activity is not a business, using the lack-of-profit-motive rationale, in a situation where the activity consistently produces net (taxable) income.

If that position is sustained by a court (which would probably happen), the activity is not considered a *business*, in which case the $70,000 of loss could not be offset against the $100,000 of income. Then, the organization would have to pay the unrelated business income tax on the entire $100,000.

All of this is happening even though the tax regulations state that the fact that a trade or business does not produce a net profit is not alone sufficient to exclude it from the definition of a trade or business.[21]

Q 6:10   What are some of the other elements being engrafted onto the definition of a *business*?

Sometimes, a business (usually an unrelated one) is deemed present solely because the charitable organization is in *competition* with one or more for-profit enterprises.[22] The existence of *profits* (net income) may lead a court to the conclusion that an undertaking is a business (again, likely an unrelated one).[23] The IRS has been known to assert the presence of unrelated business activity simply because a *fee* is charged for the product or service.[24] Moreover—and this is a growing practice—courts (and perhaps the IRS) will leap to the conclusion that an unrelated business exists where the activity is engaged in in a *commercial* manner.[25]

Q 6:11   What is a *commercial* activity?

The commerciality doctrine—which is quickly becoming one of the most important principles in the law of tax-exempt organizations—has been conceived by and is being developed by the courts, although it is not as yet well articulated. There is, with one relatively minor exception, no mention of *commerciality* in the Internal Revenue Code (Q 6:12). The same is the case with respect to the tax regulations (*id.*).

Even though a court has yet to fully explicate the doctrine, it essentially means that a tax-exempt organization is engaged in a nonexempt activity when that activity is conducted in a manner that is considered *commercial.*

NOTE: To date, the commerciality doctrine has been applied only with respect to public charities, although there is no reason as to why it could not be applied in situations involving other types of tax-exempt organizations.

An activity is a commercial one if it is undertaken in the same manner as it would be if it were being conducted by a for-profit (commercial) business. The most contemporary exposition of the commerciality doctrine sets forth these eight criteria:

1. The charitable organization sells goods or services to the general public.
2. The charity is in direct competition with one or more for-profit businesses.

3. The prices set by the charity are based on pricing formulas common in the comparable commercial business setting.

4. The charity utilizes advertising and other promotional materials and techniques to enhance sales.

5. The charity's hours of operation are basically the same as those of for-profit enterprises.

6. The management of the charity is trained in business operations.

7. The charity uses employees rather than volunteers.

8. There is an absence of charitable giving to the organization.[26]

COMMENT: Thus, the commerciality doctrine is being bred with a certain amount of ignorance as to how charitable organizations function in the modern era. While presumably not all of these eight factors are accorded equal weight in a particular assessment, it is nothing short of incredible that a charity would be found to be operating in a commercial manner because it has employees—let alone employees who may have some training to enhance their effectiveness! And Congress has specifically created a category of public charity which can receive public support that is not in the form of charitable gifts (Q 2:8).

NOTE: Commercial activity is not necessarily the equivalent of unrelated business activity. Thus, in the case of a fitness center operated by two charitable hospitals, the IRS wrote: "Competition between the [c]enter and commercial health clubs is present and several commercial health clubs have been driven out of business in the area." Yet, the fitness center was held to be a related business.[27]

Q 6:12 What are the statutory and regulatory references to the commerciality doctrine?

In 1986, Congress added to the federal tax law a rule stating that an organization cannot qualify as a tax-exempt charitable entity or social welfare entity if a substantial part of its activities consists of the provision of commercial-type insurance.[28] While that term is not defined in the statute, it generally is given this sweeping meaning: any insurance of a type provided by commercial insurance companies.[29] The reach of this aspect of commerciality is being accorded capacious interpretation in the courts.[30]

As far as the tax regulations are concerned, there is a brief mention of commerciality in the rules pertaining to whether an activity is regularly carried on (Q 6:13).[31] There, it is stated that business activities of an exempt organization will ordinarily be deemed to be regularly carried on "if they manifest a frequency and continuity, and are pursued in a manner, generally similar to comparable commercial activities of nonexempt organizations."[32]

Q 6:13   What are the rules as to whether a business activity is *regularly carried on*?

This test was derived in reflection of the fundamental purpose underlying the unrelated business rules (Q 6:6): an activity cannot be competitive with for-profit business if it is not *regularly carried on.*

Thus, income from an unrelated business is not taxable under these rules where that business is merely sporadically or infrequently conducted. The frequency and continuity of the activity, the manner in which the activity is pursued, and the continuing purpose of deriving income from the activity largely determine whether the activity is regularly carried on.[33]

NOTE: This is a most significant aspect of the law of unrelated business for the fund-raising professional. As noted, most fund-raising activities are not related businesses (Q 6:2). These activities are most likely to escape not related business income taxation, however, because they are not regularly carried on.

Q 6:14   How is this regularity measured?

There is no precise means of measurement of regularity in the unrelated business setting. It is a facts-and-circumstances test. An activity that consists of a single, one-time-only transaction or event is clearly irregular. For this reason, a sole sale of an item of property usually is not taxable. Most fund-raising special events (Q 6:23) are not taxed by reason of this rule.

Beyond that, it is a judgment call. Generally, regularity is a function of the amount of time expended in a given year. A business occupying only a few days in a year is not regularly carried on. The tax regulations offer a quaint example of this point, concerning the operation of a sandwich stand by a hospital auxiliary for two weeks at a state fair.[34] That fund-raising business is said to not be regularly carried on. But, it cannot be said with any certainty when too many days of activity cause the line to be crossed and the organization is in the realm of regularity. The regulations add that the operation of a commercial parking lot for one day of each week in a year is a business that is regularly carried on. Operation on 52 days out of 365, or operation on one day each week, obviously reflects an operation that is regularly carried on.

COMMENT: As noted, regularity is measured in terms of the amount of time expended in carrying on a business. It has nothing to do with when the payments for the business services are received. Recently, a court got itself tangled up on this point. Leasing services were provided by a charitable organization over a 4½-year period. Payments on the lease were made once annually. In deciding that the business was not regularly carried on, the court emphasized the fact that the charity was paid for its services only one time each year—a factual element that has no bearing on regularity.[35]

Q 6:15   Are there any other aspects of this level of analysis?

Yes, there are three other aspects of regularity—each of which is directly pertinent to fund-raising for charitable purposes.

One is that, where a business activity is, in the commercial sector, carried on only during a particular season, the duration of this season, rather than a full year, is the measuring period for a tax-exempt organization.[36] For example, an organization selling Christmas trees or Christmas cards is required to measure regularity against the duration of the Christmas season. Likewise, the operation of a horse-racing track would be measured in relation to the horse-racing season.

Q 6:16   What is the second aspect of regularity?

The IRS has adopted the view that there is more to the measurement of regularity than just the time expended for the event itself. The IRS takes into consideration the amount of time the organization spends in preparing for the event—known as *preparatory time*—and the time expended in connection with and subsequent to the event—*winding-down time*.[37] If an exempt organization sold a product commercially for a few days in a year, in assessing regularity the entity is—according to the IRS view—supposed to include the preparatory time of lining up the product, creating advertising, soliciting purchasers, and the like, as well as the winding-down time spent assessing the operation, arranging for the return of unsold items, and planning for resumption of the sales activity in the next year. The import of all of this, of course, is that while the time expended for the activity itself may be modest, so that taken alone it would not amount to an activity that is regularly carried on, the activity is converted into one that is regularly carried on when the preparatory time and the winding-down time are tacked on.

COMMENT: This matter of preparatory time is vexatious when it comes to special events. This factor alone can transform a fund-raising event into a taxable unrelated business. As an example, an exempt organization conducted, as a fund-raising event, a concert series two weekends each year, one in the spring and one in the fall. An activity taking place four days in the course of a year does not constitute an activity that is regularly carried on. But the organization spent much of the preceding six months planning for the concert and selling tickets. This enabled the IRS to rule that the net revenue from the concerts was taxable as unrelated business income, since these events were regularly carried on.[38]

NOTE: This position of the IRS as to the inclusion of preparatory time is not an unreasonable one. Yet, to date, it has been soundly rejected by the courts. One court, playing off the example of the operation of a sandwich stand at a state fair (Q 6:14), wrote: "The regulations do not mention time spent in planning the activity, building the stand, or purchasing the alfalfa sprouts for the sandwiches."[39]

Nonetheless, the IRS continues to assert its view in this regard,[40] notwithstanding its losses in the courts.[41]

Q 6:17   What is the third aspect of regularity?

For centuries, the law has recognized the concept of a *principal* and an *agent*. A principal is a person who hires another person to act in his, her, or its stead, for the principal's benefit; the hired person is an agent. Generally, the law considers the acts of an agent to be those of the principal. This means that the acts of the agent are attributed to, or deemed to be the acts of, the principal. Frequently, a contract will provide that one party is functioning as the agent of the other party.

In the unrelated business setting, it is common for an exempt organization to contract with a company for the performance of a service. If the company is considered an agent of the organization and the company's function is in connection with an unrelated business, the IRS may take the position that the time spent by the company is to be attributed to the exempt organization in determining whether the unrelated business was regularly carried on.[42]

TIP: Consequently, unless there is a legitimate reason to do so, it is advisable to not have a provision in a contract, entered into in the unrelated business setting, by which the company that is contracted with is designated as an agent of the tax-exempt organization.

Q 6:18 What about the third level of analysis, concerning the *substantially related* requirement?

This is where the controversy in the unrelated business area usually is: whether the business that is regularly carried on is *related* or *unrelated*.[43] The general rule is that the income derived by a tax-exempt organization from a regularly carried on trade or business is subject to tax unless the income-producing activity is substantially related to the accomplishment of the organization's tax-exempt purpose.

To determine whether an activity is related, an examination is made of the relationship between the business activity and the accomplishment of the organization's exempt purpose. The fact that the income generated by the business is used to further the organization's exempt programs does not cause the activity to be considered a related one.

A trade or business is *related* to tax-exempt purposes only where the conduct of the business has what the tax law terms a *causal relationship* to the achievement of an exempt purpose. The business is *substantially related* only if the causal relationship is recognizably large or material.[44] Thus, for the conduct of a trade or business from which a particular amount of gross income is derived to be substantially related to an exempt purpose, the production or distribution of the goods or the performance of the services from which the gross income is derived must contribute importantly to the accomplishment of these purposes. Where the production or distribution of goods or the performance of services does not contribute importantly to the accomplishment of the organization's exempt purposes, the income from the sale of the goods or services is not regarded as derived from the conduct of a related business.

Q 6:19 How is relatedness determined?

There is no mechanical test to be applied to ascertain the interrelationship between the conduct of an activity and the achievement of an exempt purpose. Judgments as to whether there is a causal relationship and whether there is substantiality are made in the context of the facts and circumstances involved.[45] There is not much that is straightforward in this area of the law; here lies complexity and murkiness.

COMMENT: Sometimes, context matters: an activity can be a taxable one in one setting and a nontaxable (related) one in another setting. Thus, a program once part of a physicians' group's medical practice was transferred to an exempt charitable organization, where it promptly became a related activity.[46] Indeed, the doctors received a charitable contribution deduction for the transfer.[47]

Q 6:20   What are some examples of these judgments?

There are hundreds of IRS rulings and court opinions finding activities to be related and unrelated. The organizations that tend to attract the most attention in this regard are colleges, universities, health care providers, and associations.

As an illustration from the realm of higher education, a fitness center operated by a university was a related business because of a range of educational programs conducted there.[48]

For example, in the health care area, the IRS concluded that a fitness center, established by two exempt hospitals, conducted exempt rehabilitation services and operated for the benefit of the general public, and thus was engaged in related business activities, even though it was conceded that the facility competed with for-profit health centers.[49] Also, even though generally the performance of diagnostic laboratory testing by a tax-exempt hospital on specimens taken from private-office patients of the hospital's staff physicians constitutes unrelated business,[50] there can be unique circumstances that transform the testing into a related business.[51]

One of the most significant issues in the unrelated business setting for associations is the tax treatment of dues paid by associate members. Where the associate member category is availed of for the principal purpose of producing unrelated business income, this type of dues will be taxed.[52] If, however, the associate member category principally has related purposes, the IRS will permit the dues to be received tax-free.[53]

There are many other instances of related and unrelated activity involving public charities generally. Here is a sampling:

- Sales of various items by an exempt museum can be related or unrelated businesses.[54]

- A school that sold 8,500 acres of farmland over a 25-year period was held by the IRS to not be engaged in an unrelated business.[55]

- The participation by a public charity—the "largest privately supported network of rehabilitation and training facilities in the world"—in a "surplus goods purchase program" was ruled to not be an unrelated business.[56]

- The IRS reviewed the travel tour activities of a religious organization, and concluded that some are exempt programs and others are unrelated businesses.[57]

- An educational organization was able to sell literature and equipment without being involved in an unrelated business.[58]

- The rental of temporary storage facilities by a charitable organization, which operates rental housing for low-income tenants, to the general public was ruled to be an unrelated business (although, if the rentals had been confined to the tenants, the activity would have been a related business).[59]

Another area of some concern (and inconsistency) is the matter of the provision of management or other administrative services (including fund-raising) by one tax-exempt organization to another. The general rule is that these services are an unrelated business, even where both exempt organizations have the same tax-exempt status.[60] That is, there is nothing inherently exempt about these types of activities.[61]

Yet, without much explanation as to when these activities may be related activities and when they may be unrelated activities, the IRS occasionally rules that the provision of administrative services is a related business. Some examples:

- An association providing management services to a related litigation entity was ruled to be engaged in a related business because the services were found to be in furtherance of the provider's exempt purposes.[62]
- A supporting organization, operating for the benefit of a university that is part of a medical center, was held to not be in an unrelated business where it owned and leased a computer system to a partnership of affiliated physicians that are the clinical faculty of the medical school in the center.[63]
- A graduate school providing administrative services (including accounting and risk management assistance) to a group of colleges was found to not be engaging in an unrelated business.[64]

There can be disagreements between the IRS and the courts in this area. Thus, in the case of a bar association selling standard legal forms to its member lawyers for their use in their law practices, the IRS ruled that the sale of the forms was an unrelated business because it did not contribute importantly to the accomplishment of the association's exempt functions.[65] There is, however, a court opinion to the contrary.[66] Another court held that the sale of preprinted lease forms and landlords' manuals by an association of apartment owners and managers was a related business.[67]

Q 6:21   Are there any other aspects of the substantially related test?

There are four subtests—tests within the substantiality test. One of them is the *size and extent test*.

In determining whether an activity contributes importantly to the accomplishment of a charitable or other exempt purpose, the size and extent of the activities should be considered in relation to the size and extent of the exempt function it purports to serve.[68] Thus, where income is realized by a tax-exempt organization from an activity that is in part related to the performance of its exempt functions, but that is conducted on a scale larger than is reasonably necessary for performance of the functions, the gross income attributable to that portion of the activities in excess of the needs of exempt functions constitutes gross income from the conduct of an unrelated business.

An example of the application of this test involved an association that had a membership of businesses in a state. One of its income-producing activities was to supply member and nonmember businesses with job injury histories on prospective employees. Rejecting the association's contention that this service contributed importantly to the accomplishment of exempt purposes, the IRS ruled that the activity was an unrelated business, in that the services went "well beyond" any mere development and promotion of efficient business practices.[69]

As an illustration of the application of this test, where the IRS concluded that the business was entirely related, the IRS considered a therapeutic program for emotionally disturbed adolescents provided by a public charity. It operated a retail grocery store that was almost completely staffed by adolescents to help secure their emotional rehabilitation. The IRS ruled that the store operation was not an unrelated business because it was operated on a scale no larger than reasonably necessary for its training and rehabilitation program.[70]

Another of these aspects is the *same state test*. As a general rule, the sale of a product that results from the performance of tax-exempt functions does not constitute an unrelated business where the product is sold in substantially the same physical state it is in upon completion of the exempt functions.[71] This rule is significant for charitable organizations that sell articles made or refurbished by disabled individuals as part of their rehabilitation training. By contrast, where a product resulting from an exempt function is exploited in business endeavors beyond what is reasonably appropriate or necessary for disposition in the state it is in upon completion of tax-exempt functions, the activity becomes transformed into an unrelated business.[72]

For example, an exempt organization maintaining a herd of dairy cows for scientific purposes may sell milk and cream produced in the ordinary course of operation of the project without unrelated income taxation. If, however, the organization were to utilize the milk and cream in the further manufacture of food items, such as ice cream and pastries, the sale of these products would likely be the conduct of an unrelated business.[73]

COMMENT: Another example of this principle was provided in the case of a tax-exempt salmon hatchery (an unlikely combination). The organization can sell a portion of its harvested salmon stock in an unprocessed condition to fish processors without incurring any tax—since the fish are sold in the same state in which the hatchery received (caught) them. Someone (who obviously spends too much time in fast food restaurants) came up with the idea of salmon nuggets (fish that was seasoned, formed into nugget shape, and breaded). The IRS ruled that when the fish was converted into nuggets, the sale of the fish in that state was an unrelated business.[74]

The third of these subtests of substantial relatedness is the *dual use test*.[75] This test comes into play in connection with a facility or other asset the use of which is necessary to the conduct of exempt functions but is also used in an unrelated endeavor. Each source of the income must be tested to see whether the activities contribute importantly to the accomplishment of exempt purposes. For example, a museum may maintain a theater for the purpose of showing educational films in connection with its program of public education in the arts and sciences; use of that theater for public entertainment in the evenings may be an unrelated business. Likewise, a school may have a ski facility that is used in its physical education program; operation of the facility for the benefit of the general public would likely be an unrelated business.

The fourth of these subtests is the *exploitation test*.[76] In certain instances, activities carried on by an exempt organization in the performance of exempt functions generate goodwill or other intangibles that are capable of being exploited in unrelated endeavors. When this is done, the mere fact that the income depended in part on an exempt function of the organization does not make it income from a related business. This type of income will be taxed as unrelated business income, unless the underlying activities themselves contribute importantly to the accomplishment of an exempt purpose. For example, income from advertising in a publication with exempt function content generally is taxable income resulting from an exploitation of an exempt resource.

COMMENT: In a sense, each of these four subtests is a variation of the fragmentation rule (Q 6:3).

Q 6:22   How do the unrelated business rules generally apply in the fund-raising context?

It is a substantial understatement to say that charitable organizations and their fund-raisers do not normally regard their fund-raising activities as unrelated businesses. Yet they often are, a fact frequently masked by the precarious relationship that has endured between the unrelated business rules and fund-raising practices for years.

Although many in the philanthropic community prefer to not think about it, the fact is that many fund-raising practices possess all the characteristics of an unrelated business. This type of activity is a business (Q 6:1), is regularly carried on (Q 6:13), and is not an effort that is inherently substantially related to the performance of charitable functions (Q 6:18). Furthermore, applying some of the tests often used by the IRS and the courts, there is no question that some fund-raising endeavors have a commercial counterpart (Q 6:11) and are being undertaken with the objective of realizing a profit (Q 6:1).

NOTE: The fact that "profits" are used in furtherance of charitable purposes but that that fact does not make the activity a related business calls to mind a court, which said of a charitable organization: "That it gave all its profits to an educational institution availeth it nothing in the mundane field of taxation, however much the children in our schools have profited from its beneficence."[77]

Treatment of a fund-raising program, such as a capital campaign or a direct mail effort, as an unrelated business may appear a rather strained outcome, and certainly is not consistent with the intent of Congress when it enacted these rules 50 years ago, but nonetheless can be a logical and technically accurate application of the rules.

As an example, the IRS reviewed the conduct by a religious organization of, as its principal fund-raising activity, bingo games and related concessions. The games were held on three nights each week, and the receipts from and expenses of the games were substantial. The IRS concluded that the "bingo games constitute a trade or business with the general public, the conduct of which is not substantially related to the exercise or the performance by the organization of the purpose for which it was organized other than the use it makes of the profits derived from the games."[78]

COMMENT: There is an exemption from unrelated business income taxation for bingo games[79] but this organization was unable to use it because, under the law of the state in which it is organized, the bingo games were illegal. Also, the above quote from the IRS does not include the finding by it that this gambling activity was regularly carried on. In a subsequent case, on similar facts, the IRS and the charitable organization stipulated that the gambling operations, conducted in the

---

name of fund-raising, were regularly carried on for purposes of unrelated income taxation.[80]

Another illustration of the application of the unrelated business income rules in the fund-raising context concerns the use of premiums. An organization offered premiums (maps, charts, calendars, and books) to potential donors as part of a semiannual direct mail solicitation. The rationale for this use of premiums was that it gained the attention of the recipients so that more initial responses were obtained or, in instances involving prior donors, the level of contributions was upgraded. Yet a court ruled that this type of fund-raising is an unrelated business because it was regularly conducted in a competitive and commercial manner.[81] The utility of the premiums as attention-getting devices did not cause the business to be related. The court wrote that "when premiums are advertised and offered only in exchange for prior contributions in stated amounts," the activity becomes a commercial one;[82] this "fund-raising" was viewed as a selling of the items. If, however, the organization "had mailed the premiums with its solicitations and had informed the recipients that the premiums could be retained without any obligation arising to make a contribution," the activity would not be a business inasmuch as it is not a competitive practice.[83]

In a comparable circumstance, the IRS ruled that the use of premiums was indeed sale of the cards.[84] The IRS observed that commercial practices were being employed, namely, payment for or return of the cards and the sending of follow-up notices. Because of these practices, the IRS concluded that the payments were not gifts because they were not "voluntary" (Q 1:13) and because the amount paid exceeded the fair market value of the cards. The receipts were thus characterized as sales of the cards at their fair market value in a competitive manner. In another like instance, the IRS said the card distribution program was "indistinguishable from normal commercial operations."[85]

A novel fund-raising scheme was held to be an unrelated business. A school consulted with a tax-shelter investment firm in search of fund-raising methods, with the result being a program in which individuals purchased various real properties from the school, which the school simultaneously purchased from third parties; both the sellers and the buyers were clients of the investment firm. There were 22 of these transactions during the years at issue, from which the school received income reflecting the difference between the sales prices and the purchase prices. Finding the "simultaneous purchase and sale of real estate . . . not substantially related to the exercise or performance of [the school's] . . .

exempt function," a court held that the net income from the transactions was unrelated business income.[86]

Only one court has squarely faced and analyzed the difference, for tax purposes, between a fund-raising activity and a business activity. Although the particular holding was overturned on appeal, the analysis nonetheless remains valid. The issue before this court was whether income, received by a charitable organization as the result of assignments to it of dividends paid in connection with insurance coverages purchased by members of a related professional association at group rates, was to be taxed as unrelated income. (The court held that there should be no taxation; the Supreme Court said there should be taxation.)

This court wrote that where the tax-exempt organization involved in an unrelated business income tax case is a charitable one, the "court must distinguish between those activities that constitute a trade or business and those that are merely fundraising."[87] Admittedly, said the court, this distinction is not always readily apparent, as "[c]haritable activities are sometimes so similar to commercial transactions that it becomes very difficult to determine whether the organization is raising money 'from the sale of goods or the performance of services' [which is the statutory definition of a *business* activity (Q 6:1)] or whether the goods or services are provided merely as an incident to a fund-raising activity." Nonetheless, the court held that the test is whether the activity in question is "operated in a competitive, commercial manner," which is a "question of fact and turns upon the circumstances of each case."[88] "At bottom," the court wrote, the "inquiry is whether the actions of the participants conform with normal assumptions about how people behave in a commercial context," and "[i]f they do not, it may be because the participants are engaged in a charitable fund-raising activity."[89]

One of the factors relied on by the lower court in finding no unrelated business activity was one that many fund-raising professionals rely on, perhaps without consciously realizing it: the activity was originally devised as a fund-raising event and was subsequently presented as such. When the Supreme Court reviewed the case, it found that to be the "only valid argument" in the charity's favor: "that the insurance program is billed as a fundraising effort."[90] But the Court summarily rejected that contention, with a rather peculiar (since hyperbole does not always lead to clarity) observation: "That fact, standing alone, cannot be determinative, or any exempt organization could engage in a tax-free business by 'giving away' its product in return for a 'contribution' equal to the market value of the product." The dissent concluded, however, that the provision of the insurance to the association's members was not competitive with commercial enterprises and that the dividend assignment program was "operated as a charitable fundraising endeavor."[91]

Q 6:23   Can a special event be an unrelated business?

Yes it can; in fact, most are—but the net income of a special event is not likely to be taxed.

A special event qualifies as a *business* (Q 6:1). It is an activity that is carried on for the production of income from the sale of goods or the performance of services. It is conducted with a profit motive (Q 6:1), although that is not likely to be the sole reason for conducting the event. A special event may be competitive with a for-profit business (as is the case with events such as bake sales and car washes) and it may be conducted in a commercial manner.

A special event is likely to be an unrelated business (Q 6:2). This is because there is rarely the requisite substantial causal relationship between the conduct of the event and the achievement of the organization's charitable purpose (Q 6:18). Yes, the event may raise money, which is used for charitable purposes, and, yes, the event may enhance the organization's standing in the community, but these are not charitable programs.

Nonetheless, due to a variety of exceptions, the net income of a special event is rarely taxed. As illustrated by a court opinion, the most common reason that a special event escapes taxation is that it is not regularly carried on (Q 6:13).

CAUTION: Again, however, this is the place to beware application of the preparatory time rule (Q 6:16).

In this case, at issue was the tax status of a membership organization for citizens' band radio operators that used insurance, travel, and discount plans to attract new members. The organization contended it was only doing what many charitable organizations do to raise contributions, analogizing these activities to fund-raising events. A court rejected this argument, defining a *fund-raising event* as a "single occurrence that may occur on limited occasions during a given year and its purpose is to further the exempt activities of the organization."[92] These events were contrasted with undertakings that are "continuous or continual activities which are certainly more pervasive a part of the organization than a sporadic event and [that are] . . . an end in themselves."

COMMENT: The court was heading in the correct direction in this regard, attempting to differentiate between sporadic fund-raising events and ongoing program or business activities. But the court got tangled up in its syntax along the way. For example, if a special event is a "sin-

---

gle occurrence," which it usually is, in the sense of once annually, how can it also "occur on limited occasions" during a year? What is the difference between "continuous" and "continual"? A variety of fund-raising programs are "continuous" and "pervasive," such as capital campaigns and planned giving programs. While fund-raising may not be an activity that is an end in itself, many charitable organizations and institutions have major, ongoing fund-raising and development programs that are permanent fixtures among the totality of the entities' activities.

Q 6:24 Can a planned giving program be considered an unrelated business?

Technically, yes. That characterization, however, is not likely to be made.

A planned giving program satisfies all of the elements of a taxable unrelated business. It is a business (Q 6:1), it is regularly carried on (Q 6:13), and it is an activity that does not have a substantial causal relationship to the achievement of charitable purposes (Q 6:18). Still, planned giving programs are just not thought of as businesses.

This matter could be left at this point, were it not for a peculiar line of law (if three court opinions constitute a line of law). These opinions involve private benefit cases (Q 1:11), rather than unrelated business income ones, yet they suggest the presence of business operations in the nature of financial and estate planning or tax advice services.

The first of these cases concerned the tax status of an organization that engaged in financial counseling by providing tax planning services (including charitable giving considerations) to wealthy individuals referred to it by subscribing religious organizations. The counseling given by the organization consisted of advice as to how a contributor might increase current or planned gifts to religious organizations, including the development of a financial plan that among other objectives, resulted in a reduction of federal income and estate taxes.

The position of the IRS was that this organization could not qualify for federal income tax exemption because it served the private interests of individuals by enabling them to reduce their tax burden. The organization's position was that it was merely engaging in activities that charitable organizations may themselves undertake without loss of their tax exemption. The court agreed with the government, finding that the organization's "sole financial planning activity, albeit an exempt purpose furthering ... [exempt] fund-raising efforts, has a nonexempt purpose of offering advice to individuals on tax matters that reduces an individual's personal and estate tax liabilities."[93] As the court dryly stated, "[w]e do not find within the scope of the word charity that the financial planning for wealthy individuals described in this case is a charitable purpose."[94]

In this opinion, the court singled out the planned giving techniques for portrayal as methods that give rise to unwarranted private benefit. The court made the following observation—which should chill the heart of every charitable gift planner:

> For example, when [this organization] advises a contributor to establish a charitable unitrust gift, the contributor ultimately forfeits the remainder. Nevertheless, this loss is voluntarily exchanged for considerable lifetime advantages. Unitrusts generate substantial income and estate and gift tax benefits, such as retained income for life, reduced capital gains tax, if any, on the exchange of appreciated investments, favorable tax rates for part or all of the income payments on certain investments, and lower probate costs. Consequently, there are real and substantial benefits inuring to the contributors by the [organization's] activities.[95]

Concluded the court: "We think the tax benefits inuring to the contributors are . . . substantial enough to deny exemption."[96]

In the second of these cases, a religious organization was held to not be tax-exempt because it engaged in a substantial nonexempt purpose, which was the counseling of individuals on the purported tax benefits accruing to those who become ministers of the organization.[97] The court found the organization, by the name of The Ecclesiastical Order of the Ism of Am, to be akin to a "commercial tax service, albeit within a narrower field (i.e., tax benefits to ministers and churches) and a narrower class of customers (i.e., petitioner's ministers)," and thus said that it served private purposes.[98] The many detailed discussions, in the organization's literature, of ways to maximize tax benefits led the court to observe that "although petitioner may well advocate belief in the God of Am, it also advocates belief in the God of Tax Avoidance."[99] The court wrote that a "substantial nonexempt purpose does not become an exempt purpose simply because it promotes the organization in some way."[100]

In the third of these opinions, a court held that an organization, the membership of which was religious missions, was not entitled to tax-exempt status as a religious organization because it engaged in the substantial nonexempt purpose of providing financial and tax advice.[101] Once again, the court was concerned about the "efforts of taxpayers to hide behind the cover of purported tax-exempt religious organizations for significant tax avoidance purposes."[102]

As the court envisioned the facts of this case, each member mission was the result of individuals attempting to create churches involving only their families so as to "convert after-tax personal and family expenses into tax deductible contributions."[103] The central organization provided sample incorporation papers, tax seminars, and other forms of tax advice and assistance to those creating the missions. Consequently, the court was persuaded that the "pattern of tax avoidance activities which appears to be present at the membership level, combined with . . . [the organization's] admitted role as a tax advisor to its members," justified the conclusion that the organization was ineligible for tax exemption.[104]

COMMENT 1: These opinions are truly extraordinary. Activities to promote an organization are seen as nonexempt purposes. The provision of tax advice concerning deductible charitable giving, which charities do around the country countless times daily, is cast as impermissible tax planning counseling—if not outright furthering of tax avoidance. Explaining and implementing planned giving programs is portrayed as according contributors substantial private benefit. Watch out for those tax seminars.

NOTE: In the second of these opinions, the court seemed to comprehend the extremes it was sketching and to attempt to narrow the scope of its sweep by noting that the court was "not holding today that any group which discusses the tax consequences of donations to and/or expenditures of its organization is in danger of losing or not acquiring tax-exempt status."[105]

COMMENT 2: What is to be made of these three court opinions? Surely they are not to be applied literally, for if that was done nearly every church, school, college, university, hospital, and dozens of other types of public charities would lose their tax-exempt status. Maybe it means that organizations that have charitable gift planning as their sole or principal function are not eligible for exemption. Still, as those who run fund-raising foundations will attest, the opinions strike very close to home. On balance, probably the best—perhaps the only—thing to do is to regard this "line of law" as an aberration, and ignore it.

Q 6:25   What types of activities are exempt from unrelated business income taxation?

The federal tax law exempts many activities from unrelated business income taxation; several of these, however, are outside the scope of fundraising. Nonetheless, the applicable exceptions are critical to the fund-raising process because they are the principal way that fund-raising activities are able to sidestep the unrelated business income tax.

Foremost of these exceptions is the one that may be considered as construing the undertaking as something less than an *activity*: the exception for the business that is not regularly carried on (Q 6:13).

Another valuable exception is the one for a business in which substantially all of the work in carrying on the business is performed for the tax-exempt organization without compensation.[106]

Another helpful exception is for a business that is conducted by a tax-exempt charitable organization, or a state college or university, primarily for the convenience of its members, students, patients, officers, or employees.[107] This broad exception is known as the *convenience doctrine*.

Another exception is for a business that sells merchandise, substantially all of which was contributed to the exempt organization.[108] This is sometimes referred to as the *donated goods exception*.

An interesting feature of the federal tax laws is the series of *modifications* that are available in calculating unrelated business taxable income. Although these modifications largely exclude certain types of income from taxation (Q 6:27), they also exclude three types of research activities from the tax. This set of exclusions is somewhat of an oddity, in that research activities generally are exempt functions.

Still other exceptions are available for the distribution of low-cost articles incidental to the solicitation of charitable contributions (premiums),[109] the exchanging or renting of membership or donor mailing lists between tax-exempt charitable organizations,[110] the conduct of bingo games by most tax-exempt organizations,[111] the conduct of entertainment at fairs and expositions by a wide range of exempt organizations,[112] and the conduct of trade shows by most tax-exempt organizations.[113]

CAUTION 1: As to the first of these exclusions, it is the position of the IRS—asserted without citation of any authority—that the exclusion is not available if the solicitation is in competition with for-profit vendors or if it is illegal.[114]

CAUTION 2: As to the second of these exclusions, if one of the parties is not a charitable entity, the exclusion is not available. In an instance of an *exchange* of lists, it is the view of the IRS that the value of the list received is an amount that should be reported as *constructive* unrelated business income.[115]

CAUTION 3: As to the third of these exclusions, "instant bingo" is not protected.[116]

Q 6:26 How can these exemptions be utilized in the fund-raising context?

The exception for activities that are not regularly carried on (Q 6:13) salvages from taxation more fund-raising events and other fund-raising endeavors than any other tax law rule. It shields from tax nearly all sports tournaments, luncheons and dinners, theater outings, auctions, and the like. The exception is frustrated only by the unsettled rule as to preparatory time (Q 6:16).

Any unrelated business can be protected from taxation by the exception for businesses that are operated by noncompensated individuals—even the oft-taxed business of advertising.[117] This exception can be useful in shielding fund-raising special events from taxation.

TIP: The concept of *compensation* is broadly interpreted. In one instance, the revenue from gambling events operated by a tax-exempt organization was held taxable because the workers, all of whom were volunteers, were frequently tipped by the patrons.[118]

The convenience doctrine—with its references to students and patients—is relied on heavily by schools, colleges, universities, and hospitals. Much of the income from sales of items in college and university bookstores, and hospital gift shops and food courts, is rendered nontaxable because of this rule.

The exception for businesses selling donated items is generally utilized by thrift shops that sell contributed clothing, furniture, books, and the like to the general public.[119] This exception can also have utility in the case of charity auctions.

As to the three exclusions for research, one is for research for the federal government, or any of its agencies or instrumentalities, or any state or political subdivision of a state. Another exclusion is for research performed for any person; the research institution, however, must be a college, university, or hospital. The third exclusion for research is even more broad than the second: the organization must be operated primarily for the purpose of carrying on fundamental research and the results of the research must be freely available to the general public.[120]

Q 6:27 What types of income are exempt from unrelated business income taxation?

The *modifications* (Q 6:25) shield a wide variety of forms of income from unrelated income taxation. These forms of income generally are interest, dividends, rents, royalties, annuities, and capital gains. For the most part, there is little controversy in this area as to the definition of these items of income, inasmuch as the terms are amply defined throughout the federal tax law.

There is, nonetheless, an underlying festering controversy. It is the view of the IRS that this exclusion for types of income is available only where the income is investment income or is otherwise passively received. This approach to these modifications rests on the rationale for the unrelated business income rules, which is to bring parity to the economics of competitive activities involving nonprofit and for-profit organizations.[121] Passive income, by definition, is not derived from competitive activity and thus should not be taxed. But, the IRS wishes to tax net income from the active conduct of commercial business activities.

This dichotomy presents itself nicely in connection with the exclusion for rental income. Where a tax-exempt organization carries on rental activities in the nature of a commercial landlord, the exclusion is not available—the thought being the exempt organization is actively in the business of renting property.[122] This exclusion, however, is normally not voided simply because the exempt organization provides general maintenance services, although the exclusion can be lost if too much in the way of services is provided directly to tenants. In practice, this opportunity for taxation is obviated by the use of an independent management and leasing company.

CAUTION: A key ingredient for this exclusion is that the relationship between the parties be evidenced by a *lease*. In one case, the IRS concluded that a contract, by which space was acquired from a public charity for advertising purposes, was found to be not a lease but a *license*— thereby depriving the charity of the exclusion for rental income.[123]

There can be disputes as to whether an income flow is truly rent or is a share of the profits from a joint venture; revenue in the latter form is generally taxable. (The principal exception is where the joint venture is a related business.) A contemporary illustration of this distinction is the line of case law concerning crop-share leasing. The IRS has lost all of the cases brought to date; the courts have held that the funds received by the exempt charitable organization were in the form of excludable rent and not from a partnership or joint venture.[124]

Rental income is not normally regarded as revenue derived from fund-raising. Moreover, the exclusion for rental income is generally confined to the rental of real property.[125] Thus, rental income is not a likely form of revenue for a charitable organization, unless it is one of the larger institutions. Occasionally, a rental activity (even of personal property) is seen as a related activity.

NOTE: In one instance, a museum was able to lease back personal property to the donor of it and have the resulting rent cast as related business income.[126]

The contemporary battles in this context are being waged over the scope of the exclusion for royalties. This is the case, in large part, because of the fact that there are substantive disputes as to the definition of the term *royalty*. This uncertainty in the law gives exempt organizations more latitude, more so than with any other type of income, in structuring transactions to shape the resulting tax outcome. That is, the objective is to make the income fit the form of a royalty or at least dress it up to make it look like a royalty.

The IRS is persisting with its position that a royalty, to be excludable as such, must be passively received by the exempt organization. This issue has been reviewed by the U.S. Tax Court on several occasions, and the exempt organization involved has prevailed each time. The view of the Tax Court is that a royalty is a payment for the use of valuable intangible property rights; it is rejecting the passive-active dichotomy, at least in the realm of the exclusion for royalties. As discussed next, however, at least one court of appeals is in disagreement with the Tax Court on this issue—with some significant implications in the fund-raising setting.

Q 6:28 How can these exemptions be utilized in the fund-raising context?

Most income that is generated by what is conventionally called *fundraising* (Q 1:5) is received by the charitable organization in the form of gifts and grants. Almost by definition, this type of income is not taxable. The income that a charity receives from its endowment fund (interest, dividends, capital gains) is not likely to be taxed either.

These facts, coupled with the precision as to definition given most forms of excluded income, do not provide the fund-raising professional (and his or her financial advisors) with much latitude in terms of tax planning with respect to income that does not arrive as gifts or grants or from the endowment fund. There is one exception to all of this: income cast as a royalty. As to that, as noted (Q 6:27), there continues to be extensive controversy.

As noted (*id.*), the Tax Court has framed its definition of the term *royalty.* When doing so, it has decided cases of great pertinence to professional fund-raising. Some of these cases involve use of the royalty exception to shield from taxation funds derived from the rental of mailing lists.[127]

NOTE: It was said above that there is an exclusion for the exchanging or renting of membership or donor mailing lists between tax-exempt organizations (Q 6:25). However, for this exclusion to be available, the parties to the transaction must be charitable entities. (This means *charitable* as defined in the charitable giving rules,[128] rather than in the tax-exempt organization rules,[129] so it includes entities such as veterans' groups.) The mailing case involved a social welfare organization (Q 1:18), which thus cannot utilize this exclusion and is thereby forced to rely on the royalty exception to avoid tax on income generated by use of its mailing list.

Others concern use of the royalty exclusion to protect income generated from an affinity card program.

A pair of these cases—one involving use of a mailing list and one involving an affinity card program—were appealed by the IRS. The appellate court concluded that the Tax Court's definition of a *royalty* was too sweeping, in that a royalty "cannot include compensation for services rendered by the owner of the property."[130] This position, then, is a compromise on the point between the approach of the Tax Court and that of the IRS.

It is the position of the IRS that monies will be taxed, even if they are characterized as royalties (such as by means of the Tax Court's definition), when the tax-exempt organization is actively involved in the enterprise that generates the revenue; usually this entails the provision of services. The IRS may even characterize the relationship as a joint venture. The Tax Court, by contrast, was not concerned with the presence or absence of exempt organization services—its view has been that, once it is established that valuable intangible property rights are the subject of the transaction, the compensation for the use of that property is a royalty. The appellate court has basically held that incidental services supplied by the exempt organization will not defeat characterization of the payment as a royalty but that substantial services will.

Thus, the court of appeals wrote that to the extent the IRS "claims that a tax-exempt organization can do *nothing* to acquire such fees," the agency is "incorrect."[131] Yet, the court continued, "to the extent that . . . [the exempt organization involved] appears to argue that a 'royalty' is any payment for the use of a property right—such as a copyright—regardless of any additional services that are performed in addition to the owner simply permitting another to use the right at issue, we disagree."[132]

Using its middle-course definition of the term *royalty*, the appellate court affirmed the mailing list case, finding that the services provided by the exempt organization were sufficiently insubstantial so as to allow the compensation to be treated as a royalty. But, the affinity card case was remanded—sent back to the Tax Court for a trial, using the appellate court's definition of the term *royalty*. Even with that definition, the Tax Court once again opined that the mailing list revenue amounted to excludable royalties.[133]

During the pendency of this litigation, the IRS continues to adhere to its view in its letter ruling policies.[134] A common instance of this treatment is the insistence by the IRS that the funds an exempt organization receives for an endorsement are taxable, while the organization asserts that the monies are royalties, paid for the use of its name and logo.[135]

Q 6:29   How can the exclusion for royalty income be most effectively utilized in the fund-raising context?

This is a question that is somewhat difficult to answer at this time, what with the varying interpretations of the scope of the royalty exclusion. First, an organization can, at least for the time being, adhere to the IRS's view and treat as excludable royalty income only that which is passive in nature. Second, it can follow the Tax Court's approach (Q 6:28) and risk an audit and a tax assessment. Third, it can view the matter as was done on appeal (*id.*) and use that explication of the term *royalty*.

Whichever approach is taken, here is the way to look at the "big picture" in this regard. Most income generated by a fund-raising activity will be received by the charitable organization as a contribution or a grant. The next likely form of income will be exempt function income—revenue that is generated by a program activity (such as student or patient fees, or admission fees). Income may come into the charity as investment income (such as from an endowment fund).

Then there is the matter of unrelated business income. It may be that taxation of this income is unavoidable because

1. The activity is a business (Q 6:1),
2. It is regularly carried on (Q 6:13),
3. The business activity is not substantially related to the achievement of charitable purposes (Q 6:18), and
4. The activity is not exempted from unrelated business income (Q 6:27).

Before conceding any such unavoidability, however, the organization should explore a structuring (or restructuring) of the transaction or other arrangement so that the resulting income comes in the form of a royalty. This entails introducing at least one other party to the arrangement, so that the task of doing whatever it is that is to be done (such as, in the case of an affinity card program, marketing credit cards) is shifted to that party, leaving the charitable organization in the position of receiving income in a passive or nearly passive manner. For example, a charitable organization that conducted exempt function sports matches licensed its name and logo for use on souvenir items sold in connection with the contests; the IRS ruled that the revenue received by the organization from the vendors of the souvenirs was excludable royalty income.[136] Likewise, the IRS ruled that a university, which entered into sublicensing agreements as to excess television and radio channel capacity, was compensated in the form of excludable royalties.[137]

An approach in this interim, until this issue is sorted out, is to bifurcate the arrangement, to make partial use of the royalty exclusion: execute two contracts, one reflecting passive income/royalty payments and the other for the provision of services rendered.[138] The income paid pursuant to the latter contract would presumably be taxable. The charitable organization would endeavor to allocate to the royalty contract as much of the income as is reasonably possible.

CAUTION: A difficulty with this separate-contract approach is the form-over-substance rule: two contracts that are closely related can be collapsed and treated as one for tax purposes.

Q 6:30 Are there any exceptions to these rules stating these exclusions?

Yes. There are two exceptions. One pertains to the payment of otherwise excludable income from a controlled organization. As discussed, income in the form of interest, rent, royalties, annuities, and capital gain generally is not taxed as unrelated business income (Q 6:25). That type of income is taxed, however, when it is paid to the tax-exempt organization from an entity that it controls (Q 1:22). This is the case even though these forms of income are otherwise passive in nature.

NOTE: The obvious purpose of this rule is to prevent a tax-exempt organization from spinning off unrelated business activity into a subsidiary and avoiding unrelated business income taxation by the stratagem of causing the income to flow to the parent in one of the protected forms.

For this purpose, an organization controls another where the parent entity owns more than 50 percent of the interest in the other entity. There also is an indirect control (constructive ownership) test. This control element can be manifested by stock or some other like interest or by an interlocking of directors, trustees, or other representatives of the two organizations (*id.*).

COMMENT: This is an important rule in the law of tax-exempt organizations. The law in this regard was changed dramatically in 1997. Before then, this rule as to income from controlled entities was easy to sidestep. Under the old law, the control element required at least 80 percent control and that control had to extend to all classes of stock or other interests. Also, there was no constructive ownership rule. The rule was avoided by sharing ownership of the subsidiary among related exempt organizations or having two tiers of subsidiaries.[139]

The other exception is found in the rules concerning unrelated debt-financed property.[140] Where income is debt-financed income, the various exclusions referred to above are unavailable.

Q 6:31   Are there any exceptions to these exceptions?

There is one. The rule concerning the taxation of income from a controlled subsidiary (Q 6:30) does not apply where the funds are paid as dividends. Correspondingly, as is not the case with respect to the other types of income from a subsidiary, dividends are not deductible by the corporation that pays them.

Q 6:32   What about the use of the Internet? Do any unrelated business issues arise?

Absolutely. Nonprofit organizations' use of the Internet is generating many unrelated business issues—and many of them pertain directly to charitable fund-raising. To date, however, there is no specific guidance from the IRS as to the law surrounding these issues.

There is one important point to be made at the outset: the fact that fund-raising or other activities are engaged in over the Internet is not relevant in applying the tax laws. Recently, the IRS make this salient statement: "[T]he use of the Internet to accomplish a particular task does not change the way the tax laws apply to that task. Advertising is still advertising and fund-raising is still fund-raising."[141] Still, there are those who think that an activity engaged in by means of the Internet is somehow different for tax law purposes.

SOME BASIC POINTS

First, some reminders as to charitable gifts of money. (Noncash gifts generally are not made directly over the Internet.) It is still necessary to be certain that the recipient of the contribution is a charity. If the donee is a charity, the gift may not be earmarked for a specific individual or for an organization that is not entitled to receive charitable contributions.

Again, the substantiation requirements apply, as do the rules as to quid pro quo contributions and appraisals. The disclosure rules for noncharitable contributions[142] are also applicable to solicitations over the Internet.

THIRD-PARTY WEBSITES

One of the issues the IRS is studying is the matter of "third-party sites." These are for-profit companies that post a list of charitable organizations. The mission statements are provided, along with a link to charities' own websites if they have one. Gifts are made by credit card. Some time may pass (such as a month) before the company remits the net gifts to the charities. The company retains a portion of the gift (such as 15 percent) as an administrative fee.

Issues arise here, even assuming the donee is a bona fide charity. Is the third-party entity an agent of the charity? (The gift is first made to it.) Is this one of these situations where there is a deductible gift, even though the initial recipient is not a charity, since the funds are earmarked for a charity? The little law there is on the point suggests that for deductibility to be available, the funds must be transferred to the charity frequently (e.g., weekly).[143] A holding of the funds for a month may preclude deductibility. Moreover, are these third parties functioning as professional fund-raisers, requiring registration and reporting under some states' laws (Q 9:4)?

Regarding marketing, merchandising, advertising, and the like, the IRS, as of late 1999, "has yet to consider many of the questions raised" by these activities.

NOTE: Considering the recent extent and growth of these activities, and the near-desperate need for guidance, it is surprising that some assistance from the IRS has not been forthcoming. As noted below, an announcement on the subject is in preparation.

Again, however, the IRS has stated that "it is reasonable to assume that as the Service position develops it will remain consistent with our position with respect to advertising and merchandising and publishing in the off-line world."[144]

LINKS

The IRS has gingerly broached the subject of charity website HyperText links to related or recommended sites. Link exchanges may be treated the same as mailing list exchanges. Compensation for a linkage may be unrelated business income. The purpose of the link may be determinative: is its purpose furtherance of exempt purposes (a referral of the site visitor to additional (educational) information) or is it part of an unrelated activity (including advertising)?

CORPORATE SPONSORSHIPS

Also involved are corporate sponsorships,[145] inasmuch as exempt organizations may seek corporate support to underwrite the production of all or a portion of the organization's website. These relationships may be short-term or continue on a long-term basis. The financial support may be acknowledged by means of display of a corporate logo, notation of the sponsor's web address and/or 800 number, a "moving banner" (a graphic advertisement, usually a moving image, measured in pixels), or a link. (The issue here is: is the support a qualified sponsorship payment, in which case the revenue is not taxable, or is it advertising income, which generally is taxable as unrelated business income?)

The IRS has recognized that there is a question as to whether the use of a link in an acknowledgment will change the character of a corporation's payment—that is, convert it from corporate sponsorship to taxable advertising income. While not yet answering this question, the IRS seems sympathetic to the view that the payment should retain its character as a mere acknowledgment since the website visitor must take an "affirmative action" (if a click can be called that) to reach the corporation's website. A moving banner is more likely to be considered advertising.

Another problem relates to the rule that qualified sponsorship payments do not include payments that entitle the sponsors to acknowledgments to regularly printed material published by or on behalf of the tax-exempt organization. Here, the issue is the characterization of website materials. The IRS has written: "Most of the materials made available on exempt organization websites are clearly prepared in a manner that is distinguishable from the methodology used in the preparation of periodicals."[146]

Nonetheless, the IRS recognizes that there can be an on-line publication that is treated as a periodical. (When this is the case, the special rules by which unrelated business income from periodical advertising is computed become available.) Some periodicals have on-line editions and some print publications are reproduced on-line, sometimes on a subscription basis or in a members-only access portion of the website. The IRS has observed that these "materials should be and generally are sufficiently segregated from the other traditional website materials so that the methodology employed in the production and distribution methods are clearly ascertainable and the periodical income and costs can be independently and appropriately determined." The IRS adds that presumably "genuine" periodicals have an editorial staff, marketing program, and budget independent of the organization's webmaster.[147]

VIRTUAL TRADE SHOWS

Then there is the matter of the "virtual trade show," which generates income for trade associations and other exempt entities from "virtual exhibitors." This brings into play the rules by which traditional trade show income is excluded from the unrelated business income tax (Q 6:25). The IRS has observed that the extent to which the traditional rules will apply to virtual trade show income "will most likely depend in large part on whether the qualifying organization is able to demonstrate that its exhibits or displays are substantially similar to those traditionally carried on at a trade show."[148]

The IRS has hinted that the tax exclusion is not available for a mere listing of links to industry suppliers' websites. Also, the IRS is of the view that it is "highly questionable" whether income from a year-round virtual trade show is excludable from unrelated business income. Conversely, virtual trade shows with displays including educational information related to issues of interest to industry members or those that are timed to coincide with the sponsoring organization's annual meeting or regular trade show may qualify for the exclusion.

ON-LINE STOREFRONTS

Then there is the difficult issue as to on-line storefronts, complete with virtual shopping carts, on exempt organizations' websites. Again, the IRS expects to be using the same analytical methodology that it applies to sales made through stores, catalogs, and other traditional vehicles. A useful basis of comparison is likely to be the treatment of museum gift shop sales (Q 6:20). In deciding whether the unrelated business income tax applies, the IRS looks to the nature, scope, and motivation for the particular sales activities. Merchandise is evaluated on an item-by-item basis (applying the fragmentation rule (Q 6:3)) to determine whether the sales activity furthers the accomplishment of the organization's exempt purposes or is simply a way to increase revenue.

ON-LINE AUCTIONS

As to on-line auctions, the IRS is particularly concerned with charities' use of "outside auction service providers." The IRS has recognized that utilization of these providers may result in a larger audience for the auction and enable the organization to avoid credit card problems but—in a nice understatement—it cautions that the relationship "might have tax implications."[149]

Again (Q 2:30, Q 4:36), the focus is on control. The IRS will consider how much control the charity exercises over the marketing and conduct of the auction. The IRS wants the charity to have "primary responsibility" in this regard. Otherwise, the IRS "may be more likely to view income from such auction activities as income from classified advertising rather than as income derived from the conduct of a fund-raising event."[150]

CAUTION: The IRS has stated that these service providers are "essentially professional fund-raisers" (with implications as to state charitable solicitation acts (Q 9:4)), and thus their functions and fees should be scrutinized using the doctrines of private inurement (Q 1:10) and private benefit (Q 1:11).

AFFILIATION WITH MERCHANTS

Finally, the IRS is addressing affiliate and other co-venture programs with merchants. Of particular note are arrangements with large, on-line booksellers. Some exempt organizations make book recommendations that are displayed on their website; others have a link to the bookseller. The exempt organization earns a percentage of sales of recommended materials and perhaps also a commission on purchases sold through the referring link. The principal issue here is whether the resulting income is a tax-excludable royalty (Q 6:27).

On this point, the IRS analogizes to the litigation involving the tax treatment of mailing list and affinity card income (Q 6:28). The IRS is persisting in its view that the marketing of a credit card by an exempt organization constitutes services typically provided by a commercial company. At the same time, this view has not prevailed in the many cases contested in court.

NOTE: The Treasury/IRS 1999 business plan contemplates the issuance of a request for comments on the application of the tax law to the Internet activities of exempt organizations. In addition to the unrelated business income issues, there are matters to be resolved in the realms of lobbying (Q 1:16) and political campaign intervention (Q 1:17). The IRS has written: "It is hoped that all members of the exempt organizations [community] will be involved in the development of new policies which will build upon principles developed over time and adapt to allow exempt organizations to take advantage of the technological innovations of the new millennium."[151]

Q 6:33   How is the unrelated business income tax calculated?

In general, the unrelated business income tax is determined in the same manner used by for-profit entities to ascertain taxable income. The unrelated income tax rates payable by most tax-exempt organizations are the rates applicable to for-profit corporations.[152] Some organizations, such as trusts, are subject to the individual income tax rates.[153] There is a specific deduction of $1,000.[154]

This tax falls on *net* unrelated business income. An exempt organization is allowed to subtract its business expenses from gross unrelated business income in arriving at taxable (net) unrelated business income. The law generally states that to be deductible, the expense must be *directly connected* with the carrying on of the business.[155] That is, an item of deduction must have a proximate and primary relationship to the carrying on of the business.[156]

COMMENT: This standard is more rigorous than the comparable one applied to for-profit and individual taxpayers, where the law allows the deductibility of expenses that are reasonably connected with the taxable endeavor. In practice, however, exempt organizations often follow the standard of reasonableness, particularly when allocating expenses. Because of flabby language in the tax regulations, this approach has been upheld in the courts.[157]

There is one exception to the directly connected test. This exception is for the charitable contribution deduction allowed in computing taxable unrelated business income. In general, this deduction cannot exceed 10 percent of the unrelated business taxable income otherwise computed.[158]

Q 6:34   How is the unrelated business income tax reported?

Tax-exempt organizations must make quarterly estimated payments of the unrelated business income tax.[159]

The return filed by nearly all tax-exempt organizations with the IRS on an annual basis is an *information* return (Chapter 8). This type of return is not used to report unrelated business taxable income. For that purpose, a *tax* return is required. The IRS has devised a tax return for reporting unrelated business taxable income. This form—Form 990-T—must be filed in addition to the annual information return.[160]

CHAPTER 7

Fund-Raisers' Compensation

Professional fund-raisers can be compensated for their services. The basic standard is that the compensation amount must be *reasonable*.

There is, however, much more to this matter of fund-raisers' compensation. Several aspects of the federal tax law may be involved in this regard, not the least of which are the doctrines of private inurement and private benefit, and the rules as to intermediate sanctions.

This component of the law can have major implications for the charitable organization that is compensating the professional fund-raiser.

Here are the questions most frequently asked by professional fund-raisers (or that should be asked by them) about their compensation—and the answers to them.

Q 7:1   What does the term *professional fund-raiser* mean?

For purposes of compensation issues, the definition of the term *professional fund-raiser* is that principally used in the state law setting. That is, a professional fund-raiser is a person who, for compensation, performs for a charitable organization any service in connection with which contributions are, or will be, solicited in the state by the compensated person or any other person that person employs or otherwise engages to solicit; it also embraces any person who, for compensation, plans, manages, advises, consults, or prepares material for, or with respect to, the solicitation in the state of contributions for a charitable organization (Q 1:1).

Q 7:2 Does it make any difference whether the fund-raiser is an employee or an independent contractor?

First, although this may seem obvious, it is important that these terms be defined. An *employee* is an individual who is hired by an employer—in this context, a charitable organization. The work of an employee is usually performed on the premises of and in the facilities of the employer, using equipment, furniture, and supplies furnished by the employer. The hours and conditions of work are usually set by the employer. The compensation of an employee is usually cast as a *salary*. The compensation of an employee is subject to income tax and other types of tax withholdings.

There can be an issue as to whether an individual is an employee or an independent contractor (see below). This issue can be posed to the IRS. This agency will almost always rule, however, that the individual is an employee.

As part of the audit process, the IRS is likely to examine the practices of a tax-exempt organization, including a charitable one, to determine if it is properly classifying individuals as employees.

An *independent contractor* is a person who provides services to another person under circumstances where the relationship is not that of employer-employee. For example, while a charitable organization may have a lawyer who is an employee (in-house legal counsel), a lawyer in private practice (usually with a law firm) who is working for that organization is an independent contractor.

Likewise, a charitable organization may have a professional fund-raiser on its staff (such as a vice-president for advancement or a director of development). This individual is serving as an employee. By contrast, the charitable organization may enter into a contract with a professional fund-raiser for fund-raising services, under circumstances where there is not an employment relationship. Then, the professional fund-raiser—individual or company—is an independent contractor.

Now to the question. For the most part, it will not make much of a difference for compensation purposes as to whether the fund-raiser is an employee or an independent contractor. As will be discussed, the standard in either instance is that the compensation be reasonable (Q 7:5). At the same time, the likelihood that the fund-raiser will be considered an insider (Q 1:10) or a disqualified person[1] may be reduced if the fund-raiser is an independent contractor.

Also, the manner in which the compensation is reported to the IRS on the annual information return will vary as to whether the fund-raiser is an employee or an independent contractor. In the latter instance, the charitable organization will not be withholding on the payments of compensation made to the fund-raiser.

Q 7:3   The definition of a professional fund-raiser includes the element of compensation. Are there limits as to the amount of compensation paid to a fund-raiser?

There are limits on the amount of compensation a charitable organization may pay to a professional fund-raiser. These bounds, however, are no different from the restriction on compensation that may be paid to any provider of services to a charity. In a word, the compensation must be *reasonable.*

A charitable organization must, among other requirements, be operated so that it does not cause any inurement of its net earnings to a person who is an insider with respect to it (Q 1:10) or otherwise confer an impermissible amount of private benefit to a person (Q 1:11). Either of these rules—the *private inurement doctrine* or the *private benefit doctrine*—can be violated by the payment of excessive (or unreasonable) compensation. A sanction for transgressing the limits of either doctrine is loss or denial of the charitable organization's tax-exempt status.

NOTE: Another sanction for the payment of unreasonable compensation is imposition of the intermediate sanctions penalties. For this to occur, the recipient of the compensation must be a disqualified person (Q 7:2).

Thus, payments to a fund-raiser can trigger the private inurement doctrine or the private benefit doctrine. Whether a fund-raiser is an insider with respect to a charitable organization is a subject explored elsewhere (Q 1:10).

If the fund-raiser is an employee of a charitable organization (Q 7:2), his or her complete compensation package (Q 7:4) will be tested against the standard of reasonableness. If the fund-raiser is an independent contractor with respect to a charitable organization (*id.*), the focus as to reasonableness will be on the amount of fees paid. In either instance, there may also be questions raised about reimbursement of expenses.

COMMENT: Both of these rules may be implicated in the same set of facts. In one case, ministers of a church were found to be excessively compensated when their church salaries were aggregated with payments received by them from a direct mail company they owned which was hired by the church.[2]

To summarize (and emphasize): a charitable organization may not, without endangering its tax-exempt status, pay a fund-raising professional an amount that is excessive or unreasonable.

Q 7:4   What is the *compensation package* in the case of individuals?

The compensation package of an individual includes, but can go far beyond, the amount of his or her compensation paid in the form of a salary or wage. The package embraces all economic benefits paid, directly or indirectly, by the employer.

Thus, the compensation package of a fund-raiser (or any other employee) includes:

1. His or her salary or wage amount.
2. Bonuses.
3. Commissions.
4. Expense account.
5. Productivity/incentive compensation arrangements.
6. Deferred compensation arrangement(s).
7. Retirement plan(s).
8. Insurance coverage(s).
9. Value of any loan.
10. Compensation paid by one or more related entities.

Q 7:5   How is the reasonableness of compensation determined?

Basically, the matter of the reasonableness or excessiveness of an item or items of compensation is a matter of fact. That is, it is not a matter of law. Lawyers, as such, are not usually competent to pass judgment on the reasonableness of compensation. That is a task best left to accountants and others trained to evaluate employee benefit arrangements. The law, however, supplies the factors that are looked to in ascertaining reasonableness.

COMMENT: To date, nearly all of the law on this subject is found in cases concerning the reasonableness of compensation paid to employees of for-profit companies. The standard in the for-profit context is that to be deductible as a business expense,[3] the compensation amount must be *ordinary and necessary*. That standard is essentially the same as *reasonable*.

Here are seven factors that are evaluated in determining whether an individual's compensation package is reasonable:

1. Compensation amounts paid to others in comparable positions.
2. Compensation amounts paid to others in the same community.
3. Individual's training, expertise, and experience.
4. Size of the organization.
5. Scope of the individual's responsibilities.
6. Amount of compensation paid in relation to payments made to other employees of the organization.
7. Amount of time the individual devotes to the position (full-time or part-time).[4]

The foregoing pertains to factors that are looked to when the relationship is employee-employer. If the fund-raiser (individual or company) is being compensated as an independent contractor (Q 7:2), the last two of the above factors are not relevant. Other factors to be evaluated, however, in that case include the nature of the charitable cause and the type of fund-raising involved.

CAUTION: In many states, the compensation for fund-raising services—where the fund-raiser is an independent contractor—must be stated in a contract between the charitable organization and the fund-raising professional, with the agreement filed with the regulatory authorities (Q 9:11).

NOTE: The elements of a contract of this nature are discussed below (Q 7:14).

Q 7:6 Can a professional fund-raiser be paid a bonus?

Yes. A bonus, however, is more likely to be paid where the fund-raiser is an employee, rather than an independent contractor.

A *bonus* is an amount paid, usually by an employer to an employee, which is in excess of the regular amount of compensation (that is, salary or wage). It is paid in recognition of extraordinary services rendered, often measured by one or more objective goals. It is a fixed amount, generally not determined by a percentage formula.

For example, a charitable organization employs a fund-raiser, at an annual salary of $50,000. During the previous year, the organization's capital campaign ended, with the organization exceeding its publicly stated goals. The board of trustees of the organization, of the belief that the fund-raiser's extraordinary efforts during the campaign were a primary reason for the campaign's success, awarded the fund-raiser a $10,000 bonus. The fund-raiser's compensation package for that year includes the $60,000 in money payments.

A bonus amount is, of course, additional compensation. Thus, it is subject to the overall requirement of reasonableness (Q 7:5). That is, the bonus amount is part of the compensation package which, when paid by a charitable organization, must be reasonable.

Q 7:7   Can a professional fund-raiser be paid on the basis of a percentage of the contributions received by a charity?

Yes. Having said that, however, this is a controversial practice. Often, when there are questions about the propriety of compensation paid to a fund-raising professional, the issue is not the amount paid or being paid but the manner in which it is determined. This frequently concerns compensation that is ascertained on the basis of a commission or some other percentage-based arrangement.

Thus, the example in the previous answer can be altered as follows. The fund-raiser has the $50,000 base salary but the board of trustees agrees to pay him or her 2 percent of the amount received in the capital campaign in excess of the stated goal. The campaign generates $500,000 more than that goal and the fund-raiser is thus paid an additional $10,000.

In both examples, the additional amount of compensation for extraordinary services provided is $10,000. Both types of payments are subject to a test of reasonableness. Yet the second payment is far the more controversial one—solely because of the mechanism used to compute it.

One of the difficulties in this area is that a percentage-based compensation system—one where an individual's compensation is based in whole or in part on the revenue flow of the organization—comes perilously close to private inurement (Q 7:8). That is, it is or can be perceived as being an inurement of the organization's *net earnings* to one or more individuals in their private capacity. It is not surprising that the IRS tends to be suspicious of fund-raising compensation that is based on percentages of contributions received.

CAUTION: Any percentage-based compensation arrangement, where a charitable organization is making the payments, should be evaluated in light of the emerging rules concerning *revenue-sharing arrangements.*[5]

In designing a compensation plan of this nature, consideration should be given to the evolving principles as to what constitutes a permissible *gainsharing* program (Q 7:8).

Q 7:8   What is a *gainsharing* program?

There is very little law or other guidance to date as to the legal consequences of gainsharing programs. The term is being used, to date, to
define plans developed in the health care setting, where physicians receive compensation for achieving cost efficiencies in the operation of
their departments in a hospital.

   The guidance that is available so far from the IRS is in the form of a
gainsharing plan private letter ruling (officially unpublished). On that
occasion, the IRS ruled that the plan does not give rise to private inurement with respect to the participating physicians and thus does not endanger the tax-exempt status of the hospital maintaining the plan.

FACTS

This plan is sponsored by a tax-exempt teaching hospital (Hospital)
that offers a broad range of inpatient and outpatient medical, surgical,
and diagnostic services. These services include cardiac care, cardiac in-
tensive care, and cardiac rehabilitation services.

   There is a physician group (Physicians) consisting of cardiologists,
cardiologists/electrophysiologists, primary care physicians, and cardiovascular surgeons. The offices of the Physicians are located on the Hospital's campus. These physicians are on the Hospital's medical staff, as
well as on the staffs of other hospitals in the region. None of the physicians is on the Board of Directors of the Hospital.

   The Hospital and the Physicians want to improve clinical outcomes
and the quality of cardiovascular care in the delivery of comprehensive
heart care services. The Hospital also wants to reduce costs in the delivery of comprehensive cardiac care services. To achieve the goal of better cardiovascular care with lower costs, the parties researched various
demonstration projects of the Health Care Financing Administration.

   Based on this research, the Hospital wants to create incentives for
physicians to assist the Hospital in—in the language of the ruling—the
"development and implementation of more efficient practice patterns
which should ultimately lead to the more cost-effective utilization of
hospital resources." The Hospital is of the belief that substantial improvements in the quality of patient care and in the delivery of efficient
patient care can be achieved through cooperative efforts that "align"
Physicians and Hospital incentives. To that end, the parties entered
into a Cardiovascular Quality and Process Improvement Program Participation Agreement (Agreement).

   Under the Agreement, the Physicians will participate with the Hospital in a Cardiovascular Quality and Process Improvement Program

(Program) to maintain or improve the quality of cardiovascular services delivered. The Program will also develop and implement "process improvement initiatives" (Initiatives) to better manage the costs of inpatient and outpatient cardiovascular services. The Physicians are to provide ongoing input, consultation, analysis, and other services in connection with the design and implementation of the Initiatives. (The Initiatives in this instance were redacted.)

Under the Program, the Physicians must satisfy certain preestablished threshold criteria relating to the quality of patient care and patient satisfaction. (The criteria are not disclosed.) If the criteria are met, the Physicians will be eligible to receive a portion of the cost savings realized by the Hospital.

Once there are reductions in the Hospital's costs of providing selected cardiology services, the savings will be used to fund a Process Improvement Award Pool (Pool). The portion of the Pool to be paid to the Physicians will depend on the level of achievement by the Physicians in relation to the Initiatives.

If the Pool is funded, the performance of the Physicians under the Initiatives will be measured. Points (between 5 and 15) have been assigned to each Initiative based on an assessment of the level of effort required by the Physicians to develop and implement the particular Initiative and, if applicable, to comply with the particular Initiative. There is a total of 110 points for all of the Initiatives.

The Hospital will review on a quarterly basis the Physician's efforts and accomplishments with respect to the Initiatives. The number of points awarded to the Physicians for an Initiative will be determined, by the Hospital, by measuring the Physicians' efforts and accomplishments against the evaluation criteria assigned to the Initiative.

Should there be a dispute between the parties as to the Hospital's point assignment, the matter will be referred to an independent consultant, who will determine the number of points to be awarded. This decision will be binding on the parties. The total number of points achieved by the Physicians will determine the amount of the award for which the Physicians will be eligible in connection with services provided by the Physicians under the Program.

The parties understand that these process improvement awards must be consistent with the concept of fair market value. Thus, once an award amount has been determined, that amount will be analyzed by an independent appraiser to confirm that the amount reflects the fair market value of the efforts of the Physicians. If the proposed award amount is "inconsistent with" (read: higher than) the fair market value of the Physicians' efforts and services, as ascertained by the appraiser, the award amount for the period will be "adjusted accordingly" (read: lowered).

An independent appraisal obtained by the Hospital determined that if the methodology described in the Agreement is utilized, the resulting award will result in reasonable compensation for the Physicians' participation in the Program. Also, at the end of each 12-month period during the term of the Agreement, an independent appraiser will evaluate the actual awards calculated to confirm their reasonableness and the award(s) will be adjusted if necessary.

The parties have committed to certain "program integrity requirements" (Requirements) designed to ensure that the Physicians' participation in the Program will not lead to undesirable and unintended consequences with respect to the delivery of cardiovascular services to patients. The Physicians will agree to make admissions decisions and provide medical services to patients without regard to (1) a patient's race, creed, color, religion, gender, sexual orientation, national origin, health status, age, disability, income level, or ability to pay, (2) whether a patient is covered by Medicare, Medicaid, or other federal health care program, or (3) financial incentives under the Program. The Physicians will agree to provide the Hospital with a certification as to these factors signed by each of the physicians prior to the effective date of the Agreement. This certification will include an agreement by each Physician to provide requested information and submit to periodic audits to ensure compliance.

The Hospital will monitor the Physicians' compliance with the Requirements on a regular basis. The Physicians will grant the Hospital's case managers and corporate compliance officer reasonable access to patients' charts and medical records, and other Program-related information, to ensure that each Physician is in compliance with the Requirements.

If the Hospital determines that a physician has failed to comply with the Requirements, it will notify a Cardiovascular Coordinating Team (Team) and the matter will be reviewed by the Team. The Team will make a recommendation to the Hospital as to whether to exclude a Physician, for failing to comply with the Requirements, from further participation in the Program. If the Physician is excluded, the Physicians will become ineligible to receive any portion of the process improvement award.

The Team will "provide an interdisciplinary approach to the evaluation of cardiovascular outcomes and patient care as well as evaluate additional opportunities for quality care delivery and process improvement across all cardiovascular patient rate areas" within the Hospital's system. The Team will also be responsible for making recommendations to the Hospital's other service lines as to any service that can be impacted by an improvement idea or application beyond the cardiovascular line.

The IRS noted that the terms of the Agreement were arrived at in arm's-length negotiations between the Hospital and the Physicians. It observed that these terms are intended to provide reasonable, fair market value compensation to the Physicians.

ANALYSIS

The IRS observed that a compensation plan of an exempt organization does not result in private inurement if the plan (1) is not inconsistent with exempt status (such as by being a device to distribute profits to principals or transforming the organization's principal activity into a joint venture), (2) is the result of arm's-length bargaining, and (3) results in reasonable compensation.

In this case, the IRS accepted the proposition that the purpose of the Agreement is to improve cardiovascular care while reducing the costs of delivering that care. The terms of the Plan were acceptable to the IRS; it was persuaded that the Agreement was negotiated at arm's-length and that the amounts to be received by the Physicians in the form of process improvement awards will be reasonable.

Consequently, the plan was held to not constitute inurement of net earnings and thus not jeopardize the tax exemption of the Hospital.

COMMENT: This plan serves as an example of an incentive compensation plan that qualifies for tax purposes.[6] The purpose of the plan is to advance exempt functions (promotion of health). The IRS was satisfied that the award criteria are objective and that adequate mechanisms are in place to ensure that the incentive compensation is reasonable.

This approved gainsharing arrangement has implications beyond its formal bounds, including in the charitable fund-raising setting. It is to be noted that the Agreement is designed to further charitable ends, the criteria are preestablished and presumably objective, and there are mechanisms in place for outside competent persons to determine what is reasonable (fair market value). The plan does not entail a monetary cap (Q 7:9), yet the IRS found sufficient the facts that the Hospital will benefit from tangible cost savings and that the amount of the awards will be tested against independent analyses.

Q 7:9   Is there any law on the subject of percentage-based fund-raising compensation arrangements?

Yes, there are some court opinions on the point. Indeed, the courts have been quite tolerant of these compensation arrangements.

Actually, in the first of these cases, the court found private inurement.[7] The facts in the case were, however, rather egregious on the point of excessive compensation. Thus, a compensation arrangement based on a percentage of gross receipts was held by the court to constitute private inurement, with the court making much of the fact that the terms of the arrangement did not include an upper limit, or cap, as to total compensation. This opinion, then, suggests that one way to avoid private inurement (or impermissible private benefit) when using percentage compensation arrangements is to place a ceiling on the total amount to be paid—assuming, of course, that the total amount is not excessive.

Yet, this same court, in a subsequent opinion, restricted the import of the prior decision by holding that private inurement did not take place when a tax-exempt organization paid its president a commission determined by a percentage of contributions obtained by him.[8] The court held that the standard is whether the compensation is reasonable, not the manner in which it is ascertained. Using phraseology that continues to resonate throughout the fund-raising community, the court wrote that fund-raising commissions that "are directly contingent on success in procuring funds" are an "incentive well-suited to the budget of a fledgling organization."[9] In reaching this conclusion, the court reviewed states' charitable solicitation acts governing payments to professional solicitors (Q 9:5), which the court characterized as "sanction[ing] such commissions and in many cases endors[ing] percentage commissions higher than" the percentage commission paid by the exempt organization involved in the case.[10]

Thereafter, a different court found occasion to articulate a fundamental standard in this area: "there is nothing insidious or evil about a commission-based compensation system."[11] An arrangement by which those who successfully procure contributions to a charitable organization are paid a percentage of the gifts received was judged "reasonable," despite the absence of any limit as to an absolute amount of compensation.

NOTE: Percentage-based fund-raising compensation may not be insidious or evil but that did not prevent a court from finding it "unseemly."[12]

Q 7:10   How would a cap on percentage-based fund-raising compensation be determined?

In addition to an agreement between the parties as to the percentage mechanism, a determination would be made as to what amount of compensation for the fund-raising services would be reasonable under the circumstances (Q 7:5). This may be done by use of an independent consultant, as was done in the gainsharing plan (Q 7:8). An amount up to the upper limit of that range as to the reasonable amount would be the cap or ceiling on the amount of compensation actually paid, irrespective of the higher amount generated by the percentage arrangement.

Q 7:11   Aside from considerations of law, are percentage-based fund-raising compensation arrangements *ethical*?

Whether or not a fund-raising compensation arrangement is ethical is a judgment to be made by the fund-raising community, not lawyers. There certainly are good arguments against the practice, including appearances for the charitable sector (including fund-raisers), negative impact on charitable giving (due to donors' distaste for the practice), and unwarranted windfalls to fund-raisers.[13]

Attempts have been made from time to time by associations of fund-raising professionals to maintain, in their codes of ethics, prohibitions against compensation based on percentages of funds raised. These provisions are, however, violations of the antitrust laws as illegal restraints of trade and thus cannot lawfully be enforced.[14]

Q 7:12   Can this matter of fund-raising compensation have an impact on a charitable organization's tax-exempt status?

Absolutely. There are at least three ways that a charity's tax exemption can be implicated in this fashion. If the compensation paid to a professional fund-raiser—employee or independent contractor (Q 7:2)—is not reasonable, that is to say it is excessive, the payment may be a violation of the private inurement doctrine (Q 1:10) or the private benefit doctrine (Q 1:11). Under either standard, the charity's tax-exempt status may be jeopardized.

The matter of the payment of fees for fund-raising to outside consultants raises another concern, which is that the charitable organization should be careful to not get itself into the position where its fund-raising unduly dominates in relation to its program activities. The IRS is empowered to assess whether a charitable organization is maintaining a program that is commensurate in scope with its financial resources.[15] This is known as the *commensurate test*.

Precisely how the commensurate test will be applied in the fund-raising context is unclear. This is because of some recent litigation, which is discussed elsewhere (Q 1:10). It is known, nonetheless, that the IRS is interested in application of the doctrine in the fund-raising setting—and the Tax Court has expressed the view that "high" fund-raising costs can lead to loss or denial of tax-exempt status.[16]

Q 7:13   Mention was made earlier of the fund-raiser's contract. When should such a document be used?

The principal occasion for a contract in this setting is where the professional fund-raiser (individual or company) is an independent contractor (Q 7:2). Indeed, the key word here is *contractor*.

NOTE: It is unlikely that a fund-raiser, who is an employee of a charitable organization, would have a formal contract with the organization. Usually, contracts of this nature are with the chief executive officer of the entity. If the fund-raiser is functioning in that capacity, such as by being the president of a fund-raising foundation affiliated with a charitable organization, there may well be an employment contract. Some of the elements of the contract to be discussed next would be in that employment contract.

Almost all consultants have written agreements with their clients. It is axiomatic, then, that a professional fund-raiser should have a written contract with each charitable client.

NOTE: Several state laws require that the relationship between a charitable organization and a professional fund-raiser be the subject of a written contract (Q 9:11).

The reasons for a written agreement are obvious. The principal one is to state the duties and responsibilities of the parties. The hope is that with this approach, disagreements later as to what each party to the arrangement is to do or should be doing will be avoided. To shift to the other extreme, a written memorialization as to the roles of the parties provides the substantive basis for litigation, should that prove necessary. Furthermore, as noted above, another reason for a written contract may be that the law requires it.

Q 7:14   What are the basic elements of the fund-raiser's contract?

That question, basically, can be restated as this: What should a contract between a charitable organization and a professional fund-raiser contain? The place to begin in answering that question is to enumerate the elements that should be in any service contract. There are eight of them, as follows:

1. A description of the services to be provided by the party designated as the vendor of the services.

2. A statement of the fees to be paid, and the timing of the payment(s), by the party who is to be the recipient of the services.

3. A provision indicating ownership of any property that may be utilized during or created in the contractual relationship.

4. An indemnification clause, pursuant to which one party agrees to absorb the costs of certain liabilities found against the other party. (There can be cross-indemnities.)

5. A provision stating the parties' ability to amend or terminate the agreement.

6. A provision stating the state's law that governs interpretation of the terms and intents of the agreement.

7. A provision stating that the contract memorializes the entire agreement between the parties and cannot be amended except in writing by the parties.

8. A provision stating the duration of the agreement, including the effective (starting) date.

These elements should be reflected in any contract between a charitable organization and a professional fund-raiser. Many of the specific clauses will, of course, vary, depending on factors such as the type of fund-raising involved. But, irrespective of whether the fund-raising involved will utilize direct mail, special events, annual campaign, planned giving, or some other means of fund-raising, or whether the fund-raising is to be in the context of a capital campaign, the advice is the same: the professional fund-raiser and the charitable organization are best served by a reasonably detailed written statement of services to be provided, and of amounts and schedules of fees to be paid.

Q 7:15 What are the important specific elements of the fund-raiser's contract?

A full statement of services to be performed by the fund-raiser is important. It can be the trick to avoiding breach-of-contract litigation. The professional fund-raiser is likely to have to thread a way between two extremes: not promise to do more than can or should be done, yet not make the statement of services so skimpy as to cause the charitable client to wonder what it is paying for.

CAUTION: The professional fund-raiser should be careful when making verbal statements. These can heighten the expectations of the client. Worse, this type of statement may later arguably become part of the contractual relationship. Statements of this nature can lead to disappointment and set the fund-raiser up for a lawsuit. Because of the potential validity of oral agreements, a clause confining the agreement to its written form is essential (Q 7:14, element 7).

A clear statement about the amount and timing of payment of fees to the professional fund-raiser will minimize, if not eliminate, the likelihood of fee disputes. If the fees are to be paid in phases (installments), and the charitable organization is to make payment following the close of a phase, the professional fund-raiser should be certain that the charity's payment obligations along the way are clearly stated. From the charity's standpoint, the services it is to receive during the course of each phase should be stated so that the charity is not put in the position for paying for something it is not receiving.

As noted (Q 7:14, element 3), it is important to state in a contract which party owns each particular item of property that is to be used in connection with, or may be created as the result of, the provision of services. In the specific context of the professional fund-raiser's contract, the ownership of these properties, at a minimum, should be addressed: mailing list(s), copyrights, artwork, and photographs. Additional types of properties may also be the subject of a property ownership clause.

COMMENT: In one instance, a fund-raising company ostensibly so dominated the operations of a charitable organization as to utilize the charity's assets for its private ends. The principal asset that was manipulated for private purposes was the charity's donor list. The trial court held that the relationship gave rise to private inurement, although on appeal that finding was rejected on the ground that the fund-raising company was not an insider with respect to the organization.[17] Usually, contracts between charities and fund-raisers are written in such a way as to preclude this type of abuse.

NOTE 1: The analysis does not end simply because the private inurement doctrine does not apply. There is a case pending in the Tax Court, involving the relationship between a charitable organization and a fund-raising company. The court is charged with the task of determining whether the arrangement transgressed the private benefit doctrine.[18]

NOTE 2: That court has already held that a transaction that constitutes private inurement also constitutes private benefit.[19] Inasmuch as the court previously ruled that the arrangement involved private inurement, it is a good bet that it will find the presence of private benefit. In any event, that should be the outcome.

It is rarely a good idea for a professional fund-raiser to guarantee results to a charitable organization client. If this is done, however, the fund-raiser should be certain that the guarantee—and any accompanying exceptions and conditions—is clearly and fully articulated.

A charity's contract for professional fund-raising assistance is a contract for what the law terms *specific performance*. This is particularly true where the charity is contracting with one or more individuals. The charitable organization involved should insist that the contract be nontransferable, or not transferable without the charity's prior written consent. These conditions are generally present where the professional fund-raiser is a company. The charity is contracting with the particular firm and presumably has no interest in having the obligation to perform services transferred to another company (or to an individual). Indeed, the charity may demand that the contract specify the provision of services by one or more named fund-raising professionals who are employed by or otherwise affiliated with the company.

When the fund-raising professional is an individual, the contract should state that he or she is rendering services as an independent contractor, rather than as an employee—assuming that statement is true.

The contract should state that the parties are not acting together in a *joint venture*. This matter is discussed elsewhere (Q 1:25) but it may be reiterated that the form of a joint venture can be imposed by law on the relationship between the parties—even where the parties have no intention or desire to be in a joint venture. Depending on the circumstances, the involvement by a charity in a joint venture can jeopardize its tax-exempt status.[20] The IRS has been known to revoke the tax exemption of a charitable organization because of its relationship with a fund-raising company; the IRS terms the arrangement a *fund-raising joint venture*.

CHAPTER 8

Annual Information Returns

The federal tax law requires that nearly all tax-exempt organizations, including most charitable organizations, file an annual information return with the IRS. This document, which generally is accessible by the public, has become quite extensive in recent years. It is far more than a tax return (it is an information return), in that much of the information required to be submitted goes beyond financial information and involves a considerable amount of descriptive material (sentences and paragraphs).

Too many organizations devote an insufficient amount of thought and care in the preparation of the return, and too often overlook or ignore the importance of this document. Congress and the IRS are of the view that this return is all too frequently inadequately prepared, filed late, or not filed at all. Consequently, recent legislation has brought disclosure and dissemination requirements, and an increase in penalties.

There is much information in the annual return of a charitable organization that directly and indirectly relates to the organization's fund-raising program. Thus, although the return should always be carefully prepared, it should be compiled and written taking into consideration its potential impact on fund-raising.

Here are the questions most frequently asked by professional fund-raisers (or that should be asked by them) about the annual information return filing rules—and the answers to them.

Q 8:1   Do charitable organizations have to file an annual return with the IRS?

In almost all instances, yes. The federal tax law requires the filing of an annual information return by just about every type of tax-exempt organization.[1] This includes charitable organizations.[2] Also, certain nonexempt charitable trusts are required to file.[3]

NOTE: This type of trust may also have to file the tax return generally required of trusts (Form 1041). However, if the trust does not have any taxable income, Form 1041 is not required, although the annual information return still is. Even if the trust has gross receipts below $25,000 (Q 8:2), it must nonetheless file the annual return for the purpose of complying with a special requirement (*id.*).

There are, however, some organizations that are excused from the filing obligation (*id.*).

NOTE: The document involved is not an *annual report* (such as may be required under state law) and it is not a *tax return*. As to the latter, these documents are not publicly accessible. The document that must be filed is an *information return*, which means, among other things, it is a return that contains much more than financial information and it must be made available to the public.

Q 8:2   Are there charitable organizations that are not required to file an annual return?

Yes. Some tax-exempt organizations do not have to file because of their exemption classification. These are:

- Instrumentalities of the United States.[4]
- State institutions the gross income of which is excluded from income taxation.[5]
- Other governmental units and tax-exempt organizations that are affiliated with them.[6]
- Churches, interchurch organizations of local units of a church, conventions or associations of churches, and integrated auxiliaries of a church.[7]

- Church-affiliated organizations that are exclusively engaged in managing funds or maintaining retirement programs.[8]
- A school below college level affiliated with a church or operated by a religious order.[9]
- A mission society sponsored by or affiliated with one or more churches or church denominations, if more than one-half of the society's activities are conducted in, or directed at persons in, foreign countries.[10]
- An exclusively religious activity of a religious order.[11]

NOTE: Some organizations that are not required to file annual information returns because of a tax law exception may find they need to prepare them in satisfaction of state reporting requirements (Q 9:2).

Other tax-exempt organizations are excused from filing an annual return because of the size of their gross receipts. There are two categories in this regard: organizations normally receiving $25,000 or less in gross receipts annually[12] and foreign organizations the annual gross receipts of which from sources within the United States are normally $25,000 or less.[13]

TIP: An organization with gross receipts that are normally not more than $25,000 should consider filing with the IRS anyway. This is done by completing the top portion of the return (name, address, and the like) and checking the box on line K. The purpose of this is to be certain that the IRS has the organization's correct address and realizes that the organization is not filing because it is not required to, rather than because it is unaware of or is ignoring the requirement. Also, the IRS requests that when an organization of this type receives a Form 990 Package in the mail, the top portion of the return be filed using the mailing label.

NOTE: The statute provides a filing exception only where an organization's gross receipts normally do not exceed $5,000.[14] The IRS, however, on its own initiative, increased the threshold to $25,000.

An organization that has been filing annual information returns and then becomes no longer required to file them, because of qualification under an exemption, should notify the IRS of the change in the filing status. Failure to do this is likely to result in inquiries from the IRS as to why returns are not being filed; a large expenditure of time and effort may then be required in resolving the matter.

Q 8:3   What constitutes *gross receipts*?

A distinction must be made between the term *gross receipts* and the term *gross revenue*.

NOTE: The reader may wish to have a copy of Form 990 handy while reviewing the balance of this chapter. The discussions are based on the Form 990 for 1999.

On Form 990 (Q 8:6), for example, gross revenue means all revenue referenced on Part I, lines 1–12 (Q 8:10). This includes contributions, grants, exempt function revenue, investment income, and unrelated business income.

NOTE: For the most part, *gross* revenue must be taken into account in determining total revenue (that is, expenses are irrelevant). However, there are four exceptions, where only net (gross less expenses) income is taken into account for this purpose: rental income (or loss) (Form 990, Part I, lines 6a–c), gain from sale of assets (or loss) (lines 8a–d), income from special events (or loss) (lines 9a–c), and gain from sales of inventory less certain items (or loss) (lines 10a–c).

TIP: Consistency is very important when reporting these numbers. In this instance, these four net revenue items must be reported again in the context of the analysis of income-producing activities (Q: 8:23) (Form 990, Part VII, lines 97–102).

By contrast, gross receipts are the total amount the organization received from all sources during its annual accounting period, without subtraction of any costs or expenses.

NOTE: Thus, the four exceptions noted above are irrelevant in computing gross receipts. Consequently, on Form 990, gross receipts are the sum of lines 1d, 2–5, 6a, 7, 8a (both columns), 9a, 10a, and 11. Gross receipts can also be calculated by adding back the amounts subtracted in ascertaining gross revenue.

Q 8:4   What does the term *normally* mean?

The term *normally* in this context generally means an average of the most recent three tax years of the organization (including the year relating to the return). Thus, it is not necessary, to be entitled to this reporting exception, that the organization be below the $25,000 threshold each year. Specifically, an organization is considered to meet the $25,000 gross receipts test if one of the following tests apply:

- The organization has been in existence for one year and has received, or donors have pledged to give, $37,500 or less during its first year.
- The organization has been in existence between one and three years, and averaged $30,000 or less in gross receipts during each of its first two years.
- The organization has been in existence three or more years and averaged $25,000 or less in gross receipts for the immediately preceding three years (including the year for which the return would be filed).[15]

Q 8:5   What happens once this $25,000 gross receipts test is exceeded?

Once it is determined that the organization's gross receipts for the measuring period (Q 8:4) are such that it has exceeded the $25,000 threshold, it has 90 days within which to file the appropriate annual return (unless another exception is available (Q 8:2)).[16]

Q 8:6   What IRS form is this annual information return?

For most charitable organizations, it is Form 990.

NOTE: The balance of the questions and answers in this chapter will focus exclusively on that return.

Small organizations—those with gross receipts of less than $100,000 and total assets of less than $250,000—are allowed to file a simpler (two-page) version of the return, which is Form 990-EZ.

TIP: An organization that is eligible to file Form 990-EZ may nonetheless file Form 990 if it wishes (perhaps to provide more spe-

---

cific information) or if necessary (such as to meet state law reporting requirements).

Private foundations (Q 2:2) file Form 990-PF. Charitable organizations that are not private foundations are required to also file Schedule A to accompany Form 990 (or Form 990-EZ).[17]

Q 8.7   When is this annual information return due?

The annual information return is required to be filed with the IRS by the 15th day of the fifth month following the close of its accounting period.[18] Thus, for charitable organizations using the calendar year as the accounting period, the return is due by May 15. An organization with a fiscal year ending June 30 is expected to file by November 15. An organization with a fiscal year ending October 31 must file by March 15.

If the regular due date falls on a Saturday, Sunday, or legal holiday, the due date is the next business day.

NOTE: If the organization is liquidated, dissolved, or terminated, the return should be filed by the 15th day of the fifth month after the liquidation, dissolution, or termination.

Q 8:8   Are extensions of this filing due date available?

Yes. It is common for charitable organizations to obtain an extension of the annual information return due date. The proper way to request this extension is the filing of Form 2758.

Generally, the IRS will not grant an extension of time to file the annual information return for more than 90 days, unless sufficient need for an extended period is clearly shown. The IRS will not, in any event, grant an extension of more than six months to any domestic organization.

Q 8:9   Where is the annual information return filed?

All annual information returns filed by tax-exempt organizations are required to be filed with the Internal Revenue Service Center in Ogden, Utah 84201-0027.

NOTE: Historically, annual information returns were filed with the appropriate IRS key district office. Now that the IRS has centralized this function, that system has been abandoned.

Q 8:10   What are the contents of the annual information return?

That question cannot be responded to in a single answer. The best way to survey the contents of the return is to break it down by its portions. The document consists of six pages, comprising nine parts. The accompanying Schedule A also constitutes six pages, comprising seven parts. Let's proceed part by part, beginning with the basic information required on page 1, before Part I. The IRS regards this as the *heading* of the return.

Q 8:11   What items of information are required in the heading of the return, preceding Part I?

There are ten items of information that are to be supplied:

1. Identification of the organization's accounting period.
2. The nature of the return: initial, final, or amended. Any change of address is to be noted.

> **TIP:** The IRS prefers that an address change be communicated to it by the filing of Form 8822.

3. The organization's name and address.
4. The organization's employer identification number.

> **NOTE:** Presumably, the organization has been assigned this number by the time it begins filing annual information returns. If the number has not yet been obtained, the organization acquires it by the filing of Form SS-4.

5. State registration number. The state or local jurisdiction number should be entered for each jurisdiction in which the organization files the Form 990 in lieu of a state or local form.
6. The organization is required to indicate if it has an application for recognition of tax exemption pending.
7. The organization is to identify its tax status as an exempt organization (by completing the Internal Revenue Code citation) or a nonexempt charitable trust (see Q 8:1).

> **TIP:** For charitable organizations, the Code citation is 501(c)(3).

8. Information to be provided by organizations the tax exemption of which is based on a group exemption,[19] including the group exemption number.

9. The accounting method used by the organization.

10. Indication that the organization is below the $25,000 threshold (Q 8:2).

Q 8:12   What information as to revenue is required on the annual information return?

The return, in Part I, requires the reporting of all items of revenue that the organization received during the year. This requires the reporting of items of *gross* revenue, although as indicated (Q 8:3) four items of revenue are netted, in whole or in part, in this portion of the return.

1. Line 1. On this line, the organization reports revenue that it received during the year in the form of contributions, grants, and the like.

NOTE: The return references *contributions* and *gifts*. For return reporting purposes, these words mean the same thing.

This can involve distinguishing between these items and exempt function revenue. For example, an organization may have to determine whether a payment was in the form of a *grant* or made pursuant to a *contract* (Q 8:13).

TIP: Sometimes this distinction is difficult to make. The fact that the parties characterize a document as a grant or contract usually is irrelevant. It is the substance of the arrangement that is pertinent.

This financial information must be further broken down into direct and indirect public support. *Direct public support* (line 1a) means contributions to the organization from all sources: individuals, corporations, trusts, and the like; it also includes grants from private foundations. *Indirect public support* (line 1b) means a grant from a publicly supported charity; the gifts made to this grantor are deemed to be embodied in the grant, so that they are considered made indirectly to the grantee (the organization preparing the return). Government grants are also separately identified (line 1c).

This financial information is totaled (line 1d). A schedule of contributors and donors must be attached. The information on this schedule, however, need not be made accessible to the public. Also, there must be a breakdown of these items between those made in the form of cash and those that are in noncash form. These two numbers combined should be equal to the total figure (on line 1d).

NOTE: Not all noncash items are eligible to be listed as this form of revenue. Basically, the reference to *noncash* items is to tangible personal and real property, and intangible property such as securities. Items that are *not* to be reported in this portion of the return are (1) donated services or (2) the use of materials, equipment, or facilities at no charge or at substantially less than fair rental value. These items are reported elsewhere on the return (Q 8:37).

---

2. Lines 2–3. On these lines, the organization reports its *exempt function revenue*, which essentially is revenue derived from related business activities. That is, this is revenue derived from the performance of a service (such as admission to a facility or an activity pursuant to a government grant) or the sale of one or more goods (such as publications).

   The return terms this type of income *program service revenue* (line 2). These types of revenue are detailed elsewhere on the return (see Q 8:13) and the total is inserted in this portion of the return. Another type of exempt function revenue is membership dues and assessments, which is separately reported (line 3). Membership income must also be reported elsewhere on the return (*id.*).

3. Line 4. Interest on savings and temporary cash investments is reported here.

4. Line 5. Dividends and interest from securities is reported here.

5. Line 6. Gross rental income less expenses is reported here.

6. Line 7. Other investment income is reported here.

7. Line 8. Gross amounts from the sale of assets (other than inventory), including capital assets such as securities (that give rise to capital gain or loss), less their cost basis and sales expenses, are reported here. A schedule of these sales transactions must be attached.

NOTE: For organizations that engage in large numbers of securities and other sales transactions, this schedule can

---

be sizable, amounting to several inches of paper, which can cause reproduction of the return to be expensive and time-consuming.

8. Line 9. Gross income from special events, less expenses other than those for fund-raising, is reported here. A *special event* is defined in the annual return instructions as an activity the sole or primary purpose of which is to raise funds (that are not contributions) to finance the organization's activities (such as dinners, dances, carnivals, and gambling activities) (Q 6:23). A schedule of these activities must be attached.

9. Line 10. Gross sales of inventory, less returns, allowances, and costs of goods sold (yielding gross profit (or loss)) is reported here. A schedule of these sales must be attached.

10. Line 11. Other revenue is reported here. This category of revenue, which includes unrelated business income (Chapter 6), is detailed elsewhere on the return.

11. Line 12. The organization's total revenue (taking into account the four instances where a form of netting is permitted) is reported here.

TIP: The information provided as to the sources of the organization's revenue should correlate, in terms of both the accuracy of the numbers and the classification of the revenue items, with the reporting of public support (Q 2:7, Q 2:8) and the analysis of income-producing activities (see (Q 8:29)).

Q 8:13   How does an organization differentiate between *grant* revenue and *program service* revenue?

Basically, a grant is a payment that is akin to a gift, where the recipient of the money is basically free to use it as it deems appropriate. By contrast, a payment made pursuant to a contract is a purchase of services (and/or goods), with the recipient of the services (and/or goods) being the entity that paid for them.[20]

Q 8:14   What information as to expenses is required on the annual information return?

The various categories of the organization's expenses are reported on the annual information return, in Part I. Most of this information is presented in greater detail elsewhere in the return, so this portion is a summary of the four categories of expenses. The expenses of most charitable organizations are allocated across three categories: related business activities (expenditures for program), management, and fund-raising.

1. Line 13. The total of the expenses associated with the organization's program activities is reported here.

2. Line 14. The total of the expenses associated with management of the organization is reported here.

3. Line 15. The total of the expenses associated with fund-raising for the organization is reported here.

4. Line 16. Any payments to affiliated organizations are reported here. A schedule of these payments must be attached.

NOTE: An organization's expenses for program services, management and general, and fund-raising are calculated using a method by which costs are allocated across the three functions (Q 8:15).

---

5. Line 17. Expenses are totaled and reported here.

NOTE: There are two controversial matters as to an organization's expenses that are reflected elsewhere on the return. One is the issue of joint costs (Q 8:17). The other is the matter of compensation of key employees, independent contractors, and others, and the correlation of this with the intermediate sanctions rules (Q 8:27).

Q 8:15   How are an organization's fund-raising expenses reported?

Expenses of fund-raising, in the form of professional fund-raising fees, are accorded a line on the statement of expenses. Other fund-raising costs must be reported as well. There is reporting in the case of joint costs incurred in connection with an educational campaign and a fund-raising solicitation (Q 8:17).

The tax law recognizes that an expenditure may not simply be for one function. For example, payments for telephone services may all be program expenditures, or they may be part program and part management, or all management, or part program, part management, and part fund-raising, or all for fund-raising. Thus, an outlay can range over more than one function, and this has given rise to the concept of *functional expense reporting.*

However, not all tax-exempt organizations are required to report their expenses functionally. Public charities and social welfare organizations are required to do so, as are nonexempt charitable trusts. This type of reporting is optional for all other exempt entities. Every reporting exempt organization must report total expenses by category (Part II, column (A)). The return is structured to also accommodate functional reporting of expenses (columns (B)–(D)).

NOTE: There is an oddity in the return in this regard. As noted, for many categories of tax-exempt organizations, functional reporting of expenses is said to be "optional." Yet, as noted, on the face of the return, the organization is required to separately report expenses for program services, management, and fund-raising.

Q 8:16 Are fund-raising costs the only expenses that are subject to functional accounting?

No. There are 21 categories of expenses that must be so reported. They are:

CAUTION: When preparing this portion of the return, the expenses already taken into account in netting four items on the face of the return (Q 8:3) should not be repeated. Also, payments to affiliates are separately reported and thus should not be reflected here.

---

1. Grants and allocations (line 22). A schedule of these items is required. Total cash items and noncash items must be reported. These items are always allocated to program services.
2. Specific assistance to individuals (line 23). A schedule is required. These items are always allocated to program services.
3. Benefits paid to or for members (line 24). A schedule is required. These items are always allocated to program services.
4. Compensation of trustees, directors, and officers (line 25).

NOTE: Additional information in this regard is required elsewhere in the return (Q 8:26).

---

5. Other salaries and wages (line 26).
6. Pension plan contributions (line 27).
7. Other employee benefits (line 28).
8. Payroll taxes (line 29).
9. Professional fund-raising fees (line 30). This item may not be allocated to either program services or management.

10. Accounting fees (line 31).

11. Legal fees (line 32).

12. Supplies (line 33).

13. Telephone (line 34).

14. Postage and shipping (line 35).

15. Occupancy (line 36).

16. Equipment rental and maintenance (line 37).

17. Printing and publications (line 38).

18. Travel (line 39).

19. Conferences, conventions, and meetings (line 40).

20. Interest (line 41).

21. Depreciation, depletion, and the like (line 42). A schedule is required.

There is space on the return to list other expenses (line 43). An attachment may be used if necessary.

The organization's expenses are totaled (line 44). This number is carried over and inserted in the total expense line on the face of the return. If expenses are reported functionally, they are likewise carried forward and inserted in the appropriate expense line on the face of the return (Q 8:15).

Q 8:17   There is controversy about allocation of what some regard as fund-raising costs to programs. Is this reflected on the return?

Yes. The IRS refers to this situation as involving *joint costs*. Specifically, this arises where there is a combined educational campaign and a fund-raising solicitation. The organization must answer, on a "yes" or "no" basis, whether any such joint costs are being reported as part of program services expenses (Part II). If the answer is "yes," the organization must report the aggregate amount of these joint costs, the amount allocated to program, the amount allocated to management, and the amount allocated to fund-raising.

NOTE: The controversy, of course, arises when there is a perception that an organization is treating as program costs an amount of expenses that ought to be regarded as for fund-raising. This may be done to augment the size of the entity's program or reduce the amount of fund-raising outlays. Critics of this type of allocation prefer a *primary purpose rule*, which would cause all of the expenses to be regarded as fund-raising ones. The principal champions of the primary purpose rule are—as is to be expected—state regulatory agencies and the watchdog groups.[21]

Q 8:18   What about other fund-raising practices?

One of the elements of federal fund-raising regulation involves certain disclosure requirements with respect to quid pro quo contributions (Q 4:38).[22] One of the questions on the return, which requires a "yes" or "no" answer, is whether these disclosure requirements were complied with (Part VI, line 83b). Since the law requires compliance with these requirements, the organization is well advised to answer this question in the affirmative if it possibly (and truthfully) can. The answer is "yes" even if there were no quid pro quo contributions during the year. If the answer must be "no," professional assistance is advised.

Also, there are certain rules about the solicitation of gifts that are not tax deductible.[23] Basically, the law requires that the solicitation material contain an express statement that these contributions are not deductible. The return requires a "yes" or "no" answer to a question as to whether any contributions of this nature were solicited (line 84a). If the answer is "no," that is the end of the matter (assuming that answer is truthful). If the answer is "yes," the organization must answer "yes" or "no" to the question of whether the statement as to nondeductibility was included (line 85b). Of course, the desired answer to that question is "yes." Again, if this answer must be "no," professional assistance is advised.

If a public charity or nonexempt charitable trust performs fund-raising services for a tax-exempt organization (Q 6:20), certain information must be reported.

Q 8:19   What information as to net income or loss is required on the annual information return?

The reporting organization must calculate its net revenue (what the return terms *excess* revenue) or net loss (deficit) for the year. This is reported on line 18 of Part I of the return. This number is the organization's total revenue (Q 8:12) less total expenses (Q 8:14).

Q 8:20   What information as to net assets is required on the annual information return?

The reporting organization must calculate its *net assets* or *fund balances* at the beginning of the year and report this item on line 19 of Part I of the return. It must likewise calculate its net assets and fund balances at the end of the year and report this item on line 21 of the return. Any other changes in this item must be reported (on line 20), along with an explanation.

The determination as to net assets or fund balances at the beginning of the year is derived from the balance sheet that constitutes Part IV of the return. This portion of the return requires the organization to ascertain, as of the beginning of the year and the end of the year, the following:

1. Assets

    a. Cash (non-interest bearing) (line 45).

    b. Savings and temporary cash investments (line 46).

    c. Accounts receivable, less allowance for doubtful accounts (line 47).

    d. Pledges receivable, less allowance for doubtful accounts (line 48).

    e. Grants receivable (line 49).

    f. Receivables due from trustees, directors, officers, and key employees (line 50). A schedule of end-of-the-year amounts must be attached.

    NOTE: For tax-exempt organizations (other than, in some instances, private foundations), loans, advances, and the like to individuals of this nature are not prohibited (although they may be subject to special scrutiny, which is the purpose of this line). This aspect of the return verifies the point.

    ---

    g. Other notes and loans receivable, less an allowance for doubtful accounts (line 51). A schedule for end-of-the-year amounts must be attached.

    h. Inventories for sale or use (line 52).

    i. Prepaid expenses and deferred charges (line 53).

    j. Investments involving securities (line 54). A schedule for end-of-the-year amounts must be attached.

    k. Investments involving land, buildings, and equipment, less accumulated depreciation (line 55). A schedule for end-of-the-year depreciation amounts must be attached.

    l. Other investments (line 56). A schedule for end-of-the-year amounts must be attached.

    m. Land, buildings, and equipment, less accumulated depreciation (line 57). A schedule for end-of-the-year depreciation amounts must be attached.

    n. Other assets, accompanied by a description of them (line 58).

    o. Total assets (line 59).

2. Liabilities

    a. Accounts payable and accrued expenses (line 60).

    b. Grants payable (line 61).

    c. Deferred revenue (line 62).

    d. Loans from trustees, directors, officers, and key employees (line 63). A schedule for end-of-the-year amounts must be attached.

    e. Tax-exempt bond liabilities (line 64a). A schedule for end-of-the-year amounts must be attached.

    f. Mortgages and other notes payable (line 64b). A schedule for end-of-the-year amounts must be attached.

    g. Other liabilities, accompanied by a description of them (line 65).

    h. Total liabilities (line 66).

3. Net assets or fund balances for organizations that follow *Financial Statements of Not-for-Profit Organizations*, issued by the Financial Accounting Standards Board ("SFAS 117")

    a. Unrestricted (line 67).

    b. Temporarily restricted (line 68).

    c. Permanently restricted (line 69).

    d. Total net assets or fund balances (line 73). This amount for the beginning of the year (column (A)) is entered on line 19 of Part I of the return. This amount for the end of the year (column (B)) is entered on line 21 of Part I of the return.

    e. Total liabilities and net assets/fund balances (line 74).

TIP: The amount on line 74 should equal the total on lines 66 (total liabilities) and 73 (total net assets or fund balances), and should be the same as the amount on line 59 (total assets). The amount entered on line 21 of the return should also be the sum of the amounts on lines 18–20.

---

4. Net assets or fund balances for organizations that do not follow SFAS 117

    a. Capital stock, trust principal, or current funds (line 70).

    b. Paid-in or capital surplus, or land, building, and equipment fund (line 71).

    c. Retained earnings, endowment, accumulated income, or other funds (line 72).

d. Total net assets or fund balances (line 73). Again, this amount for the beginning of the year (column (A)) is entered on line 19 of Part I of the return. This amount for the end of the year (column (B)) is entered on line 21 of Part I of the return.

e. Total liabilities and net assets/fund balances (line 74).

TIP: Again, the amount on line 74 should equal the total on lines 66 (total liabilities) and 73 (total net assets or fund balances), and should be the same as the amount on line 59 (total assets). Again, the amount entered on line 21 of the return should also be the sum of the amounts on lines 18–20.

Q 8:21   Should organizations be concerned about a large amount of net assets or fund balance?

They should be somewhat concerned. There is no law that places a restriction on the amount of money or property that a charitable organization can accumulate. At the same time, a large and growing accumulation of assets can be a signal that inadequate or infrequent exempt functions are taking place.

NOTE: The IRS occasionally applies what is known as the *commensurate test*. The agency compares an organization's program activities with the extent of its financial resources to see if it is doing enough in the way of exempt functions. (So far, this test has only been applied to public charities.[24]) A large fund balance accumulation is an element that the IRS would take into consideration in applying this test.

A factor to take into account in this context is the reason for the accumulation. The organization may denominate some or all of these assets as an endowment fund, a building fund, or some other reserve. This can go a long way in dispelling concerns about what might otherwise appear to be an unreasonable accumulation.

Some organizations avoid this dilemma by transferring some or all of their fund balance to another, controlled, entity. This organization is often generically referred to as a *foundation*; it may technically be a *supporting organization* (Q 2:15). This entity can hold the funds as an endowment fund or for a similar function. Whatever the use that is made of this type of separate entity, it causes what might otherwise appear to be an excessive accumulation of funds or property to be removed from the "bottom line" of the tax-exempt organization.

Q 8:22   **It was previously noted that to be tax-exempt, a charitable organization must primarily engage in the appropriate exempt functions. Is this rule of law reflected in the annual information return?**

Very much so. One of the most important questions comprising the annual return is this: "What is the organization's primary exempt purpose?" (Form 990, Part III). The organization should be thoughtful and careful when responding to this question. This is the heart of the *operational test* as that test is applied to the organization.[25] The answer to this question provides the general framework for most of the other questions and sets the tone for the other portions of the return. The sophisticated reader of an annual information return is likely to turn to the answer to this question first.

There is not much space on the return itself for an adequate answer, so a full response will likely have to be made on an attachment. While a general answer may suffice (such as "higher education," "health care," or "museum"), the organization should go beyond very vague terminology (such as "charitable" or "educational"). Keeping in mind that this is a public document,[26] the response to this question is an opportunity to tout the organization, to cast it in the most favorable light (staying within the bounds of veracity). It is an opportunity that is frequently overlooked.

TIP: This last observation is applicable to many other portions of the annual information return.

NOTE: The annual information return now contains much factual information other than financial data. It is no longer a document to be prepared solely by an accountant. The answers to this and most of the other questions should be conscientiously considered by the organization's management, and reviewed by at least some of the volunteer leadership and the organization's lawyer, and perhaps others, such as a fund-raising and/or public relations professional.

Q 8:23   **What about the organization's programs? How should they be discussed?**

The programs of a charitable organization are the heart of the entity. The organization exists to conduct its programs. All other functions are (or should be) conducted in support of its primary activities, which are its programs. Here is one place where the annual information return should read like an annual report. The return amply provides the opportunity for the organization to summarize its programs—what the re-turn terms the organization's *program service accomplishments.*

The organization must describe its exempt purpose achievements (Part III). There is adequate room on the return to describe the four most important ones (lines a–d), although the organization should not hesitate to use one or more attachments. If more than four program ser-vice accomplishments are to be discussed, a schedule describing them should be attached (line e).

There are no bounds to creativeness here (other than accuracy). The organization should exuberantly and fully portray its programs. Specificity is in order. The return supplies some hints in this regard: the organization can state the number of clients served or publications is-sued. As the IRS puts it, the organization should also "discuss achieve-ments that are not measurable."

NOTE: In the instructions accompanying the annual information return, the IRS observes that "[s]ome members of the public rely on . . . [the annual return] as the primary or sole source of information about a par-ticular organization. How the public perceives an organization in such cases may be determined by the information presented on its return. Therefore, please make sure the return is complete and accurate and fully describes the organization's programs and accomplishments."

This portion of the return involves some financial information. This is because one way to describe program services is by citing grants and allocations to others. This financial information is manda-tory for charitable and social welfare organizations, and nonexempt charitable trusts; it is optional for all other tax-exempt organizations.

Following this descriptive and financial information, the organiza-tion's program service expenses should be totaled (line f). Of course, this number should be the same as that inserted on the face of the re-turn for program service expenses (Q 8:13).

TIP 1: Some have the attitude that the IRS should be given as little in-formation as legally possible. While in some settings this approach can be the correct one, this is not the place. Indeed, skimpy entries can be the basis for suspicions. Explicate!

TIP 2: An organization may develop excellent descriptions of its pro-grams and then simply reuse them over the years. This is fine as long as the summaries remain accurate and reflect contemporary priorities. However, there is the danger that the material facts will change, so

---

that the descriptions are no longer appropriate; they may even be false or misleading. Thus, these statements should be reviewed and considered anew each year.

Q 8:24   Are there reporting requirements for public charities that make grants to individuals?

Yes. A public charity is asked whether it makes grants for scholarships, fellowships, student loans, and the like (Form 990, Schedule A, Part III, line 3). This is a "yes" or "no" question. If the answer is "yes," the organization must attach a statement explaining how it determines that individuals receiving grants or loans from it, in furtherance of its charitable programs, qualify to receive the payments (line 4).

In addition, all organizations are required to report expenses which constitute grants (Q 8:13). Also, a grant, loan, or similar program is a program service and a statement about the program(s) is likely to be required, including the amount of the grants (*id.*). A grant payable should be identified on the organization's balance sheet (Q 8:20).

Q 8:25   There must be reporting requirements for grants to organizations as well.

Yes, although there is not a specific "yes" or "no" question on the point for all tax-exempt organizations. Nonetheless, if a public charity makes grants or loans to organizations, it must attach a statement explaining how it determines that the recipients of its support, in furtherance of its charitable programs, qualify to receive the payments (Form 990, Schedule A, Part III, line 4).

Also, a public charity may make grants or loans to other exempt organizations that are not charitable ones. If that is the case, there are other reporting requirements.

In addition, all tax-exempt organizations are required to report expenses which constitute specific assistance to individuals (Q 8:24). Also, a scholarship, loan, or similar program is a program service and a statement about the program(s) is likely to be required, including the amount of the grants (Q 8:13). As noted, a grant payable should be identified on the organization's balance sheet (Q 8:20).

Q 8:26   What about expenses for compensation?

This is another subject of great concern to the IRS. Thus, it should not be a surprise to learn that the annual information return devotes considerable space to the reporting of compensation.

As noted, as part of the listing of its expenses, the organization is required to make a line entry for the compensation of trustees, directors, and officers, as well as for other salaries and wages. In addition to those forms of compensation, the organization must report its payments for pension plan contributions and other employee benefits (Q 8:26).

Also, the organization must provide a list of its trustees, directors, officers, and key employees (Part V). This list is required even if the individual is not compensated.

Specifically, the name and address of each of these individuals must be listed, along with his or her title, the average hours per week devoted to the position, the amount of compensation, the amount contributed to employee benefit plans, the amount of deferred compensation, and information as to expense account and other allowances.

For many tax-exempt organizations, the doctrine of *private inurement* is applicable (Q 1:10). One way to have private inurement is for the exempt organization to pay an amount of compensation that is excessive. This portion of the return is used by the IRS as part of the process of ascertaining whether there may be an unreasonable compensation package.

Sometimes, a compensation package of an individual is reasonable when evaluated alone but the total compensation of the individual can be excessive when combined with compensation from a related organization. That is why the IRS asks the question, which must be answered "yes" or "no," as to whether any trustee, director, officer, or key employee received aggregate compensation of more than $100,000 from the organization and all related organizations, where more than $10,000 was provided by one or more related organizations (line 75). If the answer is "yes," an explanatory schedule must be attached.

Q 8:27   How does this matter of compensation relate to the intermediate sanctions rules?

There is a direct connection between this matter of compensation and the intermediate sanctions rules.[27]

If a public charity participates in an excess benefit transaction with a disqualified person, tax penalties are imposed on that person and on the organization managers who knew that the transaction gave rise to an excess benefit. Excessive compensation is one way to have an excess benefit transaction. Compensation arrangements involving trustees, directors, officers, and/or key employees are suspect under these rules because these individuals almost always are disqualified persons.

A public charity or a social welfare organization must answer "yes" or "no" to a question as to whether it engaged in an excess benefit transaction during the year (Part VI, line 89b). If the answer is "yes," it must attach a statement explaining each transaction. Also, the organization must report the amount of tax paid, during the year, by its organization managers or disqualified persons with respect to it (line 89c) and the amount of any of these taxes that the organization reimbursed (line 89d).

The reporting rules in this regard are more extensive for public charities. This is because these organizations are required to file Schedule A of Form 990.

This supplemental form requires much more detail as to the payment of compensation. Thus, a public charity must provide information as to the compensation of its five highest paid employees—if they were paid more than $50,000—other than trustees, directors, and officers (Schedule A, Part I). Specifically, the organization must supply the name and address of these employees, their titles, the average hours per week devoted to the position, the amount of their compensation, the amount of contributions to employee benefit plans, deferred compensation, and expense accounts and other allowances. If there are no employees of this nature, the organization should insert "None" on the first line.

NOTE: The way the schedule is constructed, the organization need only provide this information for 10 employees. It then inserts the total number of other employees paid over $50,000. If there are more than 10, there is no guidance as to which 10 to select for detailed reporting.

A public charity must also provide information as to the highest paid independent contractors for professional services. It is required to list the name and address of each independent contractor paid more than $50,000, the type of service provided, and the compensation paid. If there are no independent contractors of this nature, the organization should insert "None" on the first line.

NOTE: Again, the organization need only provide this information for 10 independent contractors. It then inserts the total number of other independent contractors paid over $50,000. As with employees, if there are more than 10, there is no guidance as to which 10 to select for detailed reporting.

A public charity is also asked whether, during the year, it, directly or indirectly, paid compensation (or paid or reimbursed expenses if more than $1,000) to any of its trustees, directors, officers, creators, key employees, or members of their families, or to any taxable organization with which any of these persons is affiliated as a trustee, director, officer, majority owner, or principal beneficiary (Schedule A, Part III, line 2d). This is a "yes" or "no" question. If the answer is "yes," a detailed explanation is required.

Q 8:28 But the intermediate sanctions rules relate to much more than excessive compensation, don't they?

Absolutely. The concept of the excess benefit transaction embraces much more than compensation arrangements. It covers the provision of excess benefits by means of sales, loans, rentals, and other transactions.

There is a set of questions on the annual return that predate the intermediate sanctions rules but that are being used to ferret out possible excess benefit transactions with public charities. These questions pertain to transactions during the year, whether direct or indirect, between the public charity and any of its trustees, directors, officers, creators, key employees, or members of their families, or with any taxable organization with which any of these persons is affiliated as a trustee, director, officer, majority owner, or principal beneficiary (Schedule A, Part III).

These transactions are the following:

1. Sales or exchanges of property (line 2a).
2. Leasing of property (line 2a).
3. Lending of money or other extension of credit (line 2b).
4. Furnishing of goods, services, or facilities (line 2c).
5. Compensation arrangements (line 2d) (Q 8:26).
6. Transfer of any part of the organization's income or assets (line 2e).

Each of these questions must be answered "yes" or "no." For each answer where the answer is "yes," a detailed explanation is required.

Q 8:29 Does the annual information return require any additional information about an organization's expenses?

Yes, much more. One of the most critical portions of the return is the analysis of income-producing activities (Part VII). This segment of the return must be prepared with considerable care and understanding of the underlying points of law.

The first step is for the organization to list each of its sources of program service revenue. This information has already been gathered and reported elsewhere on the return (Q 8:13). Here is the list:

1. Program service revenue (line 93). The return provides space for the listing of six sources; an attachment may be necessary. Fees and contracts from government agencies are expressly identified (line 93g), as are membership dues and assessments (line 94).

2. Interest on savings and temporary cash investments (line 95).

3. Dividends and interest from securities (line 96).

4. Net rental income (or loss) from real estate (line 97). There must be a differentiation between revenue derived from debt-financed property and property that is not debt-financed.

5. Net rental income (or loss) from personal property (line 98).

6. Other investment income (line 99).

7. Gain (or loss) from sales of assets other than inventory (line 100).

8. Net income (or loss) from special events (line 101).

9. Gross profit (or loss) from sales of inventory (line 102).

10. Other revenue (line 103). The return provides space for the listing of five items; an attachment may be used if necessary.

Once these sources of revenue are identified, they must be classified in accordance with the unrelated business income rules (Chapter 6). Specifically, the organization must decide whether an item of income is derived from a related business or an unrelated business, or whether the income, while not from a related business, is nonetheless not taxable because it is excluded from taxation by statute.

If the organization is reporting income as being from an exempt function, that item of income, matched up with the appropriate source (as listed above), is inserted in the appropriate line in column (E). Thus, all items that are considered related income are entered in column (E). Then, the organization must provide a written explanation as to how each of these activities is a related one, that is, how it contributed importantly to the accomplishment of the organization's exempt purposes. Of course, these explanations should be carefully thought through; this is one place where the assistance of a tax professional may well be advisable. An attachment may be required.

NOTE: It is not sufficient that the income from an activity is used for exempt purposes. The activity must inherently be an exempt function.

If the organization is reporting income from an unrelated business, this amount or these amounts must be reported in column (B).

Each unrelated business activity must be assigned a business code which is inserted in the appropriate line in column (A). These codes are found in the Form 990-T instructions.

If the organization is reporting income that is not from a related source but is sheltered from taxation by statute, this amount or these amounts must be reported in column (D). The organization must determine which section of the Internal Revenue Code provides the exclusion, correlate that exclusion with an exclusion code, and insert that code in the appropriate line in column (C). These codes are found in the Form 990 instructions.

Then, the subtotals for these three groupings of income are reported (line 104), followed by the total of them (line 105).

NOTE: As noted, most of these revenue items have been previously ascertained and reported. Thus, the total on line 105, plus the amount of any contributions and grants (Q 8:12), should equal the amount of total revenue reported on the face of the return (*id.*).

Q 8:30   What information must be reported concerning the organization's public charity status?

A charitable organization that is a public charity (Q 2:1) is required to report information about its public charity status.

There are eleven ways for a charitable organization to constitute a public charity. These ways are enumerated in the return (Form 990, Schedule A, Part IV); the organization is required to indicate which one of the categories it is in. The categories are:

1. A church, convention of churches, or association of churches (line 5).
2. A school (line 6).

NOTE: Schools are required to complete another portion of Schedule A (Part V, the Private School Questionnaire).

---

3. A hospital or a cooperative service organization (line 7).
4. A federal, state, or local government or governmental unit (line 8).
5. A medical research organization operated in conjunction with a hospital (line 9). The hospital's name, city, and state must be provided.

6. An organization operated for the benefit of a college or university that is owned or operated by a governmental unit (line 10). There is a public support requirement for these organizations; a support schedule must be completed (Part IV-A).

7. An organization that is a publicly supported charity because it is the donative type (line 11a). A support schedule must be completed (Part IV-A).

8. A community trust (or community foundation) (line 11b). A support schedule must be completed (Part IV-A).

9. An organization that is a publicly supported charity because it is the service provider type (line 12). A support schedule must be completed (Part IV-A).

10. A supporting organization (line 13). The supported organization(s) must be identified by name and public charity status (the latter by selecting the appropriate line number).

11. An organization that is organized and operated to test for public safety (line 14).

Q 8:31 Does the annual information return ask any questions about lobbying activities?

Yes. The IRS is very curious about lobbying activities by charitable organizations and this is mirrored in the amount of space the annual information return devotes to the subject. There are essentially two sets of questions about this subject. One set pertains to public charities. (The other involves membership associations, principally social welfare organizations (Q 1:18), labor organizations,[28] and business leagues (Q 1:19).)

NOTE: The portion of the annual return which focuses on an organization's expenses (Q 8:14) does not contain any express reference to lobbying expenditures.

A public charity is asked whether it, during the year, attempted to influence national, state, or local legislation, including any attempt to influence public opinion on a legislative matter or referendum (Form 990, Schedule A, Part III, line 1). This is a "yes" or "no" question. If the answer is "yes," the organization is required to report the expenses paid or incurred in this connection.

By reason of the *substantial part test* (Q 1:16), a charitable organization is prohibited from engaging in substantial amounts of lobbying activity. An organization that is subject to this test must also complete another portion of the return which requests more specific information about the lobbying activities. If a public charity has made an election and thus is bound by the rules of the *expenditure test* (*id.*), it must complete another portion of the return.

Charitable organizations that are bound by the substantial part test must answer "yes" or "no" to eight questions pertaining to lobbying activities during the year (Schedule A, Part VI-B). These activities embrace direct lobbying, grassroots lobbying, and referenda. The questions pertain to lobbying through the use of the following:

1. Volunteers (line a).
2. Paid staff or management (line b).
3. Media advertisements (line c).
4. Mailings to members, legislators, or the public (line d). The amount of these expenses must be provided.
5. Publications, or published or broadcast statements (line e). The amount of these expenses must be provided.
6. Grants to other organizations for lobbying purposes (line f). The amount of these expenses must be provided.
7. Direct contact with legislators, their staffs, government officials, or a legislative body (line g). The amount of these expenses must be provided.
8. Rallies, demonstrations, seminars, conventions, speeches, lectures, or other means (line h). The amount of these expenses must be provided.

Total lobbying expenses are reported (line i). For each type of lobbying engaged in, the organization is required to attach a statement giving a detailed description of the activities.

A charitable organization that is subject to the expenditure test must indicate if it belongs to an affiliated group (Schedule A, Part VI-A, box a) and, if so, whether the *limited control* provisions are applicable.

The focus and purpose of this portion of the return is provision of the opportunity to make the various calculations that the expenditure test requires. Thus, the charity must report the following, for the year involved, both for the organization itself and for any affiliated group:

1. Total lobbying expenditures to influence public opinion (grass roots lobbying) (line 36).
2. Total lobbying expenditures to influence a legislative body (direct lobbying) (line 37).
3. Total lobbying expenditures (line 38, which is a total of the amounts on lines 36 and 37).

4. Other exempt purpose expenditures (line 39).

5. Total exempt purpose expenditures (line 40, which is a total of lines 38 and 39).

6. Direct lobbying nontaxable amount (line 41). The return includes a table for determining that amount.

7. Grassroots lobbying nontaxable amount (line 42). This amount is 25 percent of the amount on line 41.

8. Grassroots lobbying taxable amount, if any (line 43, which is line 36 less line 42).

9. Direct lobbying taxable amount, if any (line 44, which is line 38 less line 41).

NOTE: If there is an amount in the eighth or ninth of these items, the organization must file Form 4720, which is used to pay the expenditure test tax on lobbying outlays.

Most organizations that are subject to the expenditure test must also report lobbying amounts for the current year and the three immediately previous years, because these calculations are made on the basis of four-year averaging. Thus, there must be reporting of the numbers for the four years, plus the total, for the following:

1. Direct lobbying nontaxable amount (line 45).
2. Direct lobbying ceiling amount (line 46).
3. Total direct lobbying expenditures (line 47).
4. Grassroots lobbying nontaxable amount (line 48).
5. Grassroots lobbying ceiling amount (line 49).
6. Grassroots lobbying expenditures (line 50).

In addition, a public charity must report the amount of any tax paid during the year because of lobbying expenditures (Part VI, line 89a). This involves both the tax imposed by reason of the substantial part test and the one imposed as part of the expenditure test.

Q 8:32 Does the annual information return ask any questions about political activities?

Yes. The law makes a distinction between *political activities* and *political campaign activities*. Political campaign activities are participations or interventions on behalf of or in opposition to candidates for public office (Q 1:17). Political activities include political campaign activities and also embrace efforts such as support of or opposition to nominations for public office.

Every charitable and other tax-exempt organization that files the annual information return is required, if it, directly or indirectly, made any political expenditures during the year, to enter the amount on the return (Part VI, line 81a). The organization must also state, by a "yes" or "no" answer, whether it filed the political organization tax return (Form 1120-POL) for the year (line 81b). This is because these political expenditures may be taxable and that is the form by which the tax is reported.

Public charities are prohibited from engaging in political campaign activities. One sanction that can be applied if they do this is a tax. A public charity must report the amount of any tax paid during the year because of political campaign expenditures (Part VI, line 89a).

Q 8:33   What about ownership by a charitable organization of a taxable subsidiary?

An organization must answer "yes" or "no" to the question as to whether, at any time during the year, the organization owned a 50 percent or greater interest in a taxable corporation (Part VI, line 88) (Q 1:23). If the answer is "yes," another portion of the return must be completed.

This other portion of the return (Part IX) requires reporting of the name, address, and employer identification number of the corporation. The exempt organization is also required to state the percentage of its ownership interest in the corporation, as well as state the nature of the corporation's business activities, total income, and end-of-year assets.

Remember, there is a question generally inquiring into the organization's relationship with another organization (Q 8:35). That question would be answered "yes" in the instance of ownership of a taxable subsidiary and the other information sought by that question would have to be provided.

Q 8:34   What about the involvement of a charitable organization in a partnership?

An organization filing the annual information return must answer "yes" or "no" to the question as to whether, at any time during the year, the organization owned a 50 percent or greater interest in a partnership (Part VI, line 88) (Q 1:24). If the answer is "yes," another portion of the return must be completed.

This other portion of the return (Part IX) requires reporting of the name, address, and employer identification number of the partnership. The exempt organization is also required to state the percentage of its ownership interest in the partnership, as well as state the nature of the partnership's business activities, total income, and end-of-year assets.

Again, remember, there is a question generally inquiring into the organization's relationship with another organization (Q 8:35). That question would be answered "yes" in the instance of involvement of the organization in a partnership and the other information sought by that question would have to be provided.

Q 8:35   What about relationships with other organizations?

A question on the annual information return inquires as to whether the organization is related (other than by association with a statewide or nationwide organization) through common membership, governing bodies, trustees, officers, or other means to another organization (Part VI, line 80a). If the answer is "yes," a box indicating that answer must be checked, and the name of the organization must be provided, along with an indication as to whether the other organization is tax-exempt (line 80b). Otherwise, the question is answered "no."

There are, however, other questions on this subject. These include ownership of taxable subsidiaries (Q 8:33), involvement in partnerships (Q 8:34), grants and loans by public charities to other organizations, and transactions and relationships between public charities and other tax-exempt organizations.

Public charities are additionally required to provide information regarding transfers to, and transactions and relationships with, other tax-exempt organizations that are not charities (Form 990, Schedule A, Part VII).

NOTE: For this purpose, political organizations[29] are included as tax-exempt organizations.

The public charity is required to answer "yes" or "no" to the question as to whether it, directly or indirectly, engaged in any of the following transactions with noncharitable exempt organizations:

1. Transfers of cash (line 51a(i)).
2. Transfers of other assets (line 51a(ii)).
3. Sales of assets (line 51b(i)).
4. Purchases of assets (line 51b(ii)).
5. Rental of facilities or equipment (line 51b(iii)).
6. Reimbursements (line 51b(iv)).
7. Loans or loan guarantees (line 51b(v)).
8. Performance of services or membership or fund-raising solicitations (line 51b(vi)).
9. Sharing of facilities, equipment, mailing lists, other assets, or paid employees (line 51c).

If the answer to any of these nine questions is "yes," the organization must complete a schedule. This schedule must provide in columns, for each of the transactions being reported, the amount involved, the name of the noncharitable exempt organization, and a description of the transfers, transactions, and sharing arrangements. The *amount involved* (column (b)) can be the fair market value of the goods, other assets, or services provided by the organization. If the organization received less than fair market value in any transaction or sharing arrangement, it should reflect in the description (column (d)) the value of the goods, other assets, or services received.

TIP: For purposes of the intermediate sanctions rules, a noncharitable tax-exempt organization can be a disqualified person with respect to a public charity. Thus, the information provided in this portion of the return should be evaluated from that perspective.

The organization must also answer "yes" or "no" to a question as to whether it is, directly or indirectly, affiliated with or otherwise related to one or more noncharitable tax-exempt organizations (line 52a). If the answer is "yes," a schedule must be completed (line 52b). This schedule must provide the name of the noncharitable entity, its tax-exempt status, and a description of the relationship.

Q 8:36   What about the public inspection requirements?

There is a question on the return, which must be answered "yes" or "no," inquiring as to whether the organization complied with the public inspection requirements, both with respect to applications for recognition of exemption and annual information returns (Part VI, line 83a). Inasmuch as the law requires compliance with these requirements, the organization is well advised to answer this question in the affirmative if it possibly (and truthfully) can. The answer is "yes" even if there were no requests for the documents. If the answer must be "no," the assistance of a lawyer is advised.

Q 8:37   What if the organization received a contribution of services or a gift of the use of property?

The organization must answer "yes" or "no" to the question as to whether it received donated services or the use of materials, equipment, or facilities at no charge or at substantially less than fair rental value (Part VI, line 82a). If it did, it may indicate the value of these items on the return (line 82b).

TIP: As discussed (Q 8:12), the value of gifts of this nature cannot be included as revenue. Yet, the IRS has allowed the organization to disclose this value if it can be of importance to the organization or its constituency.

Q 8:38 How does the filing of the annual information return relate to the receipt of unrelated business income?

As noted, this return is an annual information return, not a tax return (Q 8:1). Thus, the details as to unrelated business income (Chapter 6) are not reported on this return, but on the unrelated business income tax return, which is Form 990-T.

Nonetheless, the annual information return requires the tax-exempt organization to answer "yes" or "no" to the question as to whether it had unrelated business gross income of $1,000 or more during the year covered by the return (Part VI, line 78a). If the answer is truthfully "no," that is the end of the matter. If the answer is "yes," the organization must answer "yes" or "no" to the question as to whether it filed a Form 990-T for the year (line 78b). The correct answer is "yes," because that is the basic criterion for filing the unrelated business income tax return. If the organization is forced to respond to this question with a "no," it is best advised to quickly remedy the deficiency and/or seek professional assistance.

Q 8:39 Does the annual information return require any additional information concerning general operations?

Yes. The organization must identify who has the care of its books and records, this person's telephone number, and the location of these books and records (Part VI, line 91). Also, a nonexempt charitable trust that is filing this return (Q 8:1) must check a box to this effect and report the amount of any tax-exempt interest that it received or accrued during the course of the year (line 92).

Q 8:40 Don't some states require that copies of the annual information return be filed with them?

That is true. Nearly all of the states have a charitable solicitation act which, among other requirements, mandates registration and annual reporting (Chapter 9). As part of these processes, some states require the filing of a copy of this annual information return. Other states permit the filing of this return instead of all or part of separate financial information if the organization wishes to do that. The organization is required to list the states in which a copy of the annual return is filed (Part VI, line 90).

Because the IRS has developed the annual information return in conjunction with state fund-raising regulation officials, it devotes a considerable amount of space in the return instructions advising about state and local filing requirements—even though the subject has no bearing whatsoever on the federal filing obligations. For example, the IRS advises organizations to consult the appropriate officials of state and local jurisdictions in which the organization does business to determine their filing requirements there. It is the view of the IRS that *doing business* in a jurisdiction may include any of the following:

- Soliciting contributions or grants by mail or otherwise from individuals, businesses, or other charitable organizations in the jurisdiction.
- Conducting programs in the jurisdiction.
- Having employees within the jurisdiction.
- Maintaining a checking account in the jurisdiction.
- Owning or renting property in the jurisdiction.

NOTE: The IRS is acting beyond the scope of its authority in proclaiming on this subject. The states are doing enough nutty things in the realm of charitable solicitation regulation; the matter need not be exacerbated by the IRS by suggesting additional theories for even more regulation. Moreover, it is by no means clear that solicitation of gifts by mail alone constitutes doing business in a jurisdiction.

Q 8:41   What can give rise to penalties on organizations concerning annual information returns?

Penalties can be imposed for failure to file the return, or for a late filing, an incorrect filing, or an incomplete filing.

Q 8:42   What are these penalties?

The basic penalty is $20 per day, not to exceed the smaller of $10,000 or 5 percent of the gross receipts of the organization for the year. A penalty will not be imposed in an instance of reasonable cause for the violation.[30]

However, an organization with annual gross receipts in excess of $1 million is subject to a penalty of $100 for each day the failure continues. The maximum penalty per return is $50,000.[31]

These penalties begin on the due date for filing the annual return.

> **TIP:** One way to avoid penalties is to complete all applicable line items. Each question on the return should be answered "yes," "no," or "N/A" (not applicable). An entry should be made on all total lines (including a zero when appropriate). "None" or "N/A" should be entered if an entire part does not apply.

Q 8:43 Are there any other consequences for nonfiling and the like?

Yes. The IRS takes the position that it can remove an organization from its Publication 78 if an annual information return is not filed.

> **NOTE:** Publication 78 is titled "Cumulative List of Organizations Described in Section 170(c) of the Internal Revenue Code." It thus is a registry of organizations to which deductible charitable gifts can be made. This publication is often relied on by donors and grantors, so removal from it can be of dire consequence to an organization.

> **TIP:** Contributions to an organization in this position continue to be deductible until the IRS publishes a notice to the contrary in the Internal Revenue Bulletin.

Obviously, the potential of this sanction is of no consequence to organizations that are not qualified charitable donees.

Q 8:44 Are there penalties on individuals as well as organizations for nonfiling and the like?

Yes. There is a separate penalty that may be imposed on *responsible persons*. This penalty is $10 per day, not to exceed $5,000. This penalty will not be levied in an instance of reasonable cause.[32]

> **TIP:** If the organization does not file a complete return or does not furnish correct information, it is the practice of the IRS to send the organization a letter that includes a fixed time to fulfill these requirements. After that period expires, the person failing to comply will be charged the penalty.

If more than one person is responsible, they are jointly and individually liable for the penalty.

There are other penalties, in the form of fines and imprisonment, for willfully not filing returns when they are required, and for filing fraudulent returns and statements with the IRS.

Q 8:45   What role should the professional fund-raiser play in the preparation of a charitable organization's annual information returns?

At the outset, it is probably safe to say that it is the common practice for charitable organizations to prepare their annual information returns without any involvement of a professional fund-raiser.

If the professional fund-raiser is an independent contractor (Q 7:2), it is highly unlikely that he or she would be involved in the preparation of a client charitable organization's annual returns. There may be some information that needs to be derived from the fund-raiser by the charity in preparation of the return but any other involvement by the fund-raiser in the process would be unusual.

If, however, the professional fund-raiser is an employee of the charitable organization, the ideal would be for the fund-raiser to participate in the process of preparation of the charity's annual information return. One approach would be for the preparer of the return to solicit specific information from the fund-raiser about the fund-raising program as part of preparation of the return. Another approach would be for the fund-raiser to review the return, once it is prepared in draft, for comments. If possible, both approaches should be utilized.

The point is, of course, that the professional fund-raiser has specific and unique information that is needed in preparation of the annual information return. Also, the fund-raiser may have some perspectives on the overall operations of the organization that would be of utility in preparation of the return.

Even if the professional fund-raiser is not involved in preparation of the annual information return, he or she should be aware of its contents. A prospective donor may have a question about the return, and it would be to the fund-raiser's credit if he or she had, at the ready, a credible response to the inquiry.

Unfortunately, as noted at the outset, the professional fund-raiser is rarely asked to participate in the preparation of the organization's annual information return. Likewise, it rarely occurs to the fund-raiser that he or she ought to be a part of this process.

CHAPTER 9

State Law Regulation

It is not a coincidence that the chapter on state law regulation of charitable fund-raising is the last one. All too many fund-raisers elect to ignore this subject—and thus may choose to pretend that this last chapter isn't in the book, or perhaps may go so far as to chop it out.

State law regulation is the bane of the fund-raisers' existence, particularly in cases of organizations that raise funds in several states. Compliance in this area is nightmarish for charities that engage in fund-raising nationwide. This body of law can be burdensome and tricky to comply with, as it entails a variety of differing definitions, forms, due dates, accounting rules, and the like.

Although this area of the law is well-known for rampant noncompliance, the professional fund-raiser should face the reality of state regulation. While penalties are rarely imposed, or are relatively small when they are, a charitable organization can be embarrassed if its failure to comport with this body of law is made public—particularly if that occurs in the middle of an otherwise successful fund-raising campaign.

Here are the questions most frequently asked by professional fund-raisers (or that should be asked by them) about state law regulation of fund-raising—and the answers to them.

Q 9:1   How do the states regulate fund-raising for charitable purposes?

The principal way in which states regulate the process of raising funds for charitable purposes is by means of their *charitable solicitation acts* (Q 9:2). There are 47 of these laws.

In addition to the panoply of solicitation acts, however, charitable organizations soliciting gift support from the public may have to face other state statutory or other regulatory requirements. These include:

1. A state's nonprofit corporation act, which has registration and annual reporting requirements. These laws are applicable to corporations that are formed in the particular state (*domestic corporations*) as well as to out-of-state corporations (*foreign corporations*) that are *doing business* within the state.

COMMENT: Generally, it is unclear whether the solicitation of charitable contributions in a foreign state alone constitutes doing business in that state. Some states provide, by statute, that fund-raising is the conduct of business activities in their jurisdictions. If the solicitation of charitable contributions was declared, as a matter of general law, a business transaction in the states, the compliance consequences would be enormous, considering the fact that nearly every state has a nonprofit corporation act. This type of a requirement would cause a charitable organization that is soliciting contributions in every state to register and report over 90 times each year, not taking into account federal and local law requirements!

---

2. A state insurance law, which may embody a requirement that a charitable organization writing charitable gift annuity contracts (Q 5:32) obtain a permit to do so and subsequently file annual statements.

3. A state's "blue sky" statute regulating securities offerings, which may be applicable to offers to sell and to sales of interests in, and the operation of, pooled income funds (Q 5:17). These laws may also apply with respect to charitable remainder trusts (Q 5:6).

4. A state's law prohibiting fraudulent advertising or other fraudulent or deceptive practices.

5. A state's version of the Uniform Supervision of Trustees for Charitable Purposes Act, which requires a charitable trust to file with the state attorney general a copy of its governing instrument, an inventory of the charitable assets, and an annual report. Of similar scope and effect are the state laws that invest the state attorney general with plenary investigative power over charitable organizations.

6. State law concerning charitable contribution deductions and eligibility for tax-exempt status as a charitable entity.

Q 9:2   What are the elements of a typical state *charitable solicitation act*?

These laws usually open with a set of definitions. The key terms defined are *charitable, solicitation* (a term very broadly defined to capture every type of fund-raising, whether or not successful), *contribution, professional fund-raiser* (Q 1:1), *professional solicitor* (Q 1:2), and *charitable sales promotion* (Q 9:7). The ambit of these laws—which is far-reaching—is basically set by the scope of the words *charitable* and *solicitation*. Charitable in this setting includes religious, education, arts promotion, and scientific purposes.

NOTE: Charitable in this context is given a much broader definition than in settings such as the federal tax law (Q 1:8). Some state laws are applicable to fund-raising by tax-exempt social welfare organizations (Q 1:18), business and professional associations (Q 1:19), and other types of nonprofit organizations. State laws can differ on the point (for example, some expressly exclude political fund-raising), so it is necessary to check each one that is applicable.

A key feature of these laws is *registration*. They almost always require soliciting charitable organizations to register, usually annually. There often is a registration fee. The information required by this process frequently is extensive; the states have devised required registration forms. Many of the states also require the registration of professional fund-raisers and/or professional solicitors. Some states mandate a bond for fund-raisers and/or solicitors.

TIP: The registration process frequently requires charitable organizations to identify any fund-raisers or solicitors they have hired. The states use this information to determine whether the fund-raiser or solicitor has registered. Charities are often required to provide a list of other states in which they are registered. The registration form for fund-raisers and solicitors usually requires them to identify the charities they are working with. The states cross-reference this information to see whether all parties are appropriately registered and bonded.

Another feature of these laws is annual *reporting*. Each year, charitable organizations are almost always required to submit extensive financial statements, either as part of an annual report or by means of annual registration. (Some states mandate both.) Annual reports may also be required of professional fund-raisers and professional solicitors.

In a few states, the laws require solicitors to submit more frequent reports, for example, following each fund-raising campaign.

Many of the state laws contain an extensive listing of *prohibited acts*. These are rules dictating certain fund-raising practices by charitable organizations—usually in the form of practices in which they may not engage. Some of these prohibited acts go beyond the realm of fund-raising and mandate certain actions (or nonactions) by charities and others generally. It is important for charities and those who assist them in the fund-raising process to review each of the applicable sets of these prohibitions.

A growing practice is for these laws to mandate the contents of *contracts* between soliciting charitable organizations and their professional fund-raisers and/or professional solicitors (Q 7:14, Q 9:11).

Another burgeoning requirement is the presentation of *legends*. These are notices, required by law, that must prominently appear on fund-raising literature and other appeals. The typical legend must state that information about the charity is available from the charity or the state; a registration number may be needed as part of the legend.

NOTE: This requirement of legends is becoming a problem for those making charitable solicitations by mail in several states. The differences in these legends are forcing the solicitation material to become cluttered, detracting from the purpose of the mailing.

Other components of the state laws include record-keeping requirements, disclosure rules, requirements as to financial accounts and sales of tickets, investigatory and injunctive powers by the state, and a range of civil and criminal sanctions.

Q 9:3   Do these laws apply to all charitable solicitations?

Yes, unless the solicitation is expressly exempted from the statutory requirements (Q 9:9). These laws apply where the solicitation is by means of the mail, telephone (telemarketing), facsimile, television, video, and radio, as well as in-person fund-raising. The medium used to solicit is not significant; the key is whether the activity is a solicitation. The fact that interstate commerce is involved is not per se a bar to state regulation.

Q 9:4   How do these laws apply to professional fund-raisers?

They apply to professional fund-raisers in a variety of ways. The basic application of these laws is, however, dependent on the definition of the term *professional fund-raiser*. First, not all states use that term; *profes-*

sional fund-raising counsel or *paid fund-raiser* may be used instead. Second, the definition of the term can vary. The most frequent definition is, as discussed (Q 1:1), "a person who for compensation plans, manages, advises, consults, or prepares material for, or with respect to, the solicitation in this state of contributions for a charitable organization, but who does not solicit contributions and who does not employ, procure, or engage any compensated person to solicit contributions."

NOTE: The states give this term broad application. Those who work in collateral fields should be cautious: they may inadvertently become regarded as fund-raisers and be subject to penalties for noncompliance with state law. Related fields include consulting in the areas of marketing, management, and public relations.

A bona fide salaried officer, employee, or volunteer of a charitable organization is not a professional fund-raiser, nor are lawyers, investment advisors, or bankers.

It is common for a state charitable solicitation act to impose the following requirements on a professional fund-raiser working for one or more charitable organizations: registration, bonding, annual reports, recordkeeping, and a contract with the charity.

Q 9:5   How do these laws apply to professional solicitors?

They apply to professional solicitors in a variety of ways. The basic application of these laws, however, is, like those pertaining to professional fund-raisers (Q 9:4), dependent on the definition of the term *professional solicitor*. First, not all states use that term; the terminology instead may be *paid solicitor* or *fund-raiser*. Second, the definition of the term can vary. The most frequent definition is "a person who for compensation performs for a charitable organization any service in connection with which contributions are, or will be, solicited in this state by such compensated person or by any compensated person he employs, procures, or engages, directly or indirectly, to solicit." There usually is an exclusion from this definition for officers, employees, and volunteers of charitable organizations.

NOTE: The states give this term broad application—even broader than for the term *professional fund-raiser*. Many individuals and firms that consider themselves professional fund-raisers are regarded by the state as professional solicitors because of their (ostensible) direct involvement in the solicitation process. For example, a fund-raiser who assists a charity

---

in placing solicitation material into the mail may, for that reason alone, be regarded as a solicitor. Those who work in collateral fields should be cautious: they may inadvertently become regarded as solicitors and be subject to penalties for noncompliance with state law. Related fields include consulting in the areas of marketing, management, and public relations. Lawyers are usually exempted from the definition by statute.

It is common for a state charitable solicitation act to impose the following requirements on a professional solicitor working for one or more charitable organizations: registration, bonding, annual reports, postcampaign reports, the filing of solicitation notices, recordkeeping, and a contract with the charity.

COMMENT: Because of greed and other abusive conduct in their ranks, professional solicitors do not enjoy positive reputations. They are in particular disfavor with state legislators and regulators. That is one of the reasons why fund-raisers are loath to be perceived as solicitors. More important, by heaping regulatory requirements on them, the states are endeavoring to drive paid solicitors for charity out of their jurisdictions. The laws of some states are so onerous that one wonders how a solicitor can profitably function in the gift solicitation task. Anyone who can avoid classification as a professional solicitor should do so.

Q 9:6   Do these laws place limitations on the fees paid to professional fund-raisers and professional solicitors?

No. This was a popular practice in the past—particularly where the limitation was in the form of a percentage limitation on compensation. This approach has, however, been determined to be unconstitutional, as an unwarranted violation of free speech rights.[1]

In this context, the past was not that long ago. Even into the mid-1990s, from time to time, a state would enact a law placing a percentage limitation on the amount of compensation and other funds that could be paid to a professional solicitor. The most recent example occurred in California, where the state legislature passed a statute that attempted to limit solicitors' fees to a maximum of 50 percent of the contributions collected for a charity. Laws of this type are, as noted, blatantly unconstitutional; this California law was promptly voided in 1995.[2]

In another of these examples, Kentucky enacted a law that placed a 50 percent limit on the amount of fees a charitable organization could pay a professional solicitor. In 1994, this law was struck down as being unconstitutional.[3]

Q 9:7   What is a *charitable sales promotion* and how do state laws apply to it?

The phrase *charitable sales promotion* is generally defined as "an advertising or sales campaign, conducted by a commercial co-venturer, which represents that the purchase or use of goods or services offered by the commercial co-venturer will benefit, in whole or in part, a charitable organization or purpose." A business enterprise usually will state to the general public that a portion of the purchase price derived from the sale of goods or services during a particular period will be donated to a charity or charities. A commercial co-venturer is a business entity (other than a professional fund-raiser or professional solicitor) that becomes involved in a charitable sales promotion.

NOTE: The term *commercial co-venturer*, though understandable as to its derivation, is unfortunate phraseology. It suggests that the charity involved is engaged in a *commercial* undertaking, which is not favorable from the charity's standpoint (Q 6:11). It further conveys the thought that the charity is in a joint venture, which also can have adverse legal consequences (Q 1:25).

For the most part, state law mandates accurate disclosure of the arrangement between the charitable organization and the commercial co-venturer. Some states' laws require a formal accounting by the commercial enterprise; two states mandate annual reporting and bonding.

This is an advantageous way for a charitable organization to receive a substantial gift (some of these promotions result in millions of dollars for charity), for a business enterprise to obtain some positive publicity, and for the public to feel that personal consumption of a product is of benefit to charitable programs. (The purchasers do not, however, receive any charitable contribution deduction.)

TIP: It is common for a commercial co-venturer to place a limit on the amount of funds that will be transferred to a charity as the result of a particular promotion. In most states, disclosure of this cap is all that is required. In some activist states, however, the practice is deemed misleading, in that purchases made toward the close of the promotion may not, in actuality, cause any funds to pass from the business to charity.

Q 9:8   **What is the significance of the provisions of these laws concerning *prohibited acts*?**

This aspect of these laws can be very extensive, with a delineation of over 20 *prohibited acts*. Some of these prohibitions specifically apply in the fund-raising setting. For example, it can be a prohibited act to misrepresent the purpose of a charitable solicitation, solicit contributions for a purpose other than that expressed in the fund-raising material, use a name or statement of another charitable organization where its use would tend to mislead a solicited person, lead anyone to believe that registration constitutes or implies an endorsement by the state, or enter into a contract with a person who is required to register under the state's law but who has failed to do so.

    These prohibitions may, however, apply more broadly in the realm of charitable operations. For example, it can be a prohibited act to misrepresent the purpose of a charitable organization, expend contributions in a manner inconsistent with a stated charitable purpose, violate any of the applicable provisions of the state's consumer fraud law, or engage in other unlawful acts or practices as the attorney general of the state may determine.

TIP: These prohibited acts rules are applicable with respect to any solicitation in the state. A charitable organization or other person soliciting in more than one state can find that there are numerous prohibited acts with which to contend.

Q 9:9   **Are there any exceptions to these laws?**

Almost always. The exceptions largely apply with respect to charitable organizations. Some states exempt certain types of charitable organizations from the entirety of these laws; others exempt them from only the registration and reporting requirements.

    The most common exception—for religious organizations—rests primarily on constitutional law grounds.

NOTE: Ironically, many of the abuses in the field of charitable fund-raising are committed in the name of religion.

    The next most common exception is for schools, colleges, and universities. Other entities that often have some form of exemption are health care providers, membership organizations, libraries, veterans' groups, and small organizations. Some states exempt small solicitations and fund-raising for a named individual.

NOTE: These exemptions are largely predicated on the reasonable premise that the organizations can be excused from the rigors of this regulation because those whom they solicit do not need the protections of the statute, due to their close relationship with and understanding of the charitable organization. At the same time, this approach leaves the remaining regulated charities unhappy with their burdens of compliance. Exemptions from state charitable solicitation acts can cause divisiveness in the world of public charities.

TIP: There are some traps in this area:

•These exemptions are not uniform; a charitable organization can be exempt in its home state, yet not in another state where it is also soliciting gifts.

•The membership exclusion cannot be utilized simply by making a donor a "member"; the state laws usually forbid that practice.

•Some universities, health care providers, and similar organizations conduct their fund-raising through related "foundations"; not all of the states that exempt these institutions likewise expressly exempt their affiliated foundations.

•A "small" solicitation in one state is not necessarily small in another; the thresholds range from $1,500 to $25,000.

Some states exempt charitable organizations by name. These laws are of questionable constitutionality; they may be violations of the equal protection doctrine.

TIP: An exception may not be automatic. In some states, a charitable organization must make application for exemption. In other states, an otherwise applicable exemption is not available where a charitable organization uses a professional fund-raiser or a professional solicitor.

Q 9:10   Do these laws apply to charitable solicitations over the Internet?

Reading state charitable solicitation acts (as well as county and city ordinances) literally, the answer must be yes.[4] These laws define the term *solicitation* broadly, to encompass every type of charitable fund-raising. No state statute exempts Internet solicitations from its purview.

NOTE: There is the argument that a mere request for contributions by means of a website is not a solicitation, because prospective donors have to affirmatively access the site to see the message. The contention is somewhat akin to stating that a request for contributions by mail is not a solicitation, because the prospective donor must affirmatively open the envelope. In other words, that argument is not likely to prevail.

The IRS has observed that for purposes of application of the unrelated business rules, the fact that the activity takes place over the Internet does not change the applicable principles of law. Here is what the IRS recently wrote: "[T]he use of the Internet to accomplish a particular task does not change the way the tax laws apply to that task. Advertising is still advertising and fund-raising is still fund-raising."[5] The same may be said for state fund-raising regulation laws: they apply to Internet fund-raising in the same manner in which they apply to solicitations by means of television, radio, direct mail, and the like—all of which are considered *solicitations* potentially requiring registration, reporting, and other forms of compliance.

In conjunction with that observation, the IRS gave us a marvelous understatement (having said that charitable fund-raising on websites raises no "novel tax issues"): "For the charities themselves, a greater concern may be the applicability of state and local laws requiring registration before soliciting contributions. There is some concern that states and local governments will argue that if any resident of their jurisdiction can access a website and thus see a solicitation, the charity must register."[6]

That pretty much sums it up. Once a solicitation is posted on the Internet, presumably everyone with a computer with Internet access has been solicited. Among other outcomes, that would require registration, etc., pursuant to every state and local charitable solicitation act and ordinance (unless some exception was available (Q 9:9)). No state or local jurisdiction, however, has yet adopted that stance, but think of the time and financial burdens were that to happen!

Q 9:11   What provisions are generally required by these laws in a contract between a charitable organization and a professional fund-raiser or professional solicitor?

The most common provisions that a state will require, in a contract between a charitable organization and a fund-raiser or solicitor, are a statement of the respective obligations of the parties; a statement of the fees that are to be paid by the charitable organization; the projected beginning and end dates of the solicitation; a statement as to whether the fund-raiser or solicitor will have custody of contributions; a statement of the percentage of gross revenue from which the fund-raiser or solicitor will be compensated; the bank location and the number of the account in which all funds from the solicitation will be deposited; and any other information that the attorney general may prescribe.

Q 9:12   When does a charitable organization have to comply with one of these laws?

Assuming the charitable organization is not exempt from the requirement (Q 9:9), it must comply with a charitable solicitation act in a state when it is soliciting contributions in that state. At a minimum, the applicable law is that of the state in which the soliciting charitable organization is located. It is rare for a charity to solicit contributions only outside of the state in which it is headquartered. A soliciting charitable organization should first endeavor to be in compliance with the fund-raising regulation law in the state in which it is based.

NOTE: An argument that a state's law is inapplicable because the charity is only using the U.S. mail or because the fund-raising involves interstate commerce will fail. The state's police power enables it to regulate in this field as long as the forms of regulation are sufficiently narrow (Q 9:3).

Q 9:13   When does a professional fund-raiser or a professional solicitor have to comply with one of these laws?

The considerations regarding compliance are much the same as those for charitable organizations (Q 9:12). A fund-raiser or solicitor may not be assisting a charitable organization in the state where the fund-raiser or solicitor is based. Although this would be infrequent, the state law may nonetheless apply. Each state's law must be examined to see how it treats this subtlety.

Q 9:14   When does a charitable organization have to comply with more than one of these laws?

This is a subject of some confusion and frustration. Basically, the law is that a charitable organization, unless exempted from the requirement

(Q 9:9), must comply with *each* of the charitable solicitation acts in force in the states in which it is soliciting contributions. A charitable organization engaged in fund-raising in all of the states and the District of Columbia may have to comply annually with over 40 of these laws (in addition to nonprofit corporation acts and other state and local laws that may apply in the fund-raising context).

TIP: Soliciting charitable organizations also are supposed to be in compliance with the thousands of county, city, and town charitable solicitation ordinances in effect throughout the country. Some charitable organizations comply with some of these local ordinances, but, undoubtedly, no organization is in full compliance in this regard. State law compliance is difficult enough; the staff required to cope with all the local regulations would be extensive.

There is no lawful way to avoid this extent of multistate enforcement. These laws are based on the states' police power (Q 9:3) and have been generally upheld in the face of challenges as to their constitutionality. There is no legitimate authority—based on concepts of interstate commerce or other theory—for the proposition that these laws are inapplicable to charitable organizations raising funds on a multistate basis.

Q 9:15   Are solicitations of merely a few individuals subject to these state laws?

Technically, yes. Although these laws are designed to protect the *public* (Q 9:18), most of them literally apply irrespective of the number of persons solicited. An argument can be made that these laws do not apply to *private* solicitations, but there is no case law supportive of the assertion. Only a few states have addressed the subject, usually by exempting a charitable solicitation from the registration and reporting requirements where the organization does not intend to annually receive contributions from more than 10 persons. Two states exempt a solicitation where no more than 100 persons are solicited. Some states attempt to resolve this dilemma by exempting small (in terms of total funds collected) solicitations; these thresholds range from $1,500 to $25,000.

Q 9:16   When does a professional fund-raiser or professional solicitor have to comply with more than one of these laws?

The considerations here are basically the same as with charitable organizations (Q 9:14). That is, a fund-raiser or solicitor must be in compliance with these laws in every state in which it is working with a charitable organization to assist it in raising funds. Usually, however, where the charitable organization is exempt from the requirements (Q 9:9), so too is the professional fund-raiser and/or professional solicitor.

Q 9:17 What happens when a charitable organization, professional fund-raiser, or professional solicitor violates one of these laws?

The general practice—although not reflected in any statute—is that when a state regulatory office discovers a violation of the state's charitable solicitation act, the office will contact the offending party and request compliance. This approach is usually taken, for example, when a person is required to register in the state but has not. Where the violation is more egregious, such as the commission of a fraud, the reaction of the state authorities would likely be sterner.

If the violation is willful or ongoing, and persists despite polite requests to come into compliance, most of the state regulators have the authority to obtain an injunction and enjoin the practice that is contravening the law. For example, if a charitable organization is fund-raising in a state without having first registered there, the state's attorney general could enjoin the solicitation until compliance has been achieved. Likewise, a professional solicitor could find the solicitation enjoined if the solicitor's contract with the charity is not in conformity with the state's requirements.

A host of civil and criminal law penalties can come into play as well. These sanctions are civil fines and imprisonment; both can apply.

NOTE: Despite the enforcement that exists—the intensity of which varies from state to state—many charitable organizations, professional fund-raisers, and professional solicitors are not adhering to state laws or are only in partial compliance. Just as few states have the resources necessary to fully enforce these laws, most charitable organizations lack the capacity to fully comply with them. There are more outlaws in this field of the law than in any other applicable to nonprofit organizations.

Q 9:18 What is the rationale for these state laws?

The state charitable solicitation acts are intended to protect the public from fund-raising in the name of charity that is fraudulent or otherwise misrepresentative as to its purpose. Some of the preambles to this type of legislation grandly resonate with this approach to consumer protection. For example, the preamble to the statute in the California law states that "there exists in the area of solicitations and sales solicitations for charitable purposes a condition which has worked fraud, deceit, and imposition upon the people of the state." The legislature in Colorado concluded that "fraudulent charitable solicitations are a widespread practice in this state which results in millions of dollars of losses to contributors and legitimate charities each year." The latter preamble adds: "Legitimate charities are harmed by such fraud because the money available for contributions continually is being siphoned off by fraudulent charities, and the goodwill and confidence of contributors continually is being undermined by the practices of unscrupulous solicitors."

Q 9:19   Are these state laws effective?

No. The purpose of these laws is to protect people from fake charities and unscrupulous fund-raisers by deterring unlawful activity and punishing the illegalities that do occur (Q 9:18). These laws keep increasing in number and complexity, but they are having little impact on abusive practices. The chief imprint these laws are placing on the charitable sector is in the form of administrative burdens (including diversions of funds from charitable programs) on legitimate charities.

The story line that describes these laws as being effective is a myth fostered by the regulatory community. On occasion, the courts will accept the rationale. In the most recent example, a court upheld the constitutionality of a registration fee imposed on fund-raising charitable organizations on the ground that it is a "user fee." The court wrote that the charitable solicitation acts enhance "donor confidence" by "eliminating illegitimate charities."[7]

The states focus intently in this area, yet the "big picture" is often missed. Episodes such as those affecting the United Way of America and the New Era for Philanthropy Foundation unfold; state law enforcement misses them completely.

The truth is that no one knows the full extent of the ineffectiveness of these laws. More fundamentally, there are no respectable data that might reveal the magnitude of the problem these laws are supposed to rectify and prevent. It is astonishing that these laws are evolving so quickly and becoming so intricate, when there are absolutely no definitions of the reason for their existence. Research in these areas is long overdue.

Q 9:20   To be in compliance with these laws, what type of management system should a charitable organization have?

A charitable organization that is soliciting contributions in several states and wishes to be in full compliance with the law of those states needs to take several steps.

1. The organization should obtain a copy of the charitable solicitation act in effect in each of the states. It should determine, with the assistance of a lawyer if necessary, what its various obligations are under each of these laws. At a minimum, the organization should ascertain whether any exceptions are available to it, principally with respect to registration and reporting requirements (Q 9:9). Some of these laws are amplified by rules and regulations, and the charitable organization or its lawyer should have these sets of additional law to refer to in interpreting the statutes. Some court opinions may pertain to these laws as well.

2. Once the organization has determined which of these states have registration requirements that are applicable to it, it should obtain, prepare, and file the necessary registration forms. This should be done in advance of solicitation, and the organization should be certain to pay the requisite registration fee and obtain all required bonds.

3. If the organization is using the services of a professional fundraiser and/or professional solicitor, it should make a reasonable effort to see to it that each of these persons is adhering to these laws as well (Q 9:13, Q 9:16). Although, technically, the responsibility for compliance is on these persons and not the charity, the charity does not want legal difficulties to thwart a fundraising effort.

4. If the organization is subject to one or more reporting requirements, it should be certain that its financial records are properly maintained. Particular emphasis should be placed on fund-raising costs, so that the organization knows precisely what its solicitation expenses are. If the entity has costs that are allocated between fund-raising and program, it should obtain the services of an accountant who is knowledgeable as to those rules. The due dates for the state forms will vary. To remain in timely compliance with the filing requirements, the organization should have a system for self-notification as the dates draw near.

5. If the charitable organization is being assisted by a professional fund-raiser or professional solicitor, it should execute a written contract between itself and that person (or persons). Furthermore, the organization should see to it that the contract (or contracts) has all of the provisions that are required by states' laws (Q 9:11). These considerations may also apply to relationships with commercial co-venturers (Q 9:7).

6. The organization should be certain that its solicitation materials contain any and all of the applicable legends (Q 9:2).

7. The organization should review the list of prohibited acts in each of these applicable laws (Q 9:8) and be certain that it is in conformity with them.

8. The organization should endeavor to be in compliance with the applicable record-keeping requirements.

There are other aspects of these laws that the charitable organization should monitor. Among them is the receipt of copies of all materials that affiliated parties file with the states, such as the solicitation notices filed by professional solicitors and reports filed by commercial co-venturers.

Q 9:21   How does state law regulation interrelate with the oversight activities of the watch-dog agencies?

The standards promulgated by the "voluntary" watchdog agencies—such as the Philanthropic Advisory Service of the Better Business Bureaus and the National Charities Information Bureau—are not law.

NOTE: The word *voluntary* is in quotes because, despite what these agencies say, the charities caught up in standards enforcement are not doing so voluntarily. The motive of these charities is fear. The credibility these agencies have with funders and the media is such that levels of gifts and grants can plummet due to the adverse publicity that these agencies can quickly generate if their standards are not adhered to—to the letter.

Thus, since these standards are not rules of law, charities are not obligated to comply with them. As noted, however, compliance is coerced. One of the many flaws of these standards is that they can be inconsistent with legal requirements and contrary to good management practices. Attracted by the simplicity of ascertaining charities' fund-raising cost, the standards tend to highlight the subject of these costs; this seems to be where public charities are the most vulnerable, which contributes to their obsequiousness.

Also, state regulators often look to these agencies' lists to see who is compliant and who is not. Furthermore, state authorities have been known to alert one or more of the watchdog agencies as to charities who may be transgressing the law. Some argue that this form of regulation is preferable to that by government, but government regulation of fund-raising has hardly been abated by the watchdog groups (or any other force).

Endnotes

CHAPTER 1

1 See Hopkins, *The Law of Fund-Raising, Second Edition* (New York: John Wiley & Sons, 1996) (*The Law of Fund-Raising*), Chapter 4 § 1(g).

2 NSFRE Bylaws, Article IV, B.1.

3 This definition appears in the law in the state of Minnesota. Also *The Law of Fund-Raising*, Chapter 4 § 1(g).

4 *The Law of Fund-Raising*, Chapter 4 § 1(h).

5 This definition appears in the law in the state of Virginia.

6 *The Law of Fund-Raising*, Chapter 4 § 1(i).

7 This definition appears in the law in the state of New Hampshire.

8 Internal Revenue Code of 1986, as amended, section 4911(e)(1)(C). Throughout, "IRC §" is used to designate sections of the Code.

9 Income Tax Regulations (Reg.) § 56.4911-4(f)(1). Also *The Law of Fund-Raising*, Chapter 6 § 9.

10 IRC § 509(a)(2)(A)(i).

11 IRC § 509(a)(2)(A)(ii).

12 See *The Legal Answer Book for Nonprofit Organizations* (New York: John Wiley & Sons, 1996) (*LAB I*), Chapter 1. The concept of a *nonprofit organization*, and the legal and political philosophy underlying it, is summarized in Chapter 1 of Hopkins, *The Law of Tax-Exempt Organizations, Seventh Edition* (New York: John Wiley & Sons, 1998) (*The Law of Tax-Exempt Organizations*).

13 These organizations are generally described in IRC § 501(c). Exemption from the federal income tax is authorized in IRC § 501(a). Nearly all categories of tax-exempt organizations are listed in IRC § 501(c). The various types of tax-exempt organizations are summarized in *The Law of Tax-Exempt Organizations*.

14 IRC § 501(m).

15 IRC §§ 4940–4945. See Hopkins & Blazek, *Private Foundations: Tax Law and Compliance* (New York: John Wiley & Sons, 1997) (*Private Foundations*), particularly Chapters 5–10.

16 See Hopkins, *The Law of Tax-Exempt Organizations*, Chapter 5 § 3.

17 Reg. § 1.501(c)(3)-1(d)(2).

18 *Green v. Connally*, 330 F. Supp. 1150, 1160 (D.D.C. 1971), *aff'd sub nom., Coit v. Green*, 404 U.S. 997 (1971).

19 Reg. § 1.501(c)(3)-1(d)(2). Also *The Law of Tax-Exempt Organizations*, Chapter 6 § 1.

20 IRS Revenue Procedure (Rev. Proc.) 96-32. 1996-1 C.B. 717.

21 Reg. § 1.501(c)(3)-1(d)(2). Also *The Law of Tax-Exempt Organizations*, Chapter 6 § 3.

22 IRS Private Letter Ruling (Priv. Ltr. Rul.) 9530024.

23 E.g., IRS Revenue Ruling (Rev. Rul.) 76-204, 1976-1 C.B. 152.

24 Reg. § 1.501(c)(3)-1(d)(2). Also *The Law of Tax-Exempt Organizations*, Chapter 6 § 6.

25 Rev. Rul. 69-545, 1969-2 C.B. 117.

26 IRC § 170(c)(2).

27 IRC § 501(c)(3).

28 *Better Business Bureau of Washington, D.C. v. United States*, 326 U.S. 279 (1945).

29 *The Law of Tax-Exempt Organizations*, Chapter 4 § 4.

30 E.g., *The Nationalist Movement v. Commissioner*, 37 F.3d 216 (5th Cir. 1994).

31 IRS Technical Advice Memorandum (Tech. Adv. Mem.) 9711003.

32 IRC § 501(c)(25)(G)(ii).

33 IRC § 501(c)(3).

34 *United Cancer Council v. Commissioner*, 109 T.C. 326 (1997).

35 *United Cancer Council v. Commissioner*, 165 F.3d 1173 (7th Cir. 1999).

36 IRC § 4958. *The Second Legal Answer Book for Fund-Raisers (SLAB-FR)* will contain a chapter on the excess benefit transactions rules (intermediate sanctions), with emphasis on the application of them in the fund-raising context.

37 IRC § 4946.

38 IRS General Counsel Memorandum (Gen. Couns. Mem.) 38459.

39 Gen. Couns. Mem. 39862.

40 Gen. Couns. Mem. 35855.

41 E.g., *Carter v. United States*, 973 F.2d 1479 (9th Cir. 1992).

42 E.g., *Prince Edward School Foundation v. United States*, 80-1 U.S.T.C. ¶ 9295 (D.D.C. 1980), *aff'd in unpublished opinion* (D.C. Cir. 1981), *cert. den.*, 450 U.S. 944 (1981).

43 Reg. § 1.501(c)(3)-1(a)(1).

44 *American Campaign Academy v. Commissioner*, 92 T.C. 1053 (1989).

45 Reg. § 1.162-15(b).

46 Reg. § 1.170A-1(c)(5).

47 *SLAB-FR* will contain a summary of the charitable gift substantiation rules; there is a brief review of them in Q 4:37.

48 *SLAB-FR* will contain a summary of the quid pro quo contribution rules; there is a brief review of them in Q 4:38.

49 See *LAB 1*, Chapter 4.

50 IRC § 501(c)(3).

51 IRC § 4945(d)(1), (e).

52 Reg. § 1.501(c)(3)-1(c)(3)(ii).

53 IRC § 4911(d)(1)(B); Reg. § 56.4911-2(b)(1)(i).

54 IRC § 4911(d)(1)(A); Reg. § 56.4911-2(b)(2)(i).

55 See *The Law of Tax-Exempt Organizations*, Chapter 20 §§ 1(a), 2(b).

56 IRC § 4911(c)(2); Reg. § 56.4911-1 *et seq.*

57 See *The Law of Tax-Exempt Organizations*, Chapter 7.

58 IRC § 4911(d)(2)(B); Reg. § 56.4911-2(c)(3)); Rev. Rul. 70-449, 1970-2 C.B. 111.

59 IRC § 4911(d)(2).

60 IRC § 4912.

61 IRC § 4911(a)(1).

62 IRC § 501(h)(1), (2).

63 IRC § 501(c)(3).

64 Reg. § 1.501(c)(3)-1(c)(3)(iii).

65 IRC § 4945(d)(2).

66 Tech. Adv. Mem. 9609007.

67 Reg. § 1.501(c)(3)-1(c)(3)(iii).

68 *Norris v. United States*, 86 F.2d 379, 382 (8th Cir. 1936), *rev'd on other grounds*, 300 U.S. 564 (1937).

69 Reg. § 53.4946-1(g)(2)(i).

70 *Branch Ministries v. United States*, 40 F. Supp. 2d 15 (D.D.C. 1999).

71 IRC § 4955.

72 Priv. Ltr. Rul. 9725036.

73 IRC § 501(c)(4). See *The Second Legal Answer Book for Nonprofit Organizations (LAB 2)*, Chapter 6.

74 Reg. § 1.501(c)(4)-1(a)(2)(ii).

75 *Id.*

76 *Id.*
77 Reg. § 1.501(c)(4)-1(a)(2)(i).
78 See *LAB 2*, Q 6:15, Q 6:16.
79 IRC § 501(c)(6). See *LAB 2*, Chapter 5.
80 Reg. § 1.501(c)(6)-1.
81 IRC § 11.
82 IRC §§ 301-385.
83 IRC § 1361(a)(2).
84 IRC §§ 1361-1379.
85 IRC § 1362.
86 IRC § 1361(a)(1).
87 IRC § 1361(b)(1)(A), (C), (D).
88 IRC § 1361(b)(1)(B), (c)(6).
89 IRC § 1366.
90 See *LAB 1*, Chapter 4, Q 4:26.
91 See *LAB 2*, Chapter 8.
92 Gen. Couns. Mem. 39694.
93 IRC § 527(f)(1).
94 These organizations are described in IRC § 501(c)(2) and (25). See *The Law of Tax-Exempt Organizations*, Chapter 18 § 2.
95 These organizations are described in IRC § 501(c)(9), (17), and (21). See *The Law of Tax-Exempt Organizations*, Chapter 16.
96 See *LAB 1*, Chapter 11.
97 E.g., *American Society of Travel Agents v. Simon*, 435 U.S. 947 (1978).
98 The matter of travel tours is the subject of proposed regulations (REG-121268-97) and IRS pronouncements (e.g., Tech. Adv. Mem. 9702004).
99 The matter of fitness centers is the subject of IRS pronouncements (e.g., Tech. Adv. Mem. 8505002).
100 Priv. Ltr. Rul. 9335057.
101 IRC § 512(b)(1)-(3), (5). See *LAB 1*, Chapter 10, particularly Q 10:23–10:27.
102 IRC § 512(b)(13).
103 See *The Law of Tax-Exempt Organizations*, Chapters 27 § 1(n), 31.3. A summary of prior law is in *LAB 1*, Q 10:8.
104 IRC § 512(b)(13)(D)(i).
105 IRC § 318.
106 IRC § 512(b)(13)(D)(ii).
107 IRC § 512(b)(13)(A).
108 *Id.*
109 IRC § 337(b)(2).
110 IRC § 337(d); Reg. § 1.337(d)-4 (effective January 28, 1999).
111 See *LAB 2*, Chapter 3, particularly Q 3:1–3:3.

112 IRC §§ 701, 702.

113 Rev. Rul. 98-15, 1998-12 I.R.B. 6.

114 E.g., Priv. Ltr. Rul. 9722032.

115 Priv. Ltr. Rul. 8938001.

116 See *The Law of Tax-Exempt Organizations*, Chapter 32 § 2.

117 Reg. § 1.501(c)(3)-1(a)(1).

118 *Butler v. Commissioner*, 36 T.C. 1097 (1961).

119 Rev. Rul. 98-15, *supra* endnote 113.

120 Priv. Ltr. Rul. 7820058.

121 IRC § 512(c)(1).

122 IRC § 168(h)(6)(A)(i).

123 IRC § 512(c).

124 E.g., *Service Bolt & Nut Co. Profit Sharing Trust v. Commissioner*, 724 F.2d 519 (6th Cir. 1983).

125 See *LAB 2*, Chapter 3, particularly Q 3:22–3:28.

126 *Whiteford v. United States*, 61-1 U.S.T.C. ¶ 9301 (D. Kan. 1960).

127 *Commissioner v. Tower*, 327 U.S. 280, 286–287 (1946).

128 *Id.* at 287.

129 *Harlan E. Moore Charitable Trust v. United States*, 812 F. Supp. 130 (C.D. Ill. 1993), *aff'd*, 9 F.3d 623 (7th Cir. 1993).

130 *Trust U/W Emily Oblinger v. Commissioner*, 100 T.C. 114, 118 (1993).

131 *Id.*

132 *Id.*

133 *Id.* at 118–119.

134 *Id.* at 119.

135 IRC § 512(b)(2).

136 See *The Law of Tax-Exempt Organizations*, Chapter 27 § 1(a).

137 E.g., Tech. Adv. Mem. 9509002.

138 *Sierra Club v. Commissioner*, 65 T.C.M. 2582 (1993), *aff'd*, 86 F.3d 1526 (9th Cir. 1996).

139 *Sierra Club v. Commissioner*, 103 T.C. 307 (1994), *rev'd and rem'd*, 86 F.3d 1526 (9th Cir. 1996), 77 T.C.M. 1569 (1999) (where the Tax Court again found the revenue to be royalty income).

140 *United Cancer Council v. Commissioner*, *supra* endnote 34, *rev'd*, *supra* note 35.

141 Rev. Rul. 98-15, *supra* endnote 113.

142 Priv. Ltr. Rul. 9839039.

143 *Minnesota Tea Co. v. Helvering*, 302 U.S. 609, 613 (1938).

144 *Gregory v. Helvering*, 293 U.S. 465, 470 (1935).

145 *Commissioner v. Clark*, 489 U.S. 726, 738 (1989).

146 E.g., *Kornfeld v. Commissioner*, 137 F.3d 1231 (10th Cir. 1998), *cert. den.*, 119 S. Ct. 171 (1998).

147 *Greene v. United States*, 13 F.3d 577, 584 (2d Cir. 1994).

148 *Id.*

149 *Associated Wholesale Grocers, Inc. v. United States*, 927 F.2d 1517, 1523 (10th Cir. 1991).

150 *Greene v. United States, supra* endnote 147 at 583.

151 E.g., *Martin v. Machiz*, 251 F. Supp. 381 (D. Md. 1966).

152 *Humacid Co. v. Commissioner*, 42 T.C. 894, 913 (1964).

153 *Grove v. Commissioner*, 490 F.2d 241, 246 (2d Cir. 1973).

154 *Id.* at 247.

155 Reg. § 1.170A-13(c)(3)(i).

156 Reg. § 1.170A-13(c)(2).

CHAPTER 2

1 IRC §§ 508(b), 509(a).

2 IRC § 509(a)(1)-(4).

3 IRC §§ 4940–4948.

4 IRC §§ 170(b)(1)(A)(i)-(v), 509(a)(i).

5 Form 1023, Part III, questions 7–13.

6 Form 990, Part IV.

7 IRC § 4945(d)(4)(B), (h).

8 IRC § 4942.

9 IRC § 170(b).

10 IRC §§ 4941–4945. See *Private Foundations*, Chapters 5–9.

11 IRC § 4940. See *Private Foundations*, Chapter 10.

12 Form 990-PF; IRC § 6033(c). See *Private Foundations*, Chapter 12.

13 IRC § 6104(d). The law is changing in this regard, however, and in 2000 private foundations will be subject to the same document disclosure rules as other tax-exempt organizations. *SLAB-FR* will contain a summary of these rules.

14 IRC §§ 170(b)(1)(A)(vi), 509(a)(1); Reg. § 1.170A-9(e).

15 Reg. § 1.170A-9(e)(3).

16 Reg. § 1.170A-9(3)(10)-(14).

17 IRC § 509(a)(2); Reg. § 1.509(a)-3.

18 IRC § 509(d).

19 IRC § 509(a)(2)(A)(i).

20 IRC § 4946.

21 IRC § 507(d)(2).

22 IRC § 509(a)(2)(A)(ii); Reg. § 1.509(a)-3(a)(3).

23 IRC § 509(a)(2)(B).

24 Form 1023, instructions as to line 11.

25 Form 8734.

26 Form 1023, instructions as to line 11.

27 IRC § 642(c)(5)(A).

28 Reg. § 1.642(c)-5(a)(5)(iv).

29 IRC § 4942(j)(3).

30 IRC § 4940(d).

31 IRC § 509(a)(3); Reg. § 1.509(a)(4).

32 Reg. § 1.509(a)-4(c).

33 Reg. § 1.509(a)-4(e).

34 Reg. § 1.509(a)-4(f)(2).

35 Reg. § 1.509(a)-4(g).

36 Reg. § 1.509(a)-4(h).

37 Reg. § 1.509(a)-4(i).

38 Reg. § 1.509(a)-4(i)(2).

39 Reg. § 1.509(a)-4(i)(3).

40 Reg. § 1.509(a)-4(1)(3)(iii); Rev. Rul. 76-208, 1976-1 C.B. 161.

41 Reg. § 1.509(a)-4(e)(2).

42 E.g., Priv. Ltr. Rul. 8825116.

43 There are tens of IRS private letter rulings on this point (see *Private Foundations*, Chapter 15, citations accompanying note 265). Serious consideration was once given to creation of a separate category of public charity status just for entities of this nature (new IRC § 509(a)(4)).

44 Priv. Ltr. Rul. 9442025.

45 Priv. Ltr. Rul. 9438013.

46 Tech. Adv. Mem. 9847002.

47 Reg. § 1.509(a)-4(d).

48 *William F., Mable E., and Margaret K. Quarrie Charitable Fund v. Commissioner*, 70 T.C. 182 (1978), *aff'd*, 603 F.2d 1274 (7th Cir. 1979).

49 Reg. § 1.509(a)-4(e)(1).

50 IRC § 509(a)(3)(A).

51 Reg. § 1.509(a)-4(e)(1).

52 This is an organization that is tax-exempt by reason of IRC § 501(c)(5). See *The Law of Tax-Exempt Organizations*, Chapter 15 § 1.

53 IRC § 509(a)(3)(C); Reg. § 1.509(a)-4(j).

54 Rev. Rul. 80-207, 1980-2 C.B. 193.

55 Rev. Rul. 305, 1980-2 C.B. 71.

56 See *LAB 1*, Chapter 2, Q 2:41.

57 See *LAB 1*, Chapter 1, Q 1:19.

58 IRS Exempt Organization Continuing Professional Education Text for Fiscal Year 2000 (IRS CPE Text FY 2000), Technical Topic P, § D(1).

59 Langley, "Gimme Shelter—The SO [supporting organization] Trend: How to Succeed in Charity Without Really Giving," *The Wall Street Journal*, May 29, 1998.

60 IRS CPE Text FY 2000, *supra* endnote 58.
61 *Id.*
62 IRC §§ 6700, 6701.

CHAPTER 3

1 See *The Law of Tax-Exempt Organizations*, Appendix C.
2 See *The Law of Tax-Exempt Organizations*, Chapter 23 § 1.
3 IRC § 6033.
4 These are organizations that are tax-exempt by reason of IRC § 501(c)(5). See *The Law of Tax-Exempt Organizations*, Chapter 15 § 1.
5 These are organizations that are tax-exempt by reason of IRC § 501(c)(7). See *The Law of Tax-Exempt Organizations*, Chapter 14.
6 These are organizations that are tax-exempt by reason of IRC § 501(c)(19). See *The Law of Tax-Exempt Organizations*, Chapter 18 § 10.
7 Rev. Rul. 80-108, 1980-1 C.B. 119.
8 Reg. § 1.501(a)-1(a)(2).
9 Rev. Proc. 90-27, 1990-1 C.B. 514 § 3.02.
10 *Id.*
11 IRC § 6104(d). A summary of this disclosure and distribution rule will be in *SLAB-FR*.
12 Reg. § 1.508-1(a)(2)(i).
13 Rev. Rul. 80-108, *supra* endnote 7.
14 Rev. Proc. 92-85, 1992-2 C.B. 490.
15 IRC § 508(c).
16 IRC § 4940.

CHAPTER 4

1 IRC § 501(c)(3). See *The Law of Tax-Exempt Organizations*, Chapter 10 § 3.
2 IRC § 170(c).
3 IRC § 62.
4 IRC § 170(b)(1)(F). The carryback rules are the subject of IRC § 172.
5 IRC § 170(b)(1)(A).
6 IRC § 170(d)(1).
7 IRC § 68.
8 IRC § 170(b)(1)(B).
9 *Id.*
10 IRC § 170(b)(1)(A).
11 IRC § 170(b)(1)(C)(i).
12 IRC § 170(b)(1)(C)(ii).

13 See Hopkins, *The Tax Law of Charitable Giving, Second Edition* (New York: John Wiley & Sons, 2000) (*The Tax Law of Charitable Giving*), Chapter 4 § 2.

14 IRC § 1222(4). The term *capital gain property* is defined in IRC § 170(b)(1)(C)(iv).

15 IRC § 170(e)(1).

16 IRC § 170(b)(1)(C)(iii).

17 IRC § 170(b)(1)(D)(i).

18 IRC § 170(b)(1)(D)(ii).

19 IRC § 170(e)(1)(B)(ii).

20 IRC § 170(e)(5).

21 IRC § 170(b)(2).

22 IRC § 170(d)(2).

23 IRC § 170(e)(6)(F).

24 IRC § 170(e)(1)(A).

25 IRC § 170(e)(3).

26 IRC § 170(e)(3)(A).

27 IRC § 170(e)(3)(B)(i).

28 IRC § 170(e)(3)(B)(ii).

29 Abelson, "In a Wave of Balkan Charity Comes Drug Aid of Little Use," *The New York Times*, June 29, 1999, at A1, A8.

30 IRC § 1221(1).

31 *Id.*

32 IRC § 122(2).

33 *Id.*

34 Reg. § 1.170A-4A(b)(2)(ii).

35 Tech. Adv. Mem. 9631005.

36 See *supra* endnote 29.

37 IRC 170(a)(2).

38 Reg. § 1.170A-11(b)(2).

39 Priv. Ltr. Rul. 7802001.

40 IRC § 703(a)(2)(C).

41 IRC § 702(a)(4); Reg. §§ 1.702-1(a)(4), 1.703-1(a)(2)(iv).

42 Reg. § 1.170A-1(h)(7).

43 IRC § 705(a)(2).

44 IRC § 705(a)(1).

45 IRC § 705(a)(2).

46 IRC § 705(a)(1)(B), (a)(2)(B).

47 IRC § 705(a)(1)(B).

48 IRC § 705(a)(2)(B).

49 IRC § 7701(a)(2); Reg. § 7701-3.

50 IRC § 170(e)(1)(B)(i).

51 E.g., *Winokur v. Commissioner*, 90 T.C. 733 (1988).

52 *Orth v. Commissioner*, 813 F.2d 837, 843 (7th Cir. 1987).

53 Rev. Proc. 96-15, 1996-1 C.B. 185.

54 IRC § 2503(g).

55 *Anselmo v. Commissioner*, 757 F.2d 1208 (11th Cir. 1985).

56 *Rhoades v. Commissioner*, 55 T.C.M. 1159 (1988).

57 E.g., *Schacter v. Commissioner*, 51 T.C.M. 1428 (1986); *Dubin v. Commissioner*, 52 T.C.M. 456 (1985).

58 IRC § 170(e)(4).

59 IRC § 170(e)(4)(B). This second criterion is the subject of IRC § 1221(1).

60 IRC § 542.

61 IRC § 414(m)(3).

62 IRC § 41(e)(6)(A).

63 IRC § 170(e)(6).

64 IRC §§ 168(i)(2)(B), 170(e)(6)(E)(i), 197(e)(3)(B).

65 IRC § 170(f)(3)(B)(iii); Reg. § 1.170A-14(a).

66 *Satullo v. Commissioner*, 66 T.C.M. 1697 (1994).

67 IRC §§ 170(e)(1)(A), 1221(3).

68 IRC § 1256.

69 IRC § 1256(c)(1).

70 *Greene v. United States*, 864 F. Supp. 407, 414 (S.D.N.Y. 1994), *rev'd, infra* endnote 71.

71 *Greene v. United States*, 79 F.3d 1348, 1355 (2d Cir. 1996), *cert. den.*, 117 S. Ct. 582 (1996).

72 *Id.* at 1349.

73 *Id.* at 1357.

74 IRC § 408(d)(1).

75 Proposed IRC § 408(d)(8) (Taxpayer Refund and Relief Act of 1999 (H.R. 2488, vetoed on September 23, 1999) § 1009).

76 Reg. § 1.170A-1(g).

77 *Grant v. Commissioner*, 84 T.C. 809 (1985), *aff'd*, 800 F.2d 260 (4th Cir. 1986).

78 Form 990, Part VI, line 82.

79 Reg. § 1.170A-1(g).

80 Reg. § 1.170A-7(a)(1).

81 Form 990, Part VI, line 82.

82 Rev. Rul. 89-51, 1989-1 C.B. 89. The rule concerning such personal use is in IRC § 280A(d)(2)(C).

83 IRS CPE Text FY 2000, Technical Topic T, Part I.

84 IRC § 6701.

85 IRC § 6700.

86 IRC § 6701(a)(2).

87 Rev. Rul. 78-38, 1978-1 C.B. 67.

88 Rev. Rul. 68-174, 1968-1 C.B. 81.

89 *Id.*

90 E.g., *Watson v. Commissioner*, 613 F.2d 594 (5th Cir. 1980).

91 IRC § 4946.

92 IRC § 4941.

93 Priv. Ltr. Rul. 9335057.

94 Tech. Adv. Mem. 9828001.

95 Reg. § 1.170A-4(c)(2)(ii).

96 IRC § 1011(b); Reg. § 1.1011-2(a)(1).

97 IRC § 170(f)(2)(A).

98 *Id.*

99 *National Foundation, Inc. v. United States*, 87-2 U.S.T.C. ¶ 9602 (Cl. Ct. 1987); *Fund for Anonymous Gifts v. Internal Revenue Service*, 99-1 U.S.T.C. ¶ 50,440 (D.C. Cir. 1999).

100 IRS CPE Text FY 2000, Technical Topic P, Introduction.

101 *Fund for Anonymous Gifts v. Internal Revenue Service*, 97-2 U.S.T.C. ¶ 50,710 (D.D.C. 1997).

102 *Fund for Anonymous Gifts v. Internal Revenue Service, supra* endnote 99.

103 IRS CPE Text FY 2000, Technical Topic P, 2B(2).

104 *New Dynamics Foundation v. United States*, No. 90-197T (U.S. Ct. Fed. Cl.)

105 IRS CPE Text FY 2000, Technical Topic P, 2C.

106 Reg. § 1.507-2(a)(8).

107 Reg. § 1.170A-9(e)(11).

108 IRS CPE Text FY 2000, Technical Topic P, 2C.

109 IRC § 4942.

110 IRC § 4945.

111 *Fund for Anonymous Gifts v. Internal Revenue Service, supra* endnote 99. For additional information about donor-advised funds, see Chapter 16 of *Private Foundations* (2000 supp.).

112 IRC § 170(f)(8)(A). *SLAB-FR* will contain a summary of these rules.

113 IRC § 6115.

114 IRC § 6714. *SLAB-FR* will contain a summary of these rules.

115 Reg. § 1.170A-13(c). *SLAB-FR* will contain a summary of these rules.

CHAPTER 5

1 See *The Tax Law of Charitable Giving*, Chapter 5 § 3.

2 IRC § 170(f)(2)(A), (B).

3 See *supra* endnote 1.

4 IRC § 2055. *SLAB-FR* will contain a chapter summarizing the estate tax charitable deduction rules.

5 IRC § 664(c).

6 Reg. § 1.664-1(c).

7 *Lelia G. Newhall Charitable Trust v. Commissioner*, 104 T.C. 236 (1995).

8 IRC §§ 170(f)(2)(A), 664.

9 Reg. §§ 20.2031-7(d)(6), 1.642(c)-6(e)(2).

10 IRC § 664(d)(1).

11 IRC § 664(g)(4).

12 IRC § 4975(e)(7).

13 IRC § 664(g).

14 IRC § 664(d)(2).

15 Reg. § 1.664-3(a)(1)(i)(a).

16 IRC § 664(d)(3)(A).

17 Reg. § 1.664-3(a)(1)(i)(b)(1).

18 IRC § 664(d)(3)(B).

19 Reg. § 1.664-3(a)(1)(i)(b)(2).

20 Reg. § 1.664-3(a)(1)(i)(c).

21 Reg. § 1.664-3(a)(1)(i)(c)(1).

22 Reg. § 1.664-3(a)(1)(i)(d).

23 *Id.*

24 Reg. § 1.664-3(a)(1)(i)(c)(2).

25 Reg. § 1.664-1(a)(7)(ii).

26 Reg. § 1.664-3(a)(1)(i)(f)(1).

27 Reg. § 1.664-3(a)(1)(i)(f)(2).

28 IRC § 4941.

29 Reg. § 1.664-3(a)(1)(i)(f)(3).

30 IRC § 514(c).

31 E.g., Priv. Ltr. Rul. 9501004.

32 IRC § 170(a)(3).

33 IRC § 170(e)(1)(B)(i).

34 E.g., Priv. Ltr. Rul. 9452026.

35 IRC § 170(b)(1)(C)(i). The limitations on deductibility of gifts of money are in IRC § 170(b)(1)(A), (B).

36 IRS Notice 98-20, 1998-13 I.R.B. 25.

37 IRS Notice 99-17, 1999-14 I.R.B. 6.

38 IRC § 664(b).

39 This deduction may be less than the fair market value amount due to one or more of the percentage limitations on gift deductibility (Q 4:3–Q 4:7).

40 Reg. § 20.2031-7(a), (d)(2)(i).

41 Reg. § 1.664-2(c).

42 *Id.*

43 The requirement for determining this rate is in IRC § 1274(d)(1).

44 IRC § 7520(a). This rate is published monthly by the IRS in a revenue ruling. See *The Tax Law of Charitable Giving*, Appendix K, for a list of these rates.

45 Reg. § 1.7520-2(b).

46 Reg. § 1.7520-2(c).

47 IRC § 2032.

48 Reg. § 1.664-2(c).

49 Reg. § 20.2031-7(d).

50 Reg. § 20.2031-7(d)(6)(iv)(A). These actuarial tables are contained in IRS Publication 1457, Tables B (for an annuity payable for a term of years) and S (for an annuity payable for a single life).

51 Reg. § 20.2031-7(d)(6)(iv)(B).

52 Reg. § 20-2031-7(d)(6)(iv)(C).

53 See *The Tax Law of Charitable Giving*, Chapter 11.

54 Reg. § 20.2031-7(a), (d)(2)(i), (e)(1).

55 Reg. § 1.664-4(a).

56 Reg. § 1.664-4(e)(3).

57 Reg. § 1.664-4(e)(4).

58 Reg. § 1.664-4(e)(5).

59 Reg. § 1.7520-3(b).

60 Reg. §§ 1.664-3(d), 4(c).

61 Reg. § 1.170A-1(e).

62 Rev. Rul. 77-374, 1977-2 C.B. 329.

63 See *The Tax Law of Charitable Giving*, Chapter 11.

64 IRC §§ 170(f)(2)(A), 642(c)(5).

65 Reg. § 1.642(c)-6(e)(2).

66 IRC § 642(c)(5)(F).

67 IRC § 642(c)(5)(E).

68 *Id.*

69 IRC § 642(c)(5)(A).

70 Reg. § 1.642(c)-5(b)(5).

71 *Id.*

72 IRC § 642(c)(5)(A).

73 Reg. § 1.642(c)-5(b)(7).

74 Reg. §§ 20.2031-7(d)(2)(i), 1.642(c)-6(a)(1), (d), (e)(1).

75 Reg. § 20.2031-7(d)(6).

76 Reg. § 1.642(c)-6(e)(2).

77 Reg. § 1.642(c)-6(c)(1).

78 Reg. § 1.642(c)-6(e)(2).

79 Reg. § 1.642(c)-6(e)(3).

80 Rev. Rul. 98-4, 1998-2 I.R.B. 17.

81 E.g., Priv. Ltr. Rul. 9826022.

82 IRC § 170(f)(2)(A).

83 See *The Tax Law of Charitable Giving*, Chapter 14.

84 *Ritchie v. American Council on Gift Annuities*, 943 F. Supp. 685 (N.D. Tex. 1996), *appeal dis.*, *Ozee v. American Council on Gift Annuities*, 110 F.3d 1082 (5th Cir. 1997), *reh. den.*, 116 F.3d 1479 (5th Cir. 1997), *cert. gr. and judg. vac.*, *American Bible Society v. Ritchie*, 118 S.Ct. 596 (1997), *on rem.*, *Ozee v. American Council on Gift Annuities*, 143 F.3d 937 (5th Cir. 1998), *cert. den.*, *American Bible Society v. Ritchie*, 119 S.Ct. 1454 (1999). Also *Ozee v. American Council on Gift Annuities*, 110 F.3d 1082 (5th Cir. 1997), *cert. gr. and judg. vac.*, *American Council on Gift Annuities v. Ritchie*, 118 S.Ct. 597 (1997); *Ozee v. American Council on Gift Annuities*, 888 F. Supp. 1318 (N.D. Tex. 1995); *Ritchie v. American Council on Gift Annuities*, 1996 WL 743343 (N.D. Tex. 1996).

85 *SLAB-FR* will contain a chapter summarizing the antitrust and securities law rules as they apply to charitable organizations.

86 IRC § 514(c)(5).

87 IRC § 501(m)(3)(E), (5).

88 IRC § 170(f)(3)(B)(i), (ii), and (iii).

89 H.R. 572, 106th Cong., 1st Sess. (1999).

90 Taxpayer Refund and Relief Act of 1999 (H.R. 2488, 106th Cong., 1st Sess. 1999) § 1510.

91 IRC § 513(i).

CHAPTER 6

1 IRC § 513(c).

2 *American Academy of Family Physicians v. United States*, 91 F.3d 1155 (8th Cir. 1996).

3 E.g., *Clarence LaBelle Post No. 217 v. United States*, 580 F.2d 270 (8th Cir. 1978).

4 E.g., *Iowa State University of Science and Technology v. United States*, 500 F.2d 508 (Ct. Cl. 1974).

5 IRC § 513(a).

6 IRC § 513(c).

7 E.g. Tech. Adv. Mem. 9803001.

8 Tech. Adv. Mem. 9645004.

9 *United Cancer Council v. Commissioner*, 165 F.3d 1173 (7th Cir. 1999).

10 E.g., *The Nationalist Movement v. Commissioner*, 102 T.C. 558 (1994), *aff'd*, 37 F.3d 216 (5th Cir. 1994).

11 Tech. Adv. Mem. 9711003.

12 *United Cancer Council v. Commissioner, supra* endnote 9, at 1178.

13 See *LAB 1*, Chapter 11.

14 IRC § 501(c)(2), (25)(G)(ii).

15 Tech. Adv. Mem. 9847002.

16 See *The Law of Tax-Exempt Organizations*, Chapter 26 § 1.

17 Prop. Reg. § 1.513-7.

18 *Commissioner v. Goetzinger*, 480 U.S. 23 (1987).

19 E.g., *West Virginia State Medical Association v. Commissioner*, 91 T.C. 651 (1988), *aff'd*, 882 F.2d 123 (4th Cir. 1989), *cert. den.*, 493 U.S. 1044 (1990).

20 E.g., Tech. Adv. Mem. 9719002.

21 IRC § 513(c).

22 E.g., *Clarence LaBelle Post No. 227 v. United States, supra* endnote 3.

23 E.g., *National Water Well Association, Inc. v. Commissioner*, 92 T.C. 75 (1989).

24 E.g., *Consumer Credit Counseling Service of Alabama, Inc. v. United States*, 78-2 U.S.T.C. ¶ 9660 (D.D.C. 1978).

25 E.g., *Iowa State University of Science and Technology v. United States, supra* endnote 4.

26 *Living Faith, Inc. v. Commissioner*, 950 F.2d 365 (7th Cir. 1991).

27 Tech. Adv. Mem. 9803001.

28 IRC § 501(m).

29 H. Rep. 99-841, 99th Cong., 2d Sess. II-345 (1986).

30 E.g., *Florida Hospital Trust Fund v. Commissioner*, 103 T.C. 140 (1994), *aff'd*, 71 F.3d 808 (11th Cir. 1996).

31 The underlying concept is that an activity cannot rise to the level of a business that is competitive with one or more for-profit businesses if it is not actively undertaken (regularly carried on).

32 Reg. § 1.513-1(c)(1).

33 *Id.*

34 Reg. § 1.513-1(c)(2)(i).

35 *Museum of Flight Foundation v. United States*, 99-1 U.S.T.C. ¶ 50,311 (W.D. Wash. 1999).

36 Reg. § 1.513-1(c)(2)(i).

37 E.g., Tech. Adv. Mem. 9147007.

38 Tech. Adv. Mem. 9712001.

39 *National Collegiate Athletic Association v. Commissioner*, 914 F.2d 1417, 1423 (10th Cir. 1990).

40 IRS Action on Decision No. 1991-015.

41 Another loss by the government in this regard is reflected in *Suffolk County Patrolmen's Benevolent Association, Inc. v. Commissioner*, 77 T.C. 1314 (1981).

42 *National Collegiate Athletic Association v. Commissioner*, 92 T.C. 456 (1989), *aff'd, supra* endnote 39.

43 See *The Law of Tax-Exempt Organizations*, Chapter 26 § 4.

44 Reg. § 1.513-1(d)(2).

45 *Hi-Plains Hospital v. United States*, 670 F.2d 528 (5th Cir. 1982).

46 Priv. Ltr. Rul. 9710030.

47 Priv. Ltr. Rul. 9747040.

48 Priv. Ltr. Rul. 9732032.

49 Tech. Adv. Mem. 9803001.

50 Rev. Rul. 85-110, 1985-2 C.B. 166.

51 E.g., Priv. Ltr. Rul. 9739043.

52 E.g., Tech. Adv. Mem. 9751001.

53 E.g., Tech. Adv. Mem. 9742001.

54 E.g., Tech. Adv. Mem. 9550003.

55 Priv. Ltr. Rul. 9619069.

56 Priv. Ltr. Rul. 9641011.

57 Tech. Adv. Mem. 9702004.

58 Priv. Ltr. Rul. 9821063.

59 Tech. Adv. Mem. 9821067.

60 E.g., Tech. Adv. Mem. 9550001.

61 E.g., Tech. Adv. Mem. 9612003.

62 Tech. Adv. Mem. 9608003.

63 Tech. Adv. Mem. 9847002.

64 Priv. Ltr. Rul. 9849027.

65 Rev. Rul. 78-51, 1978-1 C.B. 165.

66 *San Antonio Bar Association v. United States*, 80-2 U.S.T.C. ¶ 9594 (W.D. Tex. 1980).

67 *Texas Apartment Association v. United States*, 869 F.2d 884 (5th Cir. 1989).

68 Reg. § 1.513-1(d)(3).

69 Rev. Rul. 73-386, 1973-2 C.B. 191, 192.

70 Rev. Rul. 76-94, 1976-1 C.B. 171.

71 Reg. § 1.513-1(d)(4)(ii).

72 *Id.*

73 *Id.*

74 Priv. Ltr. Rul. 9320042.

75 Reg. § 1.513-1(d)(4)(iii).

76 Reg. § 1.513-1(d)(4)(iv).

77 *SICO Foundation v. United States*, 295 F.2d 924, 925 (Ct. Cl. 1961), *reh. den.*, 297 F.2d 557 (Ct. Cl. 1962).

78 Priv. Ltr. Rul. 7946001.

79 IRC § 513(f).

80 *Executive Network Club v. Commissioner*, 69 T.C.M. 1680 (1995).

81 *Disabled American Veterans v. United States*, 650 F.2d 1179 (Ct. Cl. 1981).

82 *Id.* at 1187.

83 *Id.* at 1186.

84 Priv. Ltr. Rul. 8203134.

85 Priv. Ltr. Rul. 8232011.

86 *Parklane Residential School, Inc. v. Commissioner,* 45 T.C.M. 988, 992 (1983).

87 *American Bar Endowment v. United States,* 84-1 U.S.T.C. ¶ 9204 (Cl. Ct. 1984), at 83,350.

88 *Id.* at 83,351.

89 *Id.*

90 *United States v. American Bar Endowment,* 477 U.S. 105, 115 (1986).

91 *Id.* at 125.

92 *U.S. CB Radio Association, No. 1, Inc. v. Commissioner,* 42 T.C.M. 1441, 1444 (1981).

93 *Christian Stewardship Assistance, Inc. v. Commissioner,* 70 T.C. 1037, 1041 (1978).

94 *Id.* at 1043.

95 *Id.* at 1044.

96 *Id.*

97 *The Ecclesiastical Order of The Ism of Am, Inc. v. Commissioner,* 80 T.C. 833 (1983), *aff'd,* 740 F.2d 967 (6th Cir. 1984), *cert. den.,* 471 U.S. 1015 (1985).

98 *Id.,* 80 T.C. at 839.

99 *Id.* at 840.

100 *Id.* at 841.

101 *National Association of American Churches v. Commissioner,* 82 T.C. 18 (1984).

102 *Id.* at 29-30.

103 *Id.* at 30.

104 *Id.*

105 *The Ecclesiastical Order of The Ism of Am, Inc. v. Commissioner, supra* endnote 97, at 842.

106 IRC § 513(a)(1).

107 IRC § 513(a)(2).

108 IRC § 513(a)(3).

109 IRC § 513(h)(1)(A).

110 IRC § 513(h)(1)(B).

111 IRC § 513(f).

112 IRC § 513(d)(1), (2).

113 IRC § 513(d)(1), (3).

114 Tech. Adv. Mem. 9652004.

115 Tech. Adv. Mem. 9635001.

116 *Julius M. Israel Lodge of B'nai B'rith No. 2113 v. Commissioner*, 70 T.C.M. 673 (1995), *aff'd* 98 F.3d 190 (5th Cir. 1996).

117 Priv. Ltr. Rul. 9302023.

118 *Executive Network Club, Inc. v. Commissioner*, 69 T.C.M. 1680 (1995).

119 Rev. Rul. 71-581, 1971-2 C.B. 236.

120 IRC § 512(b)(7), (8), and (9).

121 See *The Law of Tax-Exempt Organizations*, Chapter 26 § 1.

122 Reg. § 1.512(b)-1(c)(5).

123 Priv. Ltr. Rul. 9740032.

124 See *The Law of Tax-Exempt Organizations*, Chapter 26 § 5(h).

125 IRC § 512(b)(3)(A)(i).

126 *Museum of Flight Foundation v. United States, supra* endnote 35.

127 E.g., *Sierra Club, Inc. v. Commissioner*, 65 T.C.M. 2582 (1993).

128 IRC § 170(c).

129 IRC § 501(c)(3).

130 *Sierra Club v. Commissioner*, 86 F.3d 1526, 1532 (9th Cir. 1996).

131 *Id.* at 1535 (emphasis in the original).

132 *Id.*

133 *Sierra Club v. Commissioner*, 77 T.C.M. 1569 (1999).

134 E.g., Tech. Adv. Mem. 9509002.

135 Priv. Ltr. Rul. 9450028.

136 Priv. Ltr. Rul. 9821049.

137 Priv. Ltr. Rul. 9816027.

138 There is some support for this approach in *Texas Farm Bureau, Inc. v. United States*, 53 F.3d 120 (5th Cir. 1995).

139 E.g., Tech. Adv. Mem. 9338003.

140 IRC § 514.

141 IRS CPE Text FY 2000, Technical Topic I, Introduction.

142 IRC § 6113.

143 See *The Law of Tax-Exempt Organizations*, Chapter 30 § 5.

144 IRS CPE Text FY 2000, Technical Topic I, Part 2, 1A.

145 IRC § 513(i).

146 IRS CPE Text FY 2000, Technical Topic I, Part 2, 2D.

147 *Id.*

148 *Id.*, E.

149 *Id.*, 3B.

150 *Id.*

151 *Id.*, Conclusion.

152 IRC § 11.

153 IRC § 1(d).

154 IRC § 512(b)(12).

155 IRC § 512(a)(1).

156 Reg. § 1.512(a)-1(a).

157 E.g., *Rensselaer Polytechnic Institute v. Commissioner*, 732 F.2d 1058 2d Cir. 1984).
158 IRC § 512(b)(10).
159 IRC § 6655(a)-(d).
160 IRC § 6012(a)(2), (4).

CHAPTER 7

1 IRC § 4958.
2 *Church By Mail, Inc. v. Commissioner*, 765 F.2d 1387 (9th Cir. 1985).
3 IRC § 162.
4 E.g., *Rapco, Inc. v. Commissioner*, 85 F.3d 950 (2d Cir. 1990).
5 Proposed Reg. § 53.4958-5. *SLAB-FR* will contain a summary of these rules as part of the chapter on intermediate sanctions.
6 See *The Law of Tax-Exempt Organizations*, Chapter 19 § 4(a), text accompanied by notes 70–79.
7 *People of God Community v. Commissioner*, 75 T.C. 127 (1980).
8 *World Family Corporation v. Commissioner*, 81 T.C. 958 (1983).
9 *Id.* at 970.
10 *Id.* at 969.
11 *National Foundation, Inc. v. United States*, 87-2 U.S.T.C. ¶ 9602 (Ct. Cl. 1987).
12 *Kushnir v. American Medical Center at Denver*, 492 P.2d 906 (Col. App. 1971).
13 See *The Law of Fund-Raising*, Chapter 6 § 12.
14 *SLAB-FR* will contain a summary of the antitrust law as it applies in the fund-raising context.
15 See *The Law of Tax-Exempt Organizations*, Chapter 4 § 7.
16 *United Cancer Council v. Commissioner*, 109 T.C. 326 (1997), *rev'd and rem'd.* 165 F.3d 1173 (7th Cir. 1999).
17 *Id.*
18 *Id.*
19 *American Campaign Academy v. Commissioner*, 92 T.C. 1053 (1989).
20 Rev. Rul. 98-15, 1998-12 I.R.B. 6.

CHAPTER 8

1 IRC § 6033. This rreference to *tax-exempt organizations* is to organizations that are exempt from tax under IRC § 501(a) and described in IRC § 501(c)(3).
2 That is, organizations described in IRC § 501(c)(3), including those referenced in IRC § 501(e), (f), (k), and (n).
3 These are entities that are the subject of IRC § 4947(a)(1).
4 That is, organizations described in IRC § 501(c)(1).

5 IRC § 115; Reg. § 1.6033-2(g)(1)(v).
6 Rev. Proc. 95-48, 1995-2 C.B. 418. E.g., Priv. Ltr. Rul. 9825030.
7 IRC § 6033(a)(2)(A)(i); Reg. § 1.6033-2(g)(1)(i).
8 Rev. Proc. 96-10, 1996-1 C.B. 577.
9 Reg. § 1.6033-2(g)(1)(vii).
10 Reg. § 1.6033-2(g)(1)(iv).
11 IRC § 6033(a)(2)(A)(iii); Reg. § 1.6033-2(g)(1)(iii).
12 IRS Announcement (Ann.) 82-88, 1982-25 I.R.B. 23.
13 Rev. Proc. 94-17, 1994-1 C.B. 579.
14 IRC § 6033(a)(2)(A)(ii).
15 Ann. 82-88, *supra* endnote 12.
16 *Id.*
17 IRC § 6033(b).
18 IRC § 6072(e).
19 See *The Law of Tax-Exempt Organizations*, Chapter 23 § 6.
20 Reg. § 1.509(a)-3(g).
21 See *The Law of Fund-Raising*, Chapter 9 § 8.
22 IRC § 6115. *SLAB-FR* will contain a discussion of these rules. See *LAB 1*, Chapter 7, Q 7:9.
23 IRC § 6113. *SLAB-FR* will contain a discussion of these rules.
24 See *The Law of Tax-Exempt Organizations*, Chapter 4 § 7.
25 *Id.*, Chapter 4 § 5.
26 IRC § 6104(d). *SLAB-FR* will contain a discussion of these rules.
27 IRC § 4958. *SLAB-FR* will contain a discussion of these rules. See *LAB 2*, Chapter 1.
28 These are organizations that are tax-exempt by reason of IRC § 501(c)(5). See *The Law of Tax-Exempt Organizations*, Chapter 15 § 1.
29 These are organizations that are tax-exempt by reason of IRC § 527. See *LAB 2*, Chapter 8.
30 IRC § 6652(c)(1)(A).
31 *Id.*
32 IRC § 6652(c)(1)(B).

CHAPTER 9

1 *Village of Schaumberg v. Citizens for a Better Environment*, 444 U.S. 620 (1980); *Secretary of State of Maryland v. Joseph H. Munson Co., Inc.*, 467 U.S. 947 (1984); *Riley v. National Federation of the Blind of North Carolina, Inc.*, 487 U.S. 781 (1988). See *The Law of Fund-Raising*, Chapter 5.
2 *National Federation of Nonprofits v. Lungren* (N.D. Cal., order issued March 29, 1995).

3 *Kentucky State Police Professional Association v. Gorman*, 870 F. Supp. 166 (E.D. Ky. 1994).

4 See *The Law of Fund-Raising*, Chapter 8 § 15B (in cumulative supplement).

5 IRS CPE Text FY 2000, Technical Topic I, Introduction.

6 *Id.* 4A.

7 *Center for Auto Safety v. Athey*, 37 F.3d 139, 144, note 9 (4th Cir. 1994).

Index

Visit us on the World Wide Web

www.wiley.com/nonprofit

Our nonprofit website features:

• **A nonprofit catalogue** where you can order and search for titles online. View book and author information about our management, law/tax, fund-raising, accounting and finance titles.

• **A threaded discussion forum**, which will provide you and your colleagues with the chance to ask questions, share knowledge, and debate issues important to your organization and the sector.

• **Over 500 free forms and worksheets** to help run any nonprofit organization more efficiently and effectively. Forms are updated monthly to cover a new key area of nonprofit management.

• **Useful links** to many nonprofit resources online.

The Wiley Nonprofit Series brings together an extraordinary team of experts in the fields of nonprofit management, fund raising, law, accounting, and finance. This website highlights our new books, which present the best, most innovative practices being used in the nonprofit sector today. It also highlights our established works, which through their use in the day-to-day operations of thousands of nonprofits, have proven themselves to be invaluable to any nonprofit looking to raise more money or improve their operations, while still remaining in compliance with all rules and regulations.

For nearly 200 years, Wiley has prided itself on being a publisher of books known for thoroughness, rigor, and readability. Please browse the website. You are sure to find valued titles that you need to navigate the new world of nonprofit action.

WILEY

Wiley Nonprofit Series